the
arrange
ment

the arrange ment

a love story

Memoir by
David Winkler

RARE BIRD

LOS ANGELES, CALIF.

RARE BIRD

THIS IS A GENUINE RARE BIRD BOOK

Rare Bird Books
6044 North Figueroa Street
Los Angeles, California 90042
rarebirdbooks.com

FIRST PAPERBACK EDITION 2024

Set in Minion Pro
Printed in the United States

Cover Design by Lisa Brewster
Cover Floral Arrangement and Photography by Camilla Vergani
Author Photo by Next Exit Photography

10 9 8 7 6 5 4 3 2 1

Library of Congress Cataloging-in-Publication Data available upon request.

CONTENTS

1
ONCE UPON A TIME IN BEVERLY HILLS

I SPILLED A LITTLE champagne in the Uber!

Jordan's text lit up my iPhone on the bed as I dressed for the evening.

Well, there's an amusing start to a first date, I thought.

I laced up my black Prada sneakers, the final touch of my characteristically casual outfit—slim fit Levi's and a black cashmere crew neck—then picked up the device.

Started without me, did you?

She responded with a laughing face emoji. Swear I'm not an alcoholic! I just get nervous meeting men this way.

Can't blame you for that! I answered. After all, we had met—virtually speaking—on a dating site, and if that wasn't nerve-inducing enough, it was on SeekingArrangement.com, where beautiful young women and successful older men seek "mutually beneficial arrangements."

(That collective gasp of shock would be coming from most of my family and friends, because on the night of January 9, 2019, few knew this fifty-two-year-old, divorced Hollywood film producer was, as they say, a "sugar daddy.")

✤

DAMPENED PAPER TOWELS IN hand, I pulled shut the front door to my house—a rosy, cream-plastered two-story with that maroon Spanish tile roof common in my neighborhood of Westwood, California.

Finally stopped raining! I thought. It was such a nice, warm night, I didn't even need a jacket, a welcome change after a winter so wet that Southern California meteorologists were calling it "drought-ending."

I walked to the curb and looked west. I'd ordered the Uber for Jordan, so I knew it would be coming from Venice. (Lux option, of course. *Can't be cheap when you're a sugar daddy!*) But not seeing a single car approaching, I took a deep breath and exhaled slowly—I made a practice of stealing moments to meditate and reflect.

I felt gratitude wash over me. This wasn't uncommon. I often joked to friends that I'd been "born lucky."

In fact, in many ways, my life had been a veritable fairy tale. *Once upon a time in Beverly Hills, there lived a prince*…it might have been written.

I certainly *looked* like the embodiment of the phrase "Jewish American Prince." At five foot eight and 170 pounds (on a good day) I kept the remains of my brown hair clipped so its recession blended with my tan forehead. Perched below my hazel eyes was that ancestral crook in my nose. (As a teenager, while all my friends were having rhinoplasty, I proudly refused to have my birthright straightened.)

And the royal family was admired throughout the kingdom…

My parents were often called "Hollywood Royalty." My father, one of the most successful and respected film producers in the industry, and his wife of nearly sixty years raised my two brothers and me in an eight-bedroom Beverly Hills mansion. With nearly three acres of sculptured gardens, a tennis court, and an Olympic-length pool, all surrounded by a tall stone wall, it was a moat shy of a castle. More impressive still, my parents had forged a harmonious clan—especially in the fame, fortune, and ego-plagued lands of Beverly Hills. My two brothers and our families got along famously, often traveling to Europe and spending weekends together at our Malibu beach house.

*But the prince had prospered in his own right…*the fairy tale would have described my own royal quests.

Though I'd recently partnered with my father to produce a few critically acclaimed and financially blockbusting movies, I was just as proud of the screenplays, independent films, and television movies I wrote and directed on my own. I'd traveled the globe, flown airplanes and jumped out of them, surfed giant waves, become an ace tennis player, reached near-scratch golfer, and rode motorcycles to my heart's content. And, of course, I'd embarked on the biggest adventure of all—marriage and children. The former ended in disappointment—come March, it would be four years since my divorce—but the latter was my greatest accomplishment. My two beautiful children were the pride of my royal existence.

*So the prince again sought true love's kiss…*would be the next logical passage in this fairy tale.

If I were in any hurry to turn the page, that is. Which I was not. Don't get me wrong—I didn't consider myself that cliché man in the crush of a mid-life crisis, chasing young girls to avoid the pain of divorce or of facing mortality. In fact, I considered myself a happy, content, and vibrant man. And I'd emerged from my marriage with relatively few battle scars—my ex-wife and I were not just amicable; we were great friends. But I was truly enjoying this new world of internet dating. The last time I'd been single, I was in my late thirties, and people were still embarrassed to admit they dabbled on the one site—the dial-up version of match.com. But, like a romantic Rip Van Winkle, I'd emerged to discover a world where everyone and their mother were proud to be on Bumble, Tinder, Hinge. And with so many options, who could blame me for not wanting to settle down and get married again so quickly?

As if on cue, I felt a buzzing in my jean pocket. I pulled out my phone and saw that Jordan had texted, Minute away!

Ready for ya!

Standing there like a teenager with first-date butterflies, I decided to refresh myself with Jordan's Instagram. Nearly a month had gone by since we first matched on Seeking and shared social media; our meeting delayed by a trip I took to Costa Rica with my ex-wife and kids for the Christmas holiday. (Yes, *that* amicable.)

Naturally, I'd peeked at her Instagram a few times since, but even tonight I was impressed by it. Fifty thousand plus followers strong, Jordan called herself a "Wellness Warrior." This tall dirty blonde's posts were unfiltered and un-Photoshopped pictures of her practicing yoga, modeling fitness clothes, and eating at organic restaurants around Manhattan. (In our messages she'd told me she just moved to Los Angeles.) And, unlike so many women who called themselves "influencers" but only swayed people with bikini shots and flattering selfies, Jordan's pictures were downright modest.

But there's something else about her pictures, I realized. I struggled to define what that "else" was, but the best words I could come up with were, *Jordan just fits…*where or how, I wasn't sure, but I couldn't shake the thought.

I heard a quiet buzzing and looked up to see a white Tesla Model S pulling up the street and into my driveway. I dashed forward to open the rear driver's side door.

"I'm so embarrassed," Jordan gushed as she ducked out, miniature champagne bottle in one hand, plastic cup in the other. She unfolded her frame that was an inch taller than my own and shuffled so that her blue and white-striped silk romper settled on her lithe, natural curves. Long naturally dirty blonde hair that couldn't decide if it wanted to be curled or straightened bounced past her shoulders, and she wore only the thinnest sheen of makeup. She had clear blue eyes unafraid of contact, and a small, charming bump protruded from her nose—nearly matching mine, but daintier. But it was her smiling lips that captivated me. Without even a trace of gloss or lipstick, they were invitingly full and pink.

Unable to contain how captivated I was, I blurted out, "Jesus, you're even more beautiful than your pictures!"

"Hah!" Jordan exhaled with a breathy laugh. "Thank you. And you have such an infectious smile!"

"Glad you think so." I gave her a quick hug. "Let's see what kind of mess we have here."

"Oh, right." She stepped out of the way with a conspiratorial nod to the driver's window and a whisper. "The guy's a little annoyed. But I swear, I hardly drink—this stuff's been sitting in the fridge for ages."

"I believe you," I reassured her, then whispered, "And don't worry about him, I tip big."

She laughed. "I bet you do."

I climbed into the back to find the smallest circle of spillage on the seat—certainly nothing that warranted the death stares the grumpy driver shot us—and mopped it up.

"Let me get rid of those..." Jordan leaned into the car to retrieve the sodden towels and scurried to the trash containers waiting for sidewalk collection.

I slid over in the seat and watched her dump them, the cup, and bottle into the blue recycling bins. *Thinks about the environment,* I noted—a not insignificant detail to a liberal democrat who believed in global warming.

"Crisis averted!" Jordan announced as she darted back into the car and pulled her door shut.

The car lurched backward before making a sharp turn and peeling down the street. Jordan and I exchanged comically indignant looks and quickly reached for our seat belts.

Little did I know how much we'd need them for the fairy-tale romance ahead.

2

A GENUINE ARRANGEMENT

"THIS PLACE IS SO lovely," Jordan gushed as she made the most subtle of glances around the restaurant. We sat nestled in a quiet corner table at The Ivy in West Hollywood. By day, its patio was a scene of lunching celebrities perched over the sidewalk of Robertson Boulevard, inviting paparazzi to stalk them. But in the evenings, it became one of the town's hidden romantic gems, with candles illuminating bundles of fresh flowers spilling out of Delft vases.

"And nice and quiet," I pointed out. "Call me crazy, but I actually want to hear what the person across the table has to say."

"Crazy," Jordan teased.

I smiled appreciatively and reached for my water glass. Water was all Jordan had asked of our waiter after his cocktail pitch, and being only a social drinker, I followed suit. Frankly, I was relieved—after that champagne spill, it was nice to know the girl wasn't an alcoholic.

"To finally meeting!" I toasted.

"Cheers!" she sang with an enthusiastic pitch matching the clink of our glasses. "So how was Costa Rica?" she asked.

"Amazing. Have you ever been down there?"

"I wish."

"It's truly a special place. We had an American guide who took us to all these private beaches, but it's the people I'll remember. They greet you by saying, *pura vida*. It means *the simple life*."

"Love that!" Jordan said, then flushed. "I admit I might have stalked your Instagram while you were down there."

Considering my own deep dive into *her* social media, I conceded, "I'll take it as a compliment."

"You have such beautiful children. Although, I couldn't get over seeing your ex-wife in so many of the pictures."

"Right," I said with a knowing grin. Jordan wouldn't be the first date to note my social media and ask if I was really divorced. "But trust me, we're just good friends. Check out her Instagram. You'll see she was posting about our 'conscious uncoupling' long before Gwyneth Paltrow."

"I believe you. Seriously though, I hope you don't mind my prying into your personal life. I know a lot of men on Seeking are looking for something discreet."

I shook my head. "I'm an open book. I mean, I'm publicly *very* discreet, but only because people are so judgmental. They think being a sugar daddy makes you some old lecher."

Jordan gave a comical shiver. "Oh, but don't you hate being called that? Sugar daddy, sugar baby..."

"It's a little infantilizing, but I've learned to laugh about it. If the shoe fits..."

She leaned forward and lowered her volume tactfully. "I pretty much feel the same—what consenting adults do behind closed doors is nobody's business. But I *do* think there's a difference between what I do and escorting."

I matched her lean. "Tell me."

She cocked her head to the side. "I guess I feel it's different because I'm not meeting strangers in hotel rooms. I *choose* who I date and get to know them first. And I signed up for this—literally."

I was impressed by how succinctly she'd described my own beliefs. In the perennial debate between feminists, I came down on the "sex work positive" side. Unless a woman was coerced into prostitution by human traffickers or pimps forcing her to trade tricks for drugs, I believed what any woman chose to do with her body should be legal and stigma-free.

"Anonymous encounters don't do it for me either," I said. "Jesus, half of the men in Hollywood have madams on speed dial."

"It's the same with Wall Street guys in New York."

"Right—you came to Los Angeles what, a month ago?"

"Less! Two weeks ago, I was up to my waist in dirty New York snow, and now I'm in this amazing apartment a bike ride from Muscle Beach!"

"I love Venice," I said. "What prompted the move?"

"Oh, God, I guess it was a little impulsive," Jordan sighed. "I'd been thinking of coming out here to try getting some acting work, and I mentioned as much to a friend. He said he knew a guy looking to do a swap and spend some time in Manhattan, so we linked up. He's at my spot for at least three months, maybe more if I can find some work."

"The universe provides..." I said all too casually. But in truth, her admission that she harbored dreams of acting wasn't the most appealing trait for me. First off, when I did the obligatory Google search of her, I saw that she had only a few off-off and off-off-off Broadway theater credits, but no real film or television experience to speak of. It was hard for me to get excited about a thirty-year-old inexperienced actor fresh off the proverbial bus in Hollywood. Secondly, I didn't like muddling my professional and personal life. Even before the #MeToo era, I knew bedding actresses on the "casting couch" was unethical. And this wasn't *just* a moral stance. I didn't like to believe a woman was only courting me to network. As transactional as an arrangement could be, I wanted mine to feel as genuine as possible—a real chemical attraction with an intellectual, emotional connection.

But personal reservations aside, I didn't want to sound unsupportive of Jordan's dreams, so I drummed up a standard Hollywood nicety. "By the way, I'd be happy to take a look at your reel and give you some feedback."

Jordan shook her head vehemently. "Oh, no. Absolutely not."

I raised an eyebrow. "What? You don't have one, or you don't want to share it with me?"

"No—I mean yes, of course I have a reel, and maybe I'll send it to you one day. It's just that I don't want to be a clawing actress who tries to wheedle you into getting me an agent or something. I'm an open book, too, but I'd rather we talk about anything else. If that's okay."

Okay? I wanted to leap across the table and kiss her! In one sentence she'd answered my paragraph of worry. "More than okay," I said and reached for my menu. "Let's talk food, shall we?"

"Let's! I'm guessing you've been here before, so what do you like?" she demurred.

"Well," I hesitated, thinking this fitness influencer and actress was probably more worried about caloric intake than taste. "You're probably vegan, vegetarian, paleo, something, right?"

"Nope! I eat everything."

"Really? Even carbs?"

"Please. Carbs are my soul mate."

I laughed and dared to jest, "You may be mine."

"So TELL ME ABOUT some of your arrangements?" Jordan asked as she gathered a few colorful remains from a plate of lobster tacos with her fork.

I pushed my plate of fried chicken smothered in mango chutney away while I searched my dating memory banks for a good story. "Well, last summer I dated a woman named Allison…"

I paused to let the name sink in. If there was one talent a film producer had to have, it was the ability to pitch a tale.

"Details, please!" Jordan demanded playfully, putting her fork down and perching herself on her elbows.

"We dated last summer. She was forty-two, an ex-fashion model with two kids. She'd had this horrible divorce from a famous artist, and he left her with next to nothing in support. I think it was six hundred dollars a month."

"To raise two children?"

"Obscene, right? He emptied their bank account and cut off her credit cards before he told her he wanted a divorce. Hid all his assets from the judge. Allison could barely afford a decent lawyer."

"What an asshole."

I nodded. "She lived in Atlanta, so when she didn't have custody, she'd come and spend a couple weeks here. I helped her pay for an apartment in Santa Monica, gave her an allowance, bought her a bike to tool around on…"

"Lucky girl," Jordan said with an amused laugh.

I felt silly. *Why'd I tell her about the bike?* "Anyway, we dated for five months. Then one day, Allison told me she'd fallen in love with another guy."

Jordan gave me the most sympathetic stare. "I'm sorry."

"Wait for it," I urged slyly, knowing the meat of the story was yet to come. "You see, before we met, Allison had been webcamming to get by. Apparently, one of her old clients—fans, whatever you call those guys who stay up all night online—wanted to leave his wife for her."

Jordan gasped. "No!"

"Yup. And it gets better. Allison had never even met the guy in person!"

"Oh. My. God. You must have been furious."

"For a minute, maybe. But then I realized I might have dodged a bullet—she clearly wasn't the brightest bulb in the chandelier. But we remained friends. Although, I did warn Allison that married men are a messy situation, and she should give him six months to see how things played out before uprooting her life to be with him."

"Sage advice."

I knew I had arrived at the punch line of my story. "Well, I was wrong. He ran back to his wife in six *weeks!*"

Jordan gave an animated groan. "I don't know whether to laugh or cry for the woman. And you're such a catch!"

I made a prayer gesture to thank her.

"But I guess that begs the question of why you're even on this crazy site?" she asked. "It can't be hard for a man like you to meet women, so why aren't you on normal sites like Bumble?"

I allowed myself a humble smile. "What's a nice guy like me doing in a place like this?"

"Exactly," she laughed.

"The answer is, it isn't, and I was. After my wife and I split, I tried Bumble, Tinder, Hinge, The League, you name it. And I met some great women. But they all wanted something more serious than I was ready for."

"Even on Tinder? That's a hook-up site."

"I know—it's been hijacked!"

Jordan laughed. *Yet again*, I thought. We shared a sense of humor, that was for sure.

"I guess it is for people in their twenties," I continued. "At my age, I'm more husband than friends-with-benefits material. But on Seeking, women want older men."

"That's so true. Men your age are so much more respectful and kind. But then again, I have a feeling *you* were born a gentleman."

I smiled at Jordan's compliment but had to admit, "Well, I haven't always been."

"What do you mean?"

Humility wiped my smile away. I knew I was about to reveal a proverbial skeleton in my closet. "To be honest, I wasn't the perfect husband. I went on Seeking when I was married."

"Oh."

I sensed more curiosity in her voice than judgment, but I still felt the need to clarify. "Listen, I really regret cheating on my wife. All I can say is that I'm a different person now."

"Clearly," Jordan said with a hint of astonishment. "Not many people admit to this kind of thing on a first date."

"I kind of make a habit of it," I confessed. "I want a woman to like me in spite of my failures. Warts and all, as they say."

Jordan squinted, and I imagined a thought bubble over her head with a line of questions stretching to infinity inside it.

"How long were you married?" she asked.

"Seven years."

"And when did you go on the site?"

I took a beat to summon up the CliffsNotes version of my marital history. I didn't mind being an open book, but I also didn't want to drop the whole thing on the table before we even ordered dessert.

"About two years before we split," I answered. "We'd never been all that passionate. But one day, we hadn't made love in like four months, and I saw a television special about the site. On Dateline, I think. I signed up, met a cute neuroscience major who needed money for books, and kinda never looked back."

"No sex for four months would do it for me, too," Jordan sympathized.

"Honestly, we were never all that compatible. We just both wanted kids so badly that we settled."

"Did you guys try to work things out? Go to therapy?"

"Are you kidding? We had a therapist; I had a therapist; she had a therapist. Hell, Elizabeth *is* a therapist!"

Jordan guffawed. "I'm sorry, that's too ironic."

I knew it was rich but refused to reward my bad behavior, even now. "Look, I shouldn't have started cheating. I figured paying for one-night stands was better than having full-blown affairs, but obviously that was a ridiculous rationalization. Whatever problems we had, that wasn't the right way to deal with them."

"Is it rude of me to ask how many women you cheated with?" Jordan asked.

"I don't think it's rude," I answered. "But I'd hate to turn you off on our first date."

"Believe me, I won't judge."

I smiled and relented. "I haven't actually counted, but I'm guessing a few dozen."

"Wow," she said, sounding more impressed than shocked. "How did it all come out? Did she catch you?"

"No. One day we were in couples therapy, and I was just overcome with guilt and confessed."

"That must have been some therapy session," Jordan quipped.

"Believe it or not, she wasn't even that shocked. She'd kind of suspected."

"Wait, so she wasn't even upset?"

"Oh, there were some tears," I sighed. "But looking back, I realize the fact that we dealt with it like such adults was a sign of how little passion we had for each other. Our divorce mediator said she's never had a couple who were so amicable."

"That's saying something."

"But I learned my lesson. I haven't lied to a woman since. These days I practice 'radical honesty.'"

"I love that term," she said. "Honesty and transparency are so important to me. Really, everything else is negotiable."

I couldn't help a mischievous schoolboy grin from hijacking my face. "Everything?"

"I guess that depends on how kinky you are..."

Thank God, we're back to flirting, I thought. "I'm fairly vanilla. A woman once asked me to choke her during sex. I couldn't bring myself to close my hands around her throat, and she started laughing at me."

Jordan laughed—with, not at me, I sensed. "Clearly I'm no Christian Grey," I went on. "I get off on pleasing a woman, not torturing her. Crazy idea, huh?"

"Crazy."

The space between our smiles was intruded by one busboy clearing our plates, another cleaning our tablecloth. I was so eager to turn the conversation to Jordan that I didn't even wait for them to finish—I just angled my head to the side.

"Enough about me," I said. "What got you into dating this way?"

She angled too. "I'd always been kind of intrigued by the idea. Then, ten months ago, I had a really bad breakup."

I straightened my neck as the busboys left. "I'm so sorry to hear that."

"Thank you, but I'm over it," Jordan answered with a smile that hid no PTSD. "But I was kind of an emotional train wreck for a while. We were together for two years. I thought we were going to get married. Then one day, out of the blue, I get this text from him telling me he wanted to break up, and that I had to move all my shit out of his place before he got home from work. I literally had three hours to move two years of stuff back to my place."

"Wait, back up," I said with disbelief. "He broke up with you by text?"

"Wouldn't even take my calls."

"And he didn't say why?"

"Nothing that made sense. Said he 'outgrew the relationship.' But Ray was sober for a few years before we met, so I think he may have fallen off the wagon and didn't want to admit it."

"Ohhhh," I sighed. "Still, that's cruel."

"I was a physical trainer, but I couldn't work for months, so I lost all of my clients, maxed out my credit cards. One day, I went to get on the subway and my MetroCard was empty. I had zero cash. So, I jumped the turnstiles."

Jordan made the cutest confessional face, and my mouth gaped—at once, she'd impressed and concerned me. "Couldn't you have gone to family for help?" I asked.

She rolled her eyes. "Are you kidding? My mother wouldn't be able to sleep if I told her *that*. She's a fucking lawyer."

I laughed. "Yeah, I can see how she might flip a wig. But I mean in general, wouldn't they help you?"

"They would, totally. But then I'd have to deal with her and my dad worrying and asking a million questions and begging me to give up New York and move back to Colorado."

"I get it," I answered. My parents were generous in a million ways and often gave their children and grandchildren checks as gifts on their birthdays and anniversaries, but I was proud that I'd stopped relying on their money and proved my independence in my twenties.

"I knew I'd pull my shit together eventually," Jordan continued. "I decided it was time to go on the site, meet some nice men, and maybe have a little extra cash to do some of the things I couldn't do working eleven hours a day in a gym."

I smiled inside at how Jordan said, "extra cash." Despite her tale of having once jumped turnstiles, Jordan could hold a real job. She wasn't like so many of the women on Seeking Arrangement who made being a sugar baby their full-time work.

"What else?" I asked Jordan. "Any long-term goals, dreams, ambitions…?"

"So many things," she sighed wistfully. "I've always wanted to get yoga teacher training."

"That's refreshing," I said. "I've met a lot of women on the site who were just looking for shopping sprees."

"Ha! I hate shopping. Unless it's at Target. I can spend hours there wandering the aisles."

Could this be girl be any more modest?

"Although I'm not immune to a little spoiling," she conceded. "Listen to this—the first guy I met on Seeking took me to lunch, then to Neiman Marcus—he buys me these ridiculously expensive Manolo heels and a Chanel purse. And as he's paying, he slips a thousand dollars into the damn thing."

"Just for having lunch with him?"

Jordan laughed. "Well, I did go home with him. He had this three-story townhouse on the Upper East Side. Turns out he owned a big piece of a baseball team."

"Hell of a first arrangement," I said, hiding a shade of intimidation. As generous as I was, I was a modestly successful film producer, leagues away from owning a sports team.

"Yeah, too bad he was a coke addict," Jordan deadpanned.

I cracked up—she pitched a story like a producer!

"I've heard there are a few billionaires lurking around the site," I said. "I've also heard they're the craziest, but they throw around so much money that it's hard for a girl to say no."

"Oh, I said no pretty fast," Jordan said demonstrably. "He liked to go out every night, show me off at dinner as the age-appropriate girl-friend, then go to clubs and get wasted. After five weeks of all-nighters, I was out."

"Well, you don't have to worry about *me* partying," I said. "I haven't had cocaine since my high school prom. I barely even smoke pot these days."

"Ditto. I only took sniffs here and there to make him happy. But I ran into a friend of his right before I left for LA, and he said the league made him check into rehab."

"Ejected from the game, was he?" I joked.

"Hah!" Jordan said with that signature breathy laugh again.

And I thought, *I would never get tired of listening to her laugh.*

"YOU TAKE THE LAST bite."

"No, it's yours."

"Seriously, I'm stuffed."

"So am I!"

Jordan and I stared at each other, the last morsel of blackberry crumble on a plate between us—we were in a dessert standoff, each of us more eager to please than be pleased.

"Well, it would be a gastronomical crime to not eat that," I finally pronounced, then used my spoon to part the crumble into two pieces so minuscule they seemed to float in the soup of melted salted caramel ice cream. "Carbs *and* sugar. Guess we proved you can have more than one soul mate."

We slipped our bites into our mouths and seemed to groan in blissed unison.

"We're pretty compatible, don't you think?" Jordan asked.

"Very!"

I placed my spoon down beside the espresso I'd polished off. By now, I had no doubt that Jordan and I were destined to begin an arrangement. All that was left to negotiate were a few key details. "So is there anything specific you're looking for in an arrangement?" I asked. "Beyond honesty and transparency."

"Not much. I'd be curious to know how often you might like to get together?"

"Once or twice a week would be good to start, don't you think?"

"Once or twice a week would be ideal," she said with a satisfied smile. "And you? Anything I should know about what you'd like?"

"Just what it says on the site," I answered. "No strings attached; all the perks of a relationship without the drama."

Jordan laughed. "No drama. Noted."

"And I assume you're okay with not being exclusive?" I asked.

"No problem whatsoever."

Though Jordan answered as I'd expected—people on Seeking were in no hurry to commit to monogamy on a first date—I decided to elaborate on my reasons for asking. On this point, I was pretty specific. "I guess now would be a good time to tell you that I'm not a big believer in monogamy. You know what 'ethical nonmonogamy' is?"

"Of course. Honestly, I don't think monogamy is at all practical. Every man I've dated has cheated on me."

"I don't know a man who hasn't cheated at some point in his life. Except maybe my father. I hate to sound cynical, but I guess the failure of my marriage made me, well, cynical."

Jordan chuckled. "Of?"

"It all—love, marriage, commitment. I read this interesting book called *The Monogamy Gap*. It says that statistically, people who *don't* cheat in relationships are in the minority, so we'd all be better off if we accepted that nature didn't wire us to be with just one person."

"I'll have to get it. And you're preaching to the choir. Have you read *Mating in Captivity*?"

I brightened—clearly, I'd met my existential match. "By Esther Perel, of course. The other day I watched a TED Talk she gave—she said monogamy was invented so that a farmer would know what child was his and who got the cows when he died."

Jordan laughed for the hundredth time. I smiled and decided that as long as we were being so forthcoming, now would be a good time to address the subject of safe sex—an unromantic but necessary conversation.

"Listen, I hate to ruin the moment," I said. "But since we're going to spend so much time together, would you be okay if we shared tests and agreed to wear protection with anyone else?"

"Oh, of course," Jordan answered without flinching. "I had a complete physical right before I left New York. I'll text you them now." She reached behind her chair for her purse and pulled out an iPhone wrapped in a pink silicone case, her long fingers and neat, unpolished nails tapping away.

I pulled my phone from my jeans pocket to do the same. "By the way, you don't have to worry about getting pregnant with me."

I pantomimed cutting with scissors—the universal sign for a vasectomy.

"Good to know…" she flirted.

"Yeah, I'm done," I said. "You? Want kids one day?"

Jordan slipped her phone back into her purse. "I don't know, I'm sort of a big kid myself."

I laughed, fine with her noncommittal answer. The thought of dating a woman who wanted to have her own children was a romantic dead-end for me, but then so was the idea that any *arrangement* would turn into *love*.

Then I heard, "Thank you, Mister Winkler," and saw our check placed on the table as our dessert-demolished plate was cleared.

"Thanks for the amazing dinner!" Jordan said.

"You're so welcome!"

As I took out my wallet, a sudden realization gripped me. In this little negotiation Jordan and I had exchanged, what struck me wasn't what she had asked of me, but what she *had not* asked of me. So many women I'd met on Seeking were in such a hurry to ask how much I planned to pay them. Now, I knew Jordan hadn't joined the site or accompanied me on this dinner date for my charm alone. But the fact that she hadn't even hinted at the financial aspect of our arrangement made me feel our connection was genuine.

"You've seen the outside of my house," I said. "How would you like to see the rest?"

Jordan's smile was my answer.

3

THE RARE GENTLEMAN

"HOW LONG HAVE YOU lived here?" Jordan asked as we stepped into the narrow entry that divided my living and dining room.

"Four years. It's been the perfect place for me and the kids—their mom's house is only a five-minute drive away, and I can walk them to school every morning."

"What a set-up." Jordan nodded her chin at a door under the stairwell with an impish grin. "What's in there? Secret dungeon?"

"Just a closet," I chortled, but opened the door. I knew it could be scary for a woman to go into a man's house, especially on a first date, and I wanted Jordan to feel safe. If a woman went to bed with me, I wanted more than her consent. I wanted her trust.

"You could really hurt someone with that Batman umbrella," Jordan dropped sarcastically as she peered into the closet lined with my kids' superhero-themed rain gear.

I laughed and closed the door, then walked beside her into the living room. Jordan stooped to study a picture frame on an end table beside the couch: me strolling on the beach between my son, Eli, who had my hazel eyes and brown hair, and Chloe, who shared her mother's blonde locks and blue eyes.

"Your kids are such angels," she cooed, then brightened playfully. "I want to meet them!"

Obviously, she was kidding, but I played along. "Maybe on our *second* date."

"Hogwash!" she teased.

I laughed, but in truth, I was so protective of my kids that I hadn't yet introduced them to a single woman since their mom and I split.

"Very chic…" Jordan remarked, glancing down beneath our feet at a giant area rug—a woven mural depicting dinosaurs frolicking through Jurassic fauna.

My face was getting tired of laughing at myself, but it managed one more time. "Okay, maybe it's not the sexiest of bachelor pads."

She smiled, undeterred. "Somehow it works for you, David."

I WALKED JORDAN THROUGH the rest of the downstairs—an office-turned-playroom with windows facing the small grassy backyard, and a small formal dining room, seldom used because of my less-than-average cooking skills. And finally, into the kitchen.

"Red Vines!" Jordan exclaimed at a jar filled with my kids' candy reserves.

"Help yourself," I started, but she'd already dug into them and was biting into a twisted red rope.

"They're fresh, too," she declared like a true confectionery connoisseur.

I watched her lips spread into a smile as she chewed, as if she were well aware of how damn adorable she was.

I have to kiss her before she takes another bite. I nestled up to her and slipped my arms around her waist. "May I?"

Jordan placed the candied rope on the counter and laced her hands behind my neck.

Those full lips I'd found so inviting softly met mine and our tongues merged, the taste of candy accentuating what was nothing less than a perfect kiss.

I drew Jordan's hips against mine so she could feel how hard she instantly made me. She pulled her mouth from mine and gasped, tilting her head back.

"Come with me," I whispered.

Our hands found each other's, and I led her out of the kitchen, back through the dining room, toward the stairwell.

A gentleman walks behind a woman when going upstairs, I reminded myself. *So if she falls, she falls on you.*

Jordan stepped up ahead of me but kept my hand clutched in hers.

At the top, she paused and looked to me for direction.

"This way." I guided her to the right, past the open door to my children's room, their bunk bed illuminated softly by streetlights through their windows. Jordan glanced at the room and exchanged a little smile with me, as if in silent agreement that there were more adult matters enticing us.

I let go of Jordan's hand reluctantly to draw the curtains on my glass-paned balcony doors while she walked to my bed and turned to face me. Behind her on the bedside tables were candles, but the idea of interrupting the perfect mood by lighting them seemed like a sin. And though it was completely silent in the bedroom, I couldn't risk ruining it by fumbling through my phone to find music to play.

I moved in front of Jordan, and we kissed again. She brought her hands between us to unbutton her dress.

"Let me," I softly pled and brushed her hands away. My face went to her neck to kiss and lick her skin, lowering with every button my hands released.

Jordan let out a moan, and I slid her dress off.

Then I took two steps back.

Unposed and unguarded in her black lace bra and matching panties, Jordan smiled and allowed me not just to admire her, but to imprint this vision of her into my memory. She reached behind her back, unhooked her bra, and let it fall atop her dress. I detected the slightest insecurity in her as she arched her back so the slope of her breasts would fight gravity, but all I could see was her natural beauty. If Jordan had a physical defect, it was lost on me.

I pulled my sweater over my head while she sat down and reclined herself on her elbows. Lowering myself to my knees, my head moved toward her inner thighs, and she spread her legs slightly while I kissed my way forward.

I used a finger to gently push the black lace aside and slipped my tongue inside her where a stream of wetness greeted me. She was freshly shaven or waxed, and she tasted and smelled like she'd just stepped out of a bath. Even as Jordan moaned and her body shivered, I could sense that she was deeply relaxed, allowing me to please her.

She released a guttural groan and shuddered. I knew I could stop but didn't want to until she reached down to cup my face and guide me up, rolling aside so I could lie on the bed. Her lips tapped mine, then she began kissing my cheek, then my neck, licking and nibbling.

"My weak spot…" I uttered as I felt myself lose control of my limbs and stared at the ceiling in wonder.

Jordan kissed her way to my chest and down my stomach while she unbuckled my belt. I shut my eyes and felt her warm mouth envelop me, aided by a licked-wet hand. Her head rose up and down, seldom coming up for a breath, then faster.

I grasped for the comforter, close to bursting, and gasped, "Wait… not yet."

Jordan pulled her head up, slid her body forward and then lowered herself atop me, allowing me to enter her; my body tingled as I slid deep into her warm insides. She moaned with me, perched forward so the tip of my penis was angled perfectly to the spot she wanted, then rose up and down on me rhythmically.

I raised an arm and pulled her into a kiss, but as I brought my arm around her waist to switch positions, she pushed my hand away and planted her palm on my chest.

"Do it," I urged, feeling the desire to please her take hold of me.

Jordan slipped back and forth on me, and I thrust my stomach and back up, giving her a base on which she could grind.

"*Fuck!*" she cried out as she shuddered again, this time more forcibly.

"Oh, fuck!" I allowed myself to let go, timing so we came together.

She buckled atop me, her face falling onto my shoulder.

I drew my hand to my face and covered my eyes, feeling almost embarrassed by the overwhelming rush of chemicals swirling through my head and tingling every nerve ending throughout my body.

"Amazing," Jordan whispered.

Catching my breath, I grasped for a way to describe how I felt, until one word came to mind. "Magic," I murmured back.

GOOD MORNING! I TEXTED JORDAN as I stood in the kitchen, waiting for that beautiful music my espresso machine made while brewing to stop. Call me when you're up so I can thank you properly.

I mixed half a Sweet'N Low into my coffee, thinking that Miss Wellness Warrior probably wouldn't approve of the aspartame I was ingesting, then sat at my breakfast table. I didn't expect Jordan to answer for a few hours—it was only 8:00 a.m., and she'd left at 2:00 a.m., so she was probably dead to the world. But I wanted her to wake up and see that I'd made my gentlemanly "morning-after" gesture the minute I started my day.

I also wanted to put the financial aspect of our arrangement to bed. A couple of women I'd dated told me that when they first signed up for the site, they made the newbie mistake of letting men get away with treating their first date as a "test drive." The men dangled the promise of tens of thousands of dollars, shopping trips, and luxurious vacations, got the woman to bed, then disappeared the next morning. I, on the other hand, took such pride in being a gentleman that on the occasion I didn't think I was compatible with a date, I would still thank the woman with some money, so she didn't feel taken advantage of. But after last night, I obviously had no doubt that Jordan and I were compatible.

The only question in mind was, *How much should I give her?*

Deciding I should refresh myself with Jordan's expectations, I logged onto the Seeking Arrangement app. My profile came up, my handle being "The Rare Gentleman."

I put effort into accurately portraying myself on the site. In the "About Me" section, I described myself as a "sane, happy, and healthy creative businessman." In the "What I'm Seeking" section, I wrote that I sought "an exceptional woman, who sees my support as a way to enjoy a better lifestyle than she might be able to afford on her own." I also posted very recent pictures, which was no small lure—women told me horror stories about showing up to first dates to find men had catfished them with pictures taken twenty pounds and ten years ago.

I noticed my inbox blinking with eighteen new messages, around the average number I got in a day. As ego-boosting as that might have been, the website boasted over ten million members, so it was rather a testament to its popularity. The better-known dating sites like Bumble and Tinder have twelve and eight, respectively, so this might give you an idea of how popular, if under wraps, the sugar dating lifestyle is.

I found Jordan's messages and clicked through her profile to "Lifestyle Expectations." On Seeking Arrangement, a woman checked a box to indicate what sort of monthly allowance she hoped to find. "Practical" was $1,000–$3,000 per month, "Moderate" was $3,000–$5,000, "Substantial" was $5,000–$7,000, and "High" was $7,000–$10,000. Jordan had checked "Substantial," but I knew from experience these amounts were *very* negotiable. In fact, I'd been told it was hard for a woman to get a monthly allowance at all—it was sort of the holy grail of arrangements. The website frowned on "Pay Per Meet" dates as it was too akin to straight-up prostitution, and even warned on their welcome page that they'd remove any member who was caught negotiating them, but everyone got around that by calling Pay Per Meets "short-term" allowances. I'd yet to find many women who weren't satisfied with five hundred to a thousand dollars a date. And I was happy to give it—all of my arrangements had started out as pay per date. Then, if we enjoyed each other's company, we'd switch to a monthly allowance.

From what Jordan had told me about her arrangement with the baseball team owner, I had little doubt she'd be thrilled if I gave her a thousand dollars each date, maybe even less because *I wasn't a cocaine addict*. But last night's date had gone so well, I wanted to put my best foot forward and offer Jordan a monthly allowance right away.

I did a little of my own lifestyle expectation calculating in my head. Jordan and I had discussed seeing each other twice a week, but I wasn't so rich that I'd be comfortable giving her $8,000 a month! As successful as I was, it may surprise you to learn I had no trust fund, little savings to speak of, and spent close to thirty thousand dollars a month on alimony, child support, mortgage payments, the lease on the Westwood house, and expenses. I concluded I could safely afford giving Jordan $4,000 a month.

I furtively shrank. I knew 4K would hardly pay for the gas on the private plane that baseball team owner probably flew in. And though I wasn't a "salt daddy," as some girls dubbed cheap men, I wasn't one to take girls shopping for expensive purses and shoes unless it was their birthday.

My phone buzzed in hand. I hit "Accept" and clicked on the speaker. "You're up early!"

"Hi, sweet man!" Jordan chirped. "Yeah, I dragged my ass out of bed and I'm headed to workout class."

"And what a beautiful ass it is," I complimented. "Thank you again for our night."

"I don't know where to begin..." Jordan gushed. "Safe to say we're sexually compatible."

"Beyond," I agreed. "But I don't want to make you late for your class, so let me know if there's anything you want to discuss before I send you your allowance?"

"Nothing on my end, really," she said. "What were you thinking of giving me?"

"I was thinking I could give you four thousand a month," I said quickly and far more confidently than I felt inside.

"I'm more than happy with that!" Jordan replied instantly. "To be honest, after last night I'd have taken *anything* you offered."

"That's sweet of you to say."

"It's true. I feel so lucky to have found the one decent guy on the site. Text me later and tell me your availability, and we'll schedule our next date."

"Availability?" I scoffed. "You must have me confused with those Hollywood types that say, 'I'll have my assistant call your assistant.' So... how is Friday night? I have the kids tonight and for the next few days."

"Friday night it is! But wait, I *do* have one question!"

"Shoot."

"Well, I don't know anybody out here. But if we run into any of your friends while we're out and they ask how we met, what should I say?"

I laughed. I'd never even *thought* about that little detail in an arrangement. Nobody in my family or circle had ever met anyone I'd dated, so I'd never used a cover story. "Why don't we say we met on Facebook?" I suggested. "A mutual friend posted a picture of you together, so I asked him if you were single."

"Love that!"

I could hear the dinging of Jordan's car door opening and knew I needed to wrap it up. "Send me your PayPal or Venmo."

"Doing now," she said. "Thank you so much for your generosity. And your perfect cock, by the way."

My heart skipped a beat—I did like a classy woman who wasn't afraid to talk dirty. "You're welcome to both."

We hung up, and my phone pinged with the link to Jordan's Venmo account. I typed $4,000 into the amount line and pressed send, but a pop-up commanded me to "please enter a note" in the "What's This For" section. I tried to come up with a discreet way of describing the nature and prospects of our new relationship. "TBD," I wrote as in "To Be Determined."

I put down my phone and lifted my espresso, feeling giddy. *Of course Jordan accepted my offer*, I realized. I might not be a billionaire, but I went to the ends of the earth to make a woman feel safe. A woman could trust me and count on me. And what was more attractive to a woman than that? For close to a hundred thousand years, Homo sapiens were hunter-gatherers. A man who couldn't build or provide a safe place—a cave or fire—and bring food back to the tribe had zero chance of attracting a mate.

But I, the Rare Gentleman, provided.

4
DADDY FIX-IT

As EAGER AS I WAS to see Jordan again, I had my kids for the next few days. And when I say I was "with" or "had" or my kids, I really mean that. I rarely hired nannies or babysitters, always left work early to pick them up from school, and pulled out what little hair I had left to help them with their homework. My devotion to my children was such that my friends and family regularly called me "Super Dad."

My kids, though, had a different nickname for me—one Jordan learned on our next date.

She and I decided to stay in, order sushi, and watch a movie. Jordan arrived wearing faded black jeans, a green shiny bomber jacket, a T-shirt, and Converse slip-on sneakers, no jewelry—the antithesis of what you'd expect a sugar baby would wear on any date.

Over dinner we discussed what to watch. Jordan told me her favorite film of all time was *Pretty Woman*, and that she'd seen it countless times as a young girl. I pointed out that she, with her face-wide smile and breathy laugh reminded me of Julia Roberts. I teased her that her movie selection revealed no small insight into her dating choices. "What woman wouldn't want to be a sugar baby, growing up thinking she might meet a billionaire who looks like Richard Gere?"

I had seen *Pretty Woman* a few times and loved its fairy-tale message about two people saving each other, so we rented it, kicked off our shoes, and burrowed under a giant Neapolitan-striped cashmere blanket on the couch.

As the opening credit sequence rolled up on my flatscreen, I felt like there was a magnet under my skin, pulling me toward Jordan.

"I'm literally buzzing for you," I murmured.

Jordan seemed equally perplexed by her inability to focus on the movie. "Every guy I've ever dated has told me I'm unaffectionate, but here I am snuggling with you on a second date!"

We moved in for a kiss, which quickly turned into pulling our jeans and underwear to our ankles, too eager for the delay of a full disrobing.

And so we had our first "quickie" on our second date.

After, we huddled under the blanket again, but I found myself so relaxed and content I kept drifting off to sleep. I'd catch myself and sit up to find Jordan laughing at me.

"The whole point of watching this movie was watching it with you," she said, trying to pretend she wasn't annoyed.

"I'm sorry. My kids tease me I fall asleep so early they should be putting *me* to bed."

"That's cute," Jordan cooed. "What do they call you, by the way? Dad, Daddy, Dadda?"

"They have all sorts of nicknames for me. There's Daddy Damn It—as in, when they ask why they have to eat broccoli, I say, 'Because I said so and I'm Daddy, damn it!'"

Jordan laughed. "And?"

"Well, they also call me Daddy Fix-It."

"Daddy Fix-It? Are you handy around the house?"

"Please! I can repair toys, toilets, paint walls, steam-clean carpets…I can even patch holes in drywall."

"Everything but stay awake," Jordan goaded me with a smile. Then she planted a kiss on my cheek, untangled herself from our magnetic pretzel of limbs, and began dressing. "Well, Daddy Fix-It, I'll take the hint and let you get your rest."

❧

I LEANED INTO THE nickname Daddy Fix-It with the same good humor as being called a sugar daddy, but being a man who tried to fix problems was something that went far deeper. I saw myself as a very practical, levelheaded, and optimistic man and thought of few problems in life as unsolvable. Maybe this was why I was a decent film producer—a producer is the person called to solve a problem before it becomes a crisis. The studio thinks the script sucks, the producer sequesters the writer in his office until the scenes sing. An actor doesn't get along with a director and locks himself in his trailer, the producer forces a sit-down and soothes egos. A film is running twenty minutes too long, the producer rolls up his sleeves and spends nights in the editing room going over "the cut."

But the limits of what I could fix were tested on the night of my third date with Jordan.

WE HAD CHATTED THAT morning while I made my cappuccino (it was becoming second nature to wish her "good morning" during my routine) and confirmed dinner plans. I followed up later with some restaurant suggestions to no response. Finally, I called and left a message on her voicemail, "Can't wait to see you tonight! I'll send an Uber at seven!"

Then it was seven. Then it was eight. And then it was obvious we weren't having a date.

Sitting before my television, watching Donald Trump give his daily lie about something or another, I tried to tell myself there were worse things in the world than being stood up by a woman. And this was so unlike Jordan, I assumed there *had* to be a good reason for her disappearance. Had she dropped her phone in the toilet, and it was now sitting in a bowl of rice? And of course, being a mild hypochondriac, I worried something—a horrible "something"—had happened to her.

So I sent her the obligatory Are you okay? text.

No answer.

Now, if Daddy Fix-It or Super Dad or Daddy Damn It had one weakness, one emotional kryptonite so to speak, it was his obsession with good communication. I'd once heard it said, "Love means never having to ask, *did you get my text*?" And as glib as it might sound, I applied this saying to all types of relationships. Replace the word Love with Like, Friendship, Respect, or plain Good Manners, if you will, and the statement stands. To me, the speed at which someone responds to a text or call speaks volumes not only to their respect for you, but to their enthusiasm.

But good communication was also my superhero power. (Isn't it funny how our emotional strengths are also our weaknesses?) If I had a date and *my* phone was out of order, I would have used my iPad or computer to find my date's Apple-matched contacts and let her know. And if I hadn't backed up my contacts, I'd message her on Instagram, Facebook, or on Seeking Arrangement. If a dreaded "something" happened to *me*, nothing short of having a breathing tube stuck down my throat would keep me from telling a nurse to let my date know I'd be slightly delayed!

But this night, I tried to be understanding and patient. *After all,* I told myself, *Jordan and I are just an arrangement.*

At 10:00 p.m., my phone pinged with a text from her.

I am so sorry about tonight!!

Attached was a picture of her forearm resting on a hospital gown, an IV injecting fluid into her skin.

I felt like a complete idiot. *How could I have even doubted Jordan's communication skills?*

Oh, no! What's wrong? I quickly replied.

I was vomiting all day and went to the ER. They gave me some fluids and ran some tests.

Which hospital? I'll come there now.

I'm home now. They think it was dehydration. I've had stomach issues on and off for the past few months.

What a terrible day for you, I wrote. What's going on with your stomach?

I'm not sure. Know any gastroenterologists here in Los Angeles?

Did Daddy Fix-It know a good doctor in Los Angeles? Please...

I am a member of a private Jewish Country Club, I pointed out, and sent her the names and numbers of two specialists I golfed with.

You're better than Yelp! she wrote back.

I'll leave my ringer on all night in case you need me, I promised.

❧

MY PHONE DIDN'T RING that night, so I left a "hope you're feeling better" text first thing in the morning, then took my kids to a Saturday outing at Dave & Buster's.

I stood behind them while they rode The Typhoon, perched side by side on chairs that shook and rocked as a video cast images of the rollercoaster ride from hell, when Jordan FaceTimed me.

"Be right back!" I yelled to my kids through the clatter of videogames. I slipped into a nearby room the arcade kept for private parties where I could keep an eye on them through a glass wall.

"Looks like you're on the mend!" I gasped at the vision on my screen—Jordan sat on the small lawn of her Venice apartment, wearing a black bikini and sucking on a Pedialyte pop.

"Pedialyte has magic powers," she boasted and licked a trickle of pink from her knuckle. "I want to make last night up to you."

"As soon as you're feeling romantic again."

Jordan laughed. "Well, that never goes away. I have a really high libido, even when I'm sick. I was going insane last night. I need to be fucked."

"Lord help me!" I groaned. "I have the kids till Monday."

"Damn," Jordan sulked. "I booked a flight back to New York on Monday—I have to see a doctor and figure out what's going on with my stomach."

"Why don't you see one of my doctors here?" I asked.

"I would if I could, but I talked to my GP, and she said I'll probably need a scope procedure or an MRI, which would cost a few thousand dollars. My shitty New York Medicaid won't cover anything done here."

"What insurance company expects its patients to never leave home?" I complained.

"Don't get me started on the politics of insurance," she pled. "You're probably insured through your company and can go anywhere?"

"I assume so. But honestly, I rarely get sick and can't remember ever doing so in another city."

"Lucky you," Jordan laughed. "But really, I'm kind of worried I might have a tumor or something."

"I simply won't allow you to be that sick," I answered.

Jordan raised a playful eyebrow. "Is that Daddy Fix-It or Daddy Damn It speaking?"

"Both."

I felt frustrated and had to admit to myself I'd encountered a problem I couldn't fix. Jordan's stomach issues had put her in the emergency room, and now she was headed back to New York for at least a few weeks, and there was nothing I could do to help her, short of offering to spend thousands of dollars to pay for her medical bills.

"And don't even think of offering to pay for me to see your doctors here," Jordan warned.

I had to grin—she seemed to be able to read my mind.

"And listen, I don't want you to feel like I'm taking advantage of you in any way," she furthered. "I'll be back in a week or two tops, but I'm happy to send you two weeks of the allowance you gave me."

"Are you kidding?" I answered. The thought that Jordan might be trying to cut and run with my money hadn't even occurred to me. But damn, she was showing Daddy Fix-It a thing or two—communicating and getting ahead of any possible resentment I might feel by her sudden departure.

"So we've only had two dates," I said. "If we added all the time we talked and texted, it would be like I'm only giving you minimum wage."

Jordan laughed. "You're too good to me."

5

GHOSTED FEELINGS

"SHE'S GOING TO LIVE!" declared Jordan on our FaceTime call as she walked the snowy streets of Manhattan, insulated in an indigo wool peacoat and black hoodie. "The exact diagnosis is post-bacterial IBS. Basically, my stomach hasn't fully recovered from an infection I had a few months ago."

"Great news!" I answered as I leaned back in my chair at my Beverly Hills office. (The address makes it sound lavish, but by Hollywood standards, it was a cubicle. The tight room barely fit a couch, and if it weren't for the scripts piled high on the carpet and posters of movies I'd produced on the walls, you'd never know what industry I was in—let alone "The Industry.")

"So how do you treat it?" I asked.

"More probiotics, less pizza," Jordan quipped.

I laughed. "Easy enough."

"But uch, that scope," she lamented with an adorable Yiddish accent.

"Bet you're sore."

"Yeah, my ass feels like it was probed by aliens."

I laughed again, but Jordan grimaced with comic mortification and said, "TMI?"

"With me? Hah. No such thing."

"I like that about you!" she said as she stepped off a curb and looked left and right. "God, it's gonna be impossible to find a cab during rush hour."

"Take the subway," I suggested. "You can even afford it now, won't have to jump the turnstile."

"I'll never live that down, will I?"

"Nope. Where are you headed, anyway?

"Back to my friend's place to rest up."

To rest up for what or whom? I wondered.

Mind you, I wasn't at all jealous by the idea Jordan might get her "need to be fucked" (as she'd so eloquently put it) filled. Whoever she was staying with while her Manhattan apartment was being swapped, and whoever she might be sleeping besides, was none of my business. But I was curious what Jordan's plans were for the rest of her trip, now that her health issues were out of the way.

"Speaking of friends…have any dates while you're there?" I asked.

Jordan smiled, all mystery. "I have a few invites, but *you're my priority*. I'm already looking at flights and should be back Monday or Tuesday!"

I like being called a priority, I thought. "Why don't I pick you up at the airport?"

She whistled at my romantic proposition. "God, I can't remember the last time someone did that. And you? Any exciting plans?"

"I'm still debating whether I should go to that thing on Saturday," I confessed.

Jordan squinted at the phone. "Wait, isn't your father getting an award? Why wouldn't you go?"

I realized we had our wires crossed. At one point, I'd told her I'd be attending a Producers Guild of America event because my father was being presented a lifetime achievement award. But now, I was referring to another party that happened to be occurring later that night.

"I meant the Sanctum party," I said.

"Ohhh…right," Jordan's face lit up with recognition. "Well, I get why you'd be hesitant. It's not really my scene, either. But why don't you go and try it out? Relax, have fun. Maybe I'll go to the next one."

I reached over and closed my door so nobody in my office would overhear. And even then, I lowered my voice as I said, "I don't know. After all, it would be my first *sex party*."

I SPENT THE NEXT few days vacillating on the idea of Sanctum, as I had since Tessa told me about it almost a year ago.

Living proof of the adage that one should never judge a book by its cover, Tessa was a twenty-seven-year-old, platinum-haired, naturally voluptuous swimsuit model who could talk your ear off about politics over sushi, then come home and give you the private lap dance of your life. One night, after she'd done *exactly that*, Tessa mentioned she moonlighted as a "hostess" at Sanctum's black-tie masquerade party, which was held at mansions around Beverly Hills the last Saturday of every month.

Of course, I'd always been aware my hometown was famous for its bacchanalian parties, but frankly, I had the heart of an introvert. In my teens, friends would invite me to 90210 house parties and downtown warehouse raves, but I'd pass, preferring to go to bed at nine so I could wake up for "dawn patrol" surf sessions. In my twenties, while some of my set were nightclub hopping or flying to Vegas, I was a film buff who'd bounce between movie theaters at the mall. Hell, I'd even pass on invites to those infamous Playboy Mansion parties. In my thirties, I traded surfing for flying and spent my nights solo in a single-engine Cherokee over Southern California. I'd turn off the cockpit lights and gaze in awe at the night sky, which was as close to being an astronaut as this near-sighted C-student could get. As my filmmaking career flourished in my forties, I avoided the Hollywood nightlife, rarely attending premieres or after-parties. Even at my own, I felt uncomfortable having to schmooze and became a master of the early "French exit."

And *sex clubs*? I imagined they were sleazy affairs where unattractive couples swapped partners indiscriminately, probably in cheap, disease-plagued motels, so the idea of going to one made me sick to my stomach.

But Tessa assured me Sanctum was an elite, members-only club modeled after the lavish, voyeuristic parties in the Tom Cruise movie

Eyes Wide Shut. Her job as a hostess was to wander nude except for a mask, as sexual décor. The club took anonymity so seriously, even members were required to wear masks to enter, and cell phones and cameras were confiscated at the door. Tessa showed me the Sanctum website—a password-protected site with no pictures. It only hinted at its delights, selling itself as "a place where people can safely and anonymously explore their wildest fantasies and kinky sides."

I didn't have any unfulfilled fantasies or much of a kinky side. I'd experimented with just about everything in the sexual alphabet, from Anal to Threesomes to Zip Tie cuffs, but I didn't really have a BDSM bone in my body.

"Well, maybe you'll find you have a kink or fetish you're not even aware of…?" Tessa slyly goaded me.

That did it. Tessa's suggestion was nothing short of an existential challenge. *How open-minded am I if I'm afraid to explore my sexuality?*

I applied to Sanctum the next day and set up a screening call with its owner, Damon. He and I made an instant connection. He too was amicably divorced, his kids were the same age as mine, and he was ethically nonmonogamous. The last bit was revealed when Damon asked why I thought I might be a good fit at Sanctum, and I shared my sugar daddy lifestyle. He accepted me on the phone, and I paid the $5,000 yearly fee.

But I found myself in no hurry to actually *go* to the party.

My three-month arrangement with Tessa ended (on friendly terms—she moved to Miami, where buxom swimsuit models are in even higher demand than Hollywood), and I invited Allison a couple of times, but she was never in town on the right weekend. And though I knew it wouldn't be hard to find a date to the most exclusive party in town, it seemed like going to my first sex club soiree should be with someone I trusted and wanted to share the experience with.

And going stag? Out of the question. The only thing an introvert hates more than going to parties is going to one *alone.* The idea of walking into a party by myself always filled me with dreadful insecurity, but walking into one filled with strangers fucking strangers? Forget it. Even if I was wearing a mask, I knew I'd feel like a giant loser—some middle-aged man who couldn't find a date and came trolling to get laid.

So, since then, on every fourth Saturday of the month, at around 9:00 p.m., I'd receive a text from Damon with an address where the ultra-secretive Sanctum party was being held that night. I'd stare at the text like an insecure teenager and then delete it. *I'll go to Sanctum next month.*

I DON'T WANT TO go to Sanctum tonight, I texted Jordan when I woke Saturday morning. I'd rather sit on a couch and watch a movie with you.

Lying in bed, I put the phone on my chest and wondered, *How long will it take her to answer me this time?*

Over the last few days, Jordan had been testing my "love means never having to have ask, *did you get my text?*" mantra. I'd reach out and wait hours, and when she finally did respond, it would be with little more than a curt "Jumping into a movie, talk later!" or "At a concert with friends, sorry I'm MIA."

Now, it didn't take a genius to guess Jordan's *friends* were probably of the male variety. And I had zero problems with this. In fact, it made me even more understanding of her delays. I appreciated that when she was with me, she wasn't on her phone with other men, so I wanted to offer her other dates this respect. But I'd woken up even more anxious about the idea of going to Sanctum than usual—I had this vague sense beneath my introversion laid a whole other, deeply personal objection I couldn't quite name or describe to myself. And since Jordan and I had been talking so frankly about everything up until a few days ago, I thought she might help me wrangle it from my subconscious.

Abiding by the principle that a person never gets what they need unless they ask for it, I wrote Jordan again, Can you find ten minutes to speak on the phone today?

And, to make sure she understood this was important to me, I added, well, It's really important to me.

THAT EVENING, I SMILED AND clapped, standing front and center at a table in the Beverly Hilton Ballroom as my father walked up to accept his award from titans of film Martin Scorsese and Robert DeNiro. The Producers Guild had played a highlight reel of only a few dozen of the fifty-seven movies my father produced, one of which had won an Academy Award for Best Picture.

At eighty-five, even as he was being celebrated for a lifetime of filmmaking, my dad's career was still going strong. When people asked if it was difficult growing up in his shadow, I'd answer, in all sincerity, "I see him as shade, not a shadow. He's like a giant tree that invites people to sit under it."

Clapping wildly at my table was my mother, an eighty-year-old blonde who moved from Los Angeles to New York at eighteen, worked as a secretary, then met my dad on a blind date. (At the time, she was making five dollars a week more than he was as an agent's assistant, so she clearly didn't married him for his money.) Next to her stood my older brother, also a producer, my younger brother, a law professor and author, and his wife of twenty years. And beside me was my ex-wife, Elizabeth. Eleven years younger than me, with blonde hair and blue eyes, my Oklahoma-born ex often came to these events because, as people joked, once you join the Winkler family, you never get out.

After my father's typically brief and humble speech, we settled in for the remaining hour of the awards show, and I took a moment to check my phone. I glanced through a few of my unread texts—friends congratulating my father and our family—then sighed as I realized there were none from Jordan.

It had now been almost twelve hours since I'd asked Jordan for ten minutes of her time. A few brief explanations for her absence popped into my head. *Broken phone…rice…too much pizza wreaked havoc on her stomach again so she's back in the ER…*but then popped out. No, this time I was pretty damn sure I was, as millennials say, being "ghosted."

But why, I had no clue. Jordan and I hadn't had an argument since we met. For a moment, I considered that maybe when we FaceTimed last and I reminded her about Sanctum, she might have been turned off by the idea. But if that was the case, why had she suggested she might go to the next one with me? Why would she tell me to relax and have fun there? No, I really couldn't come up with an explanation, and to my surprise, I was starting to feel rejected.

I looked up from my phone, wondering if anyone in my family would notice the frown lines etching into my forehead. On cue, my mother shot me a look I knew meant, "Put your damn phone away!" I couldn't believe it. *Fifty-two and still getting lectured on table manners.*

I slipped the phone into my tux jacket pocket. *Why would my mother, or anybody in my family for that matter, guess something was upsetting me?* As proud as I was to be part of such a regal clan, we weren't exactly an emotionally perceptive bunch. On the surface, we seemed intimate, greeting each other with hugs and kisses, and we'd have near-weekly gatherings filled with talk of politics, current events, travel plans, how the kids were faring in their schools, movies we were making or had seen, but we rarely discussed anything personal.

My father was generous with his time and career guidance and always quick to tell an amusing story, but most of the time he was stoic. Once, at lunch on a ski trip in Aspen when I was in my late twenties, I'd gathered the courage to pry a little and ask him why he was so outwardly unemotional. He shrugged and said simply, "So was my father." I pressed with questions about his childhood, but he seemed so uncomfortable with anything other than the most basic facts—his father was a poor, Orthodox Jewish fabric salesman—that I felt like I was pulling both of our teeth and gave up.

My mother was also, as they say, a "tough cookie." She hated to talk about herself. Everybody in the family loved when she told the rare story about her childhood. Her father was a bon vivant musical arranger and comedy writer who died of a heart attack in his early forties, and her mother once had a successful career on vaudeville playing violin. But whenever I asked my mom about her childhood, she'd scoff and say something like, "My mother was an alcoholic, what's more to say?" A lot, I thought, but I learned not to pry into my parents' inner lives.

A memory jutted itself into my consciousness—a prepubescent David with a mop of curly hair, in trouble with my mother for a reason I can't remember. (Did I refuse to wear a tie to Sunday dinner?) I trailed behind her through the house, arguing some point, until she finally shut herself in her room. I pounded on the door, yelling, "Can we please talk about this?" (Maybe this fostered my own obsession with communication.)

Labeled as "too sensitive," "confrontational," and "argumentative," I was sent to my first shrink when I was twelve. I recall feeling glad I had a place to vent, but I don't recall a single conversation with the man—we just built a lot of model airplanes. I quit therapy when I was fourteen but somehow never outgrew my reputation, which made me even less inclined to share *my* feelings with my family. I became like them—hiding my insecurities under a shiny armor of stoic pride.

I tried not to be too resentful of the cracks in my family's fairy-tale existence. And it was very convenient—it made it easy to hide my life as a sugar daddy. But it also left me in a bit of a lurch that night. *Who can I turn to to vent?*

I certainly couldn't talk to my ex-wife. Though we were great friends, and she was a damn good therapist, she wasn't privy to my lifestyle. What was I going to do tonight? Pull her aside and tell her I was upset because my newest sugar baby was missing in action? That would be an hours-long conversation.

I felt my phone vibrate in my tux pocket. I reached inside, where it sat nestled beside my mask, slipped it out and held it discretely in my lap under the table. I saw that I'd received a text—an address in Beverly Hills for the Sanctum party.

In Beverly Hills. Blocks from where I spent my childhood.

And in this moment, that vague, deeply personal objection to going to Sanctum wrested itself from my subconscious. The fact that the sex party was so close to home, literally and figuratively, made me realize below my existential doubt and introversion was unresolved familial, sexual shame.

I was aware mine was relatively minor—I had no sexual trauma or abuse in my history. No, it was your basic case of shame that came from growing up with parents who were a little sexually repressed. At our dinner table, the only subject more taboo than feelings was sex.

Of course, for all I knew, my parents could have had a healthy and happy sex life behind closed doors, but God help us if we cracked a sexual joke or made an innuendo at the dinner table. My father would get this sour look on his face we affectionately called "The Pickle," and that was that. For the life of me, I couldn't recall a single conversation I ever had with my parents about sex. I was certain they never had "the conversation" about safe sex and pregnancy. In fact, the *only* memory I could dredge up was from when I was maybe ten years old, sitting on the floor of the screening room in our house watching the foreign movie *Swept Away*. In the film, a female Italian castaway implores the captain with whom she's stuck on a desert island to "sodomize" her. My mother yelled, "David! Out!" and I fled the room. And though this example was obviously protective, it certainly set a tone of sexual shame that was hard to escape.

I thought I *had* escaped it. Here I was, a sexually adventurous sugar daddy, but now, I realized that joining a sex club was a whole other ball of wax. My dignified family and friends might let out a few gasps if they somehow learned I was a sugar daddy, but God knows they'd be embarrassed if it got out that I was going to kinky sex parties! The adult in me said I shouldn't care what they or anybody else might say. Hell, I wasn't famous—the Hollywood rag trade probably wouldn't even care enough about me to publish gossip. And what if it did? America these days was celebrating sex. Kim Kardashian's career had been propelled by an X-rated video that went public, and America had elected a man of infamous sexual infidelities president (may history forgive us). But my inner child was quaking in his boots, anxious that if my family discovered this new secret, I'd humiliate them and myself.

The nice Jewish prince was secretly a pervert!

I WAS STILL RUMINATING on all this after the awards show ended. My family gathered in the lobby, snapping pictures with our phones and sending them to each other on our group chat. But as they headed to valet parking for their cars or Ubers, I lingered a moment to post to Instagram.

I uploaded a picture of the Winkler men in tuxedos with the caption, "When mom insists the boys pose…we pose. Congrats to dad for the lifetime achievement." I watched it populate my very modest feed…

Right above a brand-new post of Jordan dining at some hip eatery in Soho.

To say I was disappointed would be an understatement. *Here I've been doting on this woman, but when I ask for ten minutes, she's too busy to even answer? But she has time for social media?*

And I had proof I was being ghosted!

My rejection was joined by humiliation. *Did Jordan con me? Have I given her four thousand dollars in exchange for a few dates and a best friend act?*

I laughed, defiant. *Fuck Jordan.*

I realized I needed to call my own Uber. I pulled up the app and stared at it. I started to type "Home" into the destination bar when suddenly it gripped me that Sanctum was the *perfect* place to go. Maybe my family's ability to stay on the surface emotionally was a talent to be called upon in times like this!

Where better to ghost my feelings than a sex club?

6

FINDING SANCTUM

I KNOTTED MY MASK's silk ribbons behind my head and peered through its eye slits at the driveway to a small Tudor mansion. By Beverly Hills standards, it was hardly sprawling or opulent—five or six bedrooms at most. But giant hedges obscured its facade, and I assumed privacy was more of a requisite than size for a sex party.

I stepped to the porch, where three men in black tie stood bathed in crimson light from sconces, the low vibration of bass from electronic dance music streaming from the house behind them. None of the trio wore masks, and two of them were obviously security, sporting clipboards, earpieces, and over four hundred pounds of muscle between them.

The third man had shoulder-length black hair, blue eyes, chiseled cheekbones, and a jutting chin, a less stocky Tom Cruise.

"Welcome to Sanctum," he announced with a broad smile. "I'm Damon."

I smiled back with an outstretched hand. "David Winkler."

"Of course!" He moved right past my hand and drew me into a soulful hug. "I was wondering if you'd ever come to a party!"

I laughed in lieu of excuses. "I'm excited for the experience."

Damon appraised me with devilish confidence. "You won't be disappointed. But we'll need your phone."

"Of course." I turned my phone off and handed it to one of the bouncers, who dropped it into a manila envelope before scrawling "DW" on its front with a black Sharpie.

Damon patted me on the back. "Hey brother, I really want to catch up. Go on in, and I'll find you later?"

"Sure," I obliged as one of the bouncers opened the door.

"Welcome to Sanctum, sir."

Before I had a chance to thank him, I was overwhelmed by the sight of two glorious female creatures sauntering toward me. Naked except for silver masks with the Sanctum logo (an upside-down teardrop with an eye in the center), towering black feathered headdresses, six-inch stilettos, and gold silk capes trailing behind them, it was if they were on some invisible, R-rated Victoria's Secret runway.

"Hello!" I grinned as they silently surrounded me—each lacing an arm through one of mine—and walked me into the foyer. The dance music grew louder, and through dim, erotic red and yellow lighting, I could make out a living room filled with dozens of masked members. Every man was in a perfectly tailored tux, and nearly all of the women in lingerie. And not just your basic lace bra and G-string—they'd obviously gone all out and were draped in the most elaborate, accessorized lingerie money could buy. Half of the women seemed attached to their male dates, but just as many flocked in circles, half-naked prom queens waiting to be invited to dance.

My creatures stopped and released my arms, which I guessed meant I was on my own.

"Thank you!" I called out over the music. They bowed, turned together and headed back to the front door.

Now what do I do? I spotted a bar across the room. Even if I didn't much like the taste of alcohol, busying myself with a drink would occupy a few minutes.

As I beelined to the bar through the living room, the Sanctum of it all started to present itself. A naked black woman wearing a lampshade over her head paraded by me with a handwritten sign taped to her chest, *"Touch Me."* A masked redhead in the tightest red latex bodysuit leaned against a chair back, toying a dildo strapped to her crotch. To my right, a man in a bunny mask and a plaid smoking jacket sat on a lounge chair tying Shibari ropes around a nude, blindfolded woman on her knees before him. I heard her gasp with pleasure as he tightened a knot, then a pained cry from another direction; to my left was a naked woman with a black leather hood and red ball mouth gag, handcuffed to a suspension frame, spread eagle, being spanked with a horsehair whip by a woman in a chain-bedazzled dominatrix getup.

Too self-conscious to stop and gawk, I landed at the bar behind three young women in lingerie. I caught a quick smile from one of them—a shortish, wavy-haired blonde girl in a white silk mask, her porcelain skin barely covered by white lingerie, a garter belt, and stockings. I smiled back politely as she was handed her drink and stepped out of the way. The bartender looked to me. Desperate for a prop to hide my nerves, I ordered the first thing that came to mind. "Rum and coke."

I watched him mix it and tried to adjust my mask to keep it from scratching the skin around my eyes. As I fumbled, I noticed a few men and women weren't wearing masks at all. I guessed the rule was that you had to wear it to enter, but once inside there were few rules, if any. I immediately recognized one of the unmasked faces—a late-night talk show host, then another, the long-haired singer of a classic rock band. *If they don't care who recognizes them, why should I?* I thought. *If I'm going to be a Sanctum member, I want to be a proud one.*

I tugged my mask off and dropped it into my jacket pocket. Nobody gave me a second look—until suddenly I heard a soft, high voice saying, "Excuse me, are you David?"

I hid my cringe and turned to see the blonde in white standing there as her friends wandered off. "Yeah, do we know each other?"

She seemed sweetly shy as she admitted, "Not really. I messaged you on Seeking Arrangement, but we never met."

I guffawed. "You're kidding me."

"What's so funny?"

"Just the coincidence of it all! But we never met up?"

"No, you told me I was too young for you."

I looked her up and down. "I did? I'm sorry. I hope I was nice about it?"

"You were! It's probably why I remember you. Most guys on there are rude, and they certainly don't care how young a girl is."

I couldn't recall the exchange but wasn't surprised. I generally found I had nothing to talk about with anyone under the age of twenty-five.

"How old are you?" I asked.

"Twenty-two. Here, maybe you'll recognize me without this," she said as she slipped her own mask off. "I'm Serena."

I studied her blue eyes, straight nose, and pink lips but couldn't place her. "I'm sorry. I've seen so many profiles over the years, I don't remember. But trust me, it wasn't because you're not attractive—you're stunning!"

"Thank you! And this is your first Sanctum?"

"Yes! Have you been to many?"

"A couple. A few of my friends are performers, and Damon keeps begging me to work, but I don't know. The shows are a little too raunchy for me."

"I can only imagine."

Serena looped her arm through mine. "Have you checked out the house yet?"

"No, what am I missing?"

"Well, people don't usually start hooking up until after midnight, but you never know. Want a tour?"

"Please!"

I grabbed my drink and followed Serena through the house, stopping at doorways to look into bedrooms, but they were generally empty. Every room had been cleared of the homeowner's personal effects. Each room was set up for sex—candles, duvets pulled off the bed, and jars of condoms on the bedside tables.

"The performance started," Serena whispered, as we arrived back down-stairs and joined a circle of guests surrounding a blazing fireplace. My eyes lit up. In front of me, a naked man with the physique of a Roman sculpture in a gold minotaur mask fucked not one, but two writhing women. Behind them stood three of the caped female hosts holding staffs topped by the teardrop logo, witches overseeing a Pagan ceremony.

The minotaur took his turns, moving from one performer to the next, fucking each from behind, then would direct them into position to make the girls go down on each other, or he would hand them a giant, shiny black double-headed dildo for them to use on themselves.

I was transfixed—I'd never seen any man fuck another woman in front of me, let alone this erotic theater.

The minotaur heaved as if he was orgasming inside one of the girls, then collapsed atop her. It struck me as a little staged, and I glanced at Serena, who agreed with an amused grin. Nevertheless, we applauded with the rest of the guests while the performers crawled from the room on all fours, their minotaur master behind them.

Just then, one of Serena's friends sidled up and whispered in her ear.

"Hey," my tour guide said apologetically to me. "One of my friends is having a minor crisis. I'll find you later?"

"Please," I answered. She slid away, and I swallowed my disappointment. For a few minutes there, I felt like I might have found a friend for the evening, but now I was once again looking like that middle-aged man trolling to get laid.

It was obvious the sex show had served its purpose. Couples were kissing and groping, starting to wander off to the bedrooms. I went to sip my drink but found nothing left but ice. Hardly tipsy, I approached the bar again and grabbed a prepoured champagne. Spotting my escape— double glass doors leading to the backyard—I slipped outside to find a brick patio surrounding a pool, lit up in a purple glow.

A stunningly beautiful naked woman with a red mask floated on a black flamingo raft in the pool. She had a champagne bottle in her hand and was sipping liberally while she laughed quietly, staring at the sky and swaying her head to the music coming from inside.

The Daddy Fix-It in me resolved to go find security and tell them there was a drunken guest at risk of drowning in the pool.

"Enjoying yourself?"

I turned to find Damon coming outside with a beautiful (of course) dark-haired woman. She looked no more than twenty-three, wore no lingerie or sexy dress, but instead a black pantsuit, and had little makeup on except the thinnest line of eye shadow and a touch of pink gloss on her brimming smile.

Damon glanced at the woman in the pool without concern, so I relaxed and complimented, "Quite a party."

"Just wait. David, this is Colette."

"Bonsoir," she said in a French accent as she removed a pack of Marlboros and a Bic lighter from a small leather clutch. "Want one?"

"No, thank you."

"Of course not. I love America, but this thing against smoking in any public place drives me insane. Especially since you make the best fucking cigarettes!"

"We're total hypocrites," I humored her.

"Sit down and chat for a minute," Damon suggested, pulling out chairs from a table.

We sat, and as Damon and I caught up, Colette listened and puffed elegantly on her cigarette. It had been several months since my interview, so I gave him a refresher—the kids were healthy, I was still amicable with my ex-wife, and I had a film in preproduction. Damon mentioned he was considering making a reality television show based on Sanctum and asked if I'd be interested in producing it; I told him I thought it was a great idea, but I didn't think my partners (a.k.a. my father and brother) would be open-minded about the subject matter. *(And here I am writing about my foibles—that's irony for you!)*

Unoffended, Damon switched topics, asking, "So tell me, what's going on with your love life? Seeing anybody special?"

Jordan came to mind, but I pushed her out. "I'm not tied down to anybody right now."

"That's right," Damon said to me, "You don't believe in monogamy, either. But fuck, I'm dying to fall in love again. It's just that every woman I've tried to have an open relationship with freaks out eventually. I think women are basically monogamous, even if they say they're not."

I hadn't encountered that problem in my arrangements, so I looked to Colette. "What do you think? Is it possible to be in a loving, nonmonogamous relationship?"

Colette tapped an inch of ash into a cocktail glass. "Don't look at me—I'm crazier than both of you."

"You can say that again," Damon laughed, then stood. "I need to check in and make sure everybody's playing nice."

I wondered if I should go back inside with him, but noticed Colette wasn't in a hurry to follow him. "I'll keep her company for a bit."

"Cool," Damon said, then left.

Colette bared her wide smile. "Aren't you a gentleman."

"I try," I said with a shrug. "So how are *you* crazy?"

"It's a long story."

"Please, a long story would save me from having to stand here looking like a loser without a date."

She laughed. "I like your honesty. Well, to start off with, I'm in a monogamous relationship with a *very* married man."

"I'm confused. It's monogamous because he doesn't have sex with his wife?"

"No, he fucks her too. Just not the way we fuck."

"What do you mean?"

"His wife is…vanilla. We're into more kinky stuff. Rape role play."

I stopped in the middle of a sip of champagne. *I've found the kinkiest woman at Sanctum, and she isn't even wearing lingerie or having sex.*

"It's totally consensual," Colette said with a laugh, clearly getting off on being provocative. "We have safe words, and even a sexual contract to prove it—in case some stupid tabloid outs him."

"Let me guess, he's a movie star?"

Colette drew her finger across her lips like she was zipping them up.

"Rare discretion in this town," I complimented her. "So what is it about role play that turns you guys on?"

Colette paused to consider. "This man is not like an ordinary man whose ego gets boosted when a woman wants to fuck him. *Every* woman wants to fuck him—it's ridiculous. So he gets off on how strong and powerful he feels when there's a struggle."

"Makes sense. And you?"

"I get off on the experience—learning what it's like to be someone else or be in some situation in a way you could never get reading a book or watching a movie. There's this rush of adrenaline when he attacks me that is beyond. Once, he came to my apartment, and I was angry with him because he hadn't called me in days, so I wouldn't let him in. He broke the door down and fucked me so violently I had bruises for days. But after that, no other man made me wet."

I may have gone a bit pale.

"Don't worry. The safe words. If I had wanted them, I'd have used them. There's power in being desired that much."

"Well, I certainly don't judge," I offered weakly.

"What are *you* into?" Colette probed.

"Me? I guess I'm pretty vanilla. Compared to *that*. Other than the fact that I'm what you call a sugar daddy."

She brightened. "Oh, that's interesting! I've never needed a sugar daddy. Not that I have any problem with it. It's just my parents are very rich back in France. They send me whatever I need."

"There she is!" Serena called out as she strode from the house, pointing at the girl in the pool. "Fuck, I was worried about her."

"Hiiii Serena," the drunk girl on the flamingo drawled.

Serena put her hands on her hips in amused frustration.

"You want me to swim in and pull her out?" I asked.

Serena shook her head. "No, she's safer in there. In her state if she goes inside, she might end up in a gang bang."

"Sounds fun to *me*," Colette dryly commented. "Listen, I'm going to sit out here and smoke, so I can watch her for a while if you two want to go back to the party?"

"You're not going back inside?" I asked Colette.

"Nah, once you've seen one orgy, you've seen them all."

I laughed. "I wouldn't know."

"That's so nice. Thank you!" Serena said to Colette as she took my hand. "Come inside with me. I've been thinking about you, and I have an idea on how we can make your first Sanctum something to remember."

"Who'd turn down *that* invitation?" I answered.

Colette called out, "I want a full report!"

I smiled, then realized something in our conversation was stuck in my craw. "Before I go, let me ask you something."

"Yes, darling?"

"Why be monogamous with someone who's married?"

She took a long drag, squinted, and let the smoke drift out of her mouth. "Because I love him. And love is legal insanity."

I laughed as Serena squeezed my hand and dragged me back through those glass doors.

Inside the living room, the party was in full swing. The lights had been dimmed, the music changed to an erotic trance, and in the shadows, I could see those prom queens dancing and grinding their pelvises against each other, as if they'd decided they didn't need any rich, single man to entertain them. *Touch Me* Girl was lying atop a pool table masturbating while three members ran their hands over her, taking turns kissing her. Bunny Man was getting a blow job from a girl with her hands tied behind her back, and Red Latex was in a corner plunging her dildo into someone—man or woman, I couldn't see, because a few members were crowding to watch. And I wasn't sure I wanted to see!

I downed the last of my champagne as Serena led me toward the bedrooms with a glance back. "Trust me, this will be fun." Happily tipsy, I smiled. She pulled me down the hallway and up the stairs, but this time every bedroom was a hive of sexual activity, members fucking their dates on every bed while others stood over them watching, fondling each other, waiting for the bed or an invitation to join. In one room, we saw Damon, tux pants at his ankles, thrusting into a woman who was bent over on the bed while she gave a blowjob to another member lying on his back while a beautiful Latina woman straddled his face.

I'd have been enthralled just to watch, but Serena turned me around. "Haley!" she called out.

Walking toward us was one of the creatures who'd met me at the front door, except she'd shed her cape and headdress. She wasn't wearing a mask now and had the face of an angel sticking out of long, flowing honey-brown hair. "Haley, this is David."

"Hi, handsome!" Haley said as she wrapped an arm around me and kissed my cheek.

"I thought the three of us could have some fun," Serena suggested, then added with a teasing challenge, "Unless you still think I'm too young, of course…"

I chortled. "Clearly, I was an idiot!"

Serena beamed and pressed her body against mine so she could whisper, "Will you take care of us?"

I knew *exactly* what she meant. "How much did you have in mind?"

"How is eight hundred each?"

"Perfect," I said, though I'd probably give them double that tonight.

"I know a private room," Haley suggested.

A girl hooked on each arm, I found myself walking back downstairs, only detouring by a man fucking a woman in a black cat mask against the stairwell railing, her neon pink lingerie panties dangling on the leg she'd raised like a ballerina.

Haley turned at the bottom and led us toward the kitchen, the only part of the house I hadn't seen yet. But before we could arrive there, she pushed open a hallway door and led us down a narrow flight of stairs, into a small basement room without windows, lit only by red-hued candles. The only furniture in the room was a massage table with fresh sheets, and a chair with baby oil and a basket of condoms atop it.

I climbed onto the table, watching Serena pull off her lingerie and reveal natural breasts women in town paid thousands to copy. Haley stood beside me, pressed her mouth against my face and slipped her tongue in to find mine.

Serena started unbuttoning my tux pants, so I laid back, coat and shirt still on. Haley helped her pull them down to my shoes with one hand, then deftly switched to pull Serena's white lace G-string off.

Serena climbed on the table, knees on either side of me, her ass hovering over my stomach, and leaned forward to kiss me.

I felt Haley's wet mouth on my hard cock for a few heavenly moments, then her hands sliding a tight condom on me.

Serena turned to face Haley, kissing her while she lowered herself on top, guiding me inside her. She felt tight and warm, but so wet there was no friction. She rode ever so slightly up and down on me while Haley licked and kissed her nipples.

Out of the corner of my eye, I noticed a few guests had come into the room and were watching. Between my instinctual moans, I asked myself if their gazes bothered or excited me—if I should maybe put my mask back on—but found I simply didn't give a damn who watched or might recognize me.

I felt like I was falling into a trance, and the next ten minutes were a blur...Serena moaning, "I'm fucking coming," and condoms being changed, me standing and fucking Haley from behind as she went down on Serena, more and more guests sliding into the room, crowding it with more people than I'd seen in any room so far that night, then Haley kissing me while Serena poured baby oil on my cock and stroked it faster and faster until I came on her chest.

And I heard *applause.*

"Holy fuck," I sighed and let my head fall back on the cushioned table.

SERENA, HALEY, AND I CLEANED up in the basement bathroom and walked together back up the narrow stairwell.

"That was so sexy," Haley commented.

"Who wants a drink?" Serena asked.

Elated but sobering, I thought a moment. "I'm heading home."

"Did everybody watching us freak you out?" Serena asked.

"Not at all! Honestly, tonight has been the erotic highlight of my life. I just think after that, *how can the party get any better?*"

Serena and Haley laughed in unison and then walked me to the front door. I hugged and thanked Haley, then Serena, whispering to her, "Message me again on Seeking tomorrow with your Venmo."

"Perfect."

I opened the front door and stepped outside, where the security team was waiting with a box of manilla envelopes. I gave them my name, and they handed me mine.

As my phone powered up, I basked in elation. I couldn't say I'd found having sex with two women in front of a group of strangers some new kink or fetish, as Tessa had suggested I might, but I did feel tweaked with pride—in a house full of fucking, this mild introvert with sexual shame had become an elite sex party's main event!

I ordered myself a ride home. The Uber app told me my driver was only three minutes away, so I stepped off the porch and walked down the driveway to meet the car. But as the crimson light from the sconces faded behind me, so did my high.

I knew checking my messages was pointless—Jordan was ghosting me. If I were smart, I'd put my phone back into my pocket and not even look until the morning. But I couldn't help myself; I stopped at the curb and scrolled through my phone. Of course, I found not a single message from Jordan. I was right—she was ghosting me. And suddenly that rejection and humiliation I'd managed to bury in sex was back, and it was joined by fury.

But I was done ghosting my feelings.

The words spilled out of my spiteful heart, into my arms, down my hands, and into my fingertips…

Jordan, you tell me I'm a priority, but I feel neglected. For the past two weeks I've dropped everything when you needed to talk. But when I ask for ten minutes and tell you it's very important, you don't even have the manners to answer me!

I took a breath and continued, When you told me you were going to New York and offered to give me half of the allowance back, I said no because I thought you were coming back. But now I feel like a complete fool. I guess money was all I was to you.

I hit "send" and thought, *That's the end of this damn arrangement!*

7

KISSING BRUISES

WORKING OUT THE KINKS of my golf swing on the driving range at my country club the next morning, I thought I had put Jordan out of my mind. (Okay, I *might* have imagined her face on a few golf balls as I six-ironed them.)

So naturally, when my phone vibrated in my pocket, I knew it was her. I almost didn't answer it, but then told myself, *I don't ghost people.* Even if I'm furious with a person, I communicate, for better or worse.

I set my club down by my bag and walked to the far end of the driving range. (The club was private and had a rule against using the phone on the premises unless you were a doctor, but that's where the lawyers knew they could get away with it.)

With probably only one ring left before it went to voicemail, I pressed "accept."

"You're alive," I grumbled into the phone.

"I am so, so sorry," Jordan answered, her voice unthreateningly low and soft. "I cannot believe how inconsiderate I was the last few days. I deserved everything you said in your texts last night."

I blinked. I hadn't thought I'd ever hear from Jordan again, or if I did, she'd be defensive and bitter about my insults. But she'd taken the wind out of my sails. She hadn't even given a qualifier—a "but" or a "you have to understand," which so often kills an apology.

I tried to hang onto my anger. "Jordan, what the hell happened to you?"

"Can I please tell you in person?" she pled. "I'm at JFK now, and I'll be home late tonight. Can I see you tomorrow? Please, I'll meet you wherever you want—your place, mine, it's totally up to you."

I sighed, thinking either way, this was *not* the romantic reunion I'd been expecting when I offered to pick her up at the airport the other day. But of course, I was beyond curious of what explanation she could have that needed to happen in person.

"Tomorrow night will work," I relented. "Text me your address down in Venice, and I'll come at six."

"That's great. Thank you so much for being understanding."

With only a trace of understanding in my voice, I said, "Have a safe flight."

❦

THE SUN WAS GOING down as I rang the bell at a one-story gray and white Craftsman bungalow a few blocks from Venice Beach.

"Forgive the mess!" Jordan chirped as she opened the door then quickly turned and rushed inside.

I tried not to feel too annoyed by her cheerfulness as I followed her in. The place was stylish but inviting with high, bleached wood ceilings, and a giant, white, L-shaped sectional. I certainly didn't see a mess—just laundry waiting to be folded on the white couch.

"Great place," I said politely.

"It's sooo much nicer than my studio," Jordan effused—she was across the room, rinsing off a dish, and I hadn't even seen her face yet. "Bobby, the guy I swapped with, is in the cannabis business and does well. He has a cabinet filled with every kind of edible you can imagine. My stomach was hurting last night, so I took one bite of a pot Rice Krispies treat. Really helped."

I settled onto the sofa and allowed myself a moment of small talk. "Have you been down to the Venice boardwalk yet?"

"No! And would you believe I've been here almost a month and haven't even stepped foot in the ocean—come to think of it, I've *never* been in the Pacific Ocean."

"Seems like a crime," I remarked as she walked to the couch and sat, crisscross, facing me.

"Hi," Jordan said, humility edging into her smile.

Her damn face was so disarmingly beautiful I found it nearly impossible to hold on to my anger. "Hi," I said evenly.

"So, I'm dying to hear—did you end up going to Sanctum?" Jordan asked.

I hesitated. Jordan seemed supportive when we'd first spoken about the sex club, but I wasn't sure if she'd find the actual details saucy or sick. "It was…interesting."

"I bet," she said with a half-smile. "And the Producers Guild thing for your dad?"

I couldn't take any more chitchat. I grumbled, "Great, when I wasn't checking my phone to see if you'd texted me."

Jordan looked down at her hands in her lap, then back up at me. "I'm so sorry if I ruined your night. No matter what I was going through, I should have at least shown you the courtesy of telling you I'd be MIA for a bit."

As validating as that was, I was getting worried. "What do you mean? What you were going through?"

Jordan pressed her palms on both knees and drew a breath. Her words spilled out with simplicity and earnestness. "The reason I disappeared is I had a little battle with depression."

I blinked. Over the past few days, I'd tried to guess what explanation she'd have—maybe she met another guy, or she decided to move back to New York and didn't know how to tell me—but I hadn't even *thought* she'd say this.

"Oh," was all I could say.

"Yeah. I've been dealing with depression almost all my life," she continued. "I started feeling it when I got to New York, but by Saturday, I could barely function. I shut myself in my friend's bedroom with the lights off. I couldn't even look at my phone."

She paused, and I studied her. Something about this story didn't make sense. Then I realized. "Jordan, I'm really sorry you were struggling, but you posted on Instagram at like eleven p.m...."

She squinted at me, like it took her a second to remember. "That, yeah. I literally forced myself to post an old photo of a night on the town. I guess it was my way of telling depression to 'fuck off.' But you're right. It doesn't make sense. Why couldn't I answer your texts if I can post some ridiculous shit? All I can say is when I'm in the thick of it, *nothing* makes sense. You have no idea what it was like in my head Saturday. It was misery. Disgusting."

My mouth moved to speak but words wouldn't come out. *How could I have been partying at Sanctum while she was in this state?*

Jordan's eyes welled, so she grabbed a towel from the laundry pile. "I can't remember if this is clean or dirty."

She laughed and wiped her eyes. I was struck by how Jordan could dance between the most delicate of emotions.

"I had no idea," I murmured. "I am so sorry for sending those horrible texts."

"Please, if I were you, I'd have said much worse, believe me."

"Still, I should have contained myself. How are you feeling now?"

"Fine. I woke up Sunday, and it had lifted as fast as it hit. It's so unpredictable. It can last a day or a week."

"That must be so frustrating."

She nodded. "Do you know much about depression?"

I thought before answering and felt embarrassed. I'd never dated anybody with depression, none of my family or close friends had suffered from it—or if they had, they hadn't shared it with me.

"Not much," I confessed. "When I was married, I was so unhappy I thought I might be depressed. I tried antidepressants, but I didn't feel any different and went off after a few months. My doctor and I both concluded I wasn't depressed. 'Situational,' he called it, and sure enough, the day I left my marriage, I was happy again."

"Well, you're lucky. I was born with a chemical imbalance. Major Depressive Disorder is my official diagnosis. And it's virtually treatment resistant. Antidepressants barely help, even at the highest dosages, and eventually I build a resistance to them. My psychiatrist told me I'm basically out of meds to take."

I was awed by how vulnerable she was in sharing so much detail.

"You said you were born with it?" I asked.

"I'm pretty sure it's genetic. Two of my aunts were in and out of hospitals. They had shock therapy, the works."

I bit my tongue—as brave as she was recounting all this, the idea that I was in bed with someone who might one day need shock therapy was concerning.

"I've obviously managed it better than them," Jordan continued. "It started when I was teenager but got really bad when I went off to college. And it has definitely affected my career. I had to work all these day jobs—I was a nanny, waitress, you name it—but they'd leave me too drained to go to classes or on auditions. And then there are a host of side effects—exhaustion, anxiety—it seems like I'm always battling it in one way or another."

I was overwhelmed with sympathy for Jordan. "Thank you so much for sharing this with me," I said.

Jordan put the towel down and slid her hand atop mine.

"Again, I'm so sorry I went MIA," she said. "You signed up for a relationship *without drama*, and here I am dropping a heap into your lap."

"I'm not afraid of a little drama," I insisted. "I guess if it happens again, try to give me a heads up, if you can? Send me a text and tell me you're not feeling well and you'll be unreachable, and I'll leave you alone."

"You deserve that. You're really amazing."

"I am?"

"Yeah. I mean, I almost never tell men I date this stuff. Especially so soon. I hid it from my last boyfriend for months."

"Ray, the alcoholic?"

She nodded. "In the end, I think it had a lot to do with why he left. I think he liked having this mildly Instagram-famous girl, but once I revealed a few imperfections, he couldn't deal with the reality."

"Well, I don't expect perfect. I'm anything but."

Jordan smiled appreciatively. "Are you sure this doesn't turn you off?"

I squeezed her hand. "Honestly, this makes me feel even closer to you."

⁂

LATER THAT NIGHT, JORDAN laid naked on her stomach on the queen-sized bed that seemed to take up her entire bedroom.

Licking my way down the skin of her back, I stopped suddenly, noticing she had bruises on both ass cheeks, colored mocha with hints of violet streaks, about the size of a hand.

"Someone got spanked in New York," I ventured a jovial guess.

She raised her head to look back at me. "Eek, I should have warned you."

"You never mentioned you were into BDSM."

"I'm so not," she snickered. "I saw one guy while I was there before I checked out. He got a little carried away, and I bruise easily. But fuck, I'm sorry. I'll understand if you want to stop."

"Who said anything about stopping?" I protested, then looked down at her ass. "This is how I feel about your bruises," I whispered, then began kissing the brown and purple spots on her butt ever so gingerly. With each touch of my lips to her skin, Jordan sighed louder, and her body rose and rolled with pleasure.

⁂

"DO YOU WANT TO spend the night?" Jordan asked with a weary yawn as she returned to bed after cleaning up in the bathroom.

I swallowed nervously—sleepovers had been a rare occurrence since my divorce and for good reason. "I'd like to," I answered. "But I have to tell you…I snore."

She smiled as she climbed under the covers. "Don't worry, I'm a heavy sleeper."

"No, you don't understand. Once, I downloaded an app and recorded myself. It sounded like there was an angry tiger in the room. I drove Elizabeth crazy."

Jordan laughed. "Why didn't she wear earplugs?"

"She did! I still spent most of my nights on the couch or in the kids' rooms—I desensitized them from birth."

Jordan laughed and flicked a switch by the bed to turn off the lights.

"Don't say I didn't warn you," I sighed.

She shuffled toward me, so we were spooning.

But as the minutes passed and I felt her breath slowing as she fell easily asleep, I laid there, unable to follow her; not only was I nervous about waking her with my snoring, but I also didn't *want* to go to sleep. My conversation with Jordan about her depression had been like emotional caffeine. Here I was, this fifty-two-year-old healthy and happy man who'd somehow never been touched by such a common mental health issue. I'd always considered myself fortunate, but maybe I'd been too sheltered for my own good?

And Jordan had apologized for bringing drama into our arrangement? *Hell, maybe I need more drama.*

"I MUST HAVE MEDITATED for an hour before falling asleep," I said as I took a bite of Moroccan baked eggs at Gjelina Cafe on Abbot Kinney, a Venice street known for art galleries and bohemian boutiques.

"Hang on," Jordan said, preoccupied taking a picture of the lemon ricotta pancakes in front of her. "Sorry, I hate being that girl, but if I don't keep it up, I lose followers."

"No problem."

Jordan's long fingers darted over her keyboard, expertly editing her post. "Social media is such a waste of time. Most of my posts are pointless. I tell myself I'm building a brand, but for what? I've got almost fifty thousand followers but maybe three real friends."

I laughed. "A fellow introvert."

"One of these days, I want to post about my struggles with depression. Sometimes I think nobody knows the real Jordan."

My heart skipped a small beat, thinking, hoping, that maybe *I* was receiving the honor of getting to know "the real Jordan."

"I think people would really identify with someone as beautiful as you admitting to a mental health problem," I encouraged.

"One day," she said as she planted her phone facedown on the table, poured syrup over her pancakes, and brightened. "So what's this about your snoring? I hardly noticed it last night."

"Really? That's a relief."

"Then again, I did take an Ambien."

I laughed. "Smart. I take it once in a while, but it always makes me feel like a zombie the next day."

"Have you ever tried Ambien sex?" Jordan asked.

"Ambien sex?"

"Oh, it's a total thing. Google it! Half a pill with a glass of wine right before you have sex, and you're totally in the mood. I like to use it to calm my nerves when I sleep with anybody new from the site."

My chest sank—I'd still been trying to find a better word for our sexual connection than "magic," but the idea that Jordan might have needed an Ambien to make it so special tarnished it. "Did you need it to have sex with me?" I asked.

"Just on our first date. And last night, after—because I was a little nervous about you sleeping over."

I put aside my minor insecurity and joked, "You medicated, I meditated."

Jordan chortled, started to cut her pancakes, then stopped, as if suddenly plagued by a troubling thought. "David, since we're being so radically honest, I feel like I should tell you I lied to you a little bit."

I stopped mid-bite. "What's a bit?"

She put her hand to her face and peeked through the cracks between her fingers. "Those bruises on my butt? They're not really from someone slapping me."

"They're not?"

"No. Remember how I told you I had to see a *few* doctors in New York? One of them was a plastic surgeon. He gave me injections to make my ass look fuller."

I couldn't contain my laughter. "I'll be damned."

"What's so funny?"

"Well, for one, the idea you'd think you need any plastic surgery. You're fucking perfect."

Jordan beamed, then pointed to the bridge of her nose. "I got some here, too."

"What?" I leaned forward and squinted, but failed to find any difference in her face.

"Just a little filler—it's called a non-invasive nose job. Thankfully, there was minimal bruising."

She showed me her profile—sure enough, the bump in her nose had been smoothed out a little.

"Well, I have to hand it to your doctor—it's very subtle," I complimented. "But for the record, you could have told me. I've never had any work done, but I'm all for people getting a nip and a tuck if it helps their confidence."

"I need more than confidence. I may have a little body dysmorphia." Jordan smiled cutely, poking fun at herself. "But really, I'm sorry I didn't tell you the truth last night. I'd planned to, but it seems like once we start taking our clothes off, I can't think straight."

"I know the feeling," I granted. "But listen, radical honesty only works if we're radically honest—even about the little things."

"You're so right. Lesson learned. David can handle the truth, the whole truth, and nothing but the truth."

I let out a chuckle and shook my head.

"What's so funny now?" she asked.

"I don't know, I guess it seems funny to me that you're more comfortable telling me you had your ass slapped by another guy than admitting you had a little plastic surgery."

"Look who's talking."

"What do you mean?"

"Well, is that any stranger than how you reacted? You weren't the least bit jealous another man might have had rough sex with me. I don't know many men, even sugar daddies, who could handle that."

She had me there. Suddenly I recalled the conversation from our first date, where we'd discovered that our affinity for the sugar lifestyle paired us perfectly. "We're pretty compatible, don't you think?" Jordan had asked. "Very," I'd answered.

I called back to the conversation, hoping she'd remember it. "We're very unique, aren't we?" I asked now.

Jordan smiled with warm recognition. "Very."

8

SOFT DAVID

"Should we go out or order in tonight?" I asked into the speakerphone of my Mercedes as I headed home from the office a few days later.

"Surprise me!" Jordan's voice echoed back. "I need to shower and shave my legs, then I can hop in an Uber."

Fantasizing about Jordan naked in a bathtub made it difficult to steer straight. "I have a better idea. Why don't I order in, run a bath, and shave your legs *for you*?"

"That sounds absolutely heavenly," she purred.

"But there's only one bath in the house, so I'll have to move the kids' toys."

"Don't you dare move those toys!" she barked cutely.

I laughed. *She did tell me she's a big kid.*

We ended the call, and I veered into the nearest CVS where I bought a tote full of bubble bath, bath salts, exfoliating sea sponges and pumice stones, body lotion, and oils. I was going to give Jordan the sexiest bath of her life.

I dimmed the lights in the house, put *Ol' Blue Eyes* on the speakers, and placed my favorite scented votive candles around the bathroom. I lined the kids' submarines up on the tub ledge so Jordan could see I'd respected her inner child's demands but not sit her lovely ass on them, then mixed the salts and bubbles into a thick, frothy potion.

"Stop," Jordan gasped when she saw my bathroom-turned-private-spa.

From then on, we hardly spoke.

Jordan climbed out of her clothes, and I offered my hand to steady her as she stepped into the tub. As she lowered herself into the water, I knelt beside the bath. She raised a leg out and planted her foot on the spigot, then closed her eyes—her trust made me glow inside. Right hand steering my razor, left hand cupping froth onto her skin, I shaved her slowly and beyond carefully, thinking, *I wouldn't nick her if my life depended on it.*

"Come in with me?" Jordan whispered as I set the razor aside, and she rinsed off with the hand shower.

I smiled but eyed the tub. The house was built in the 1930s and its tub could barely contain her, let alone both of us. And, filled with soap, bubbles, and floating foam dotted with stubble, the idea we might have sex in there wasn't enticing. "Let's go to the bedroom," I quietly suggested.

I wrapped Jordan in a bath towel and tucked it under her arms so I could hold her hand while leading her there. I scooted onto the bed and pulled off my jeans and shirt while Jordan shed her towel and climbed toward me. She pressed a hand on my chest to lay me on my back and went down on me. But as she worked on my cock with her hand and mouth, I felt an unusual stir of anxiety rise in my chest—it seemed like concrete was being poured over my heart and immediately drying into a wall around it.

Shit, not now, not again…

I tried to block out the voice and focus on how good Jordan's wet lips felt, but my heart started to beat fast, like it was fighting for its life.

And my cock, which usually rose to attention at Jordan's kiss and sometimes in anticipation of it, was only half erect.

Jordan inched her head up. "Tell me what you like."

I forced a reassuring smile. "You're fucking perfect at that."

"I really like how you feel in my mouth."

She gave me the sexiest of smiles and started to lick me again.

I closed my eyes and tried to find a fantasy to fixate on…Jordan in a bikini on a beach, dancing for me in lingerie, in a threesome with some faceless blonde…

"Is everything okay?" I heard Jordan ask.

I opened my eyes and saw her prop herself on her elbows. I opened my mouth to speak, but an invisible hand closed its fingers around my throat.

"Were you with someone else already today?" she asked.

I blinked—the question seemed so random—and croaked, "What made you ask *that?*"

"Well, you're usually so hard with me, so I wondered if you'd already had sex today."

I hesitated. If I had enjoyed another woman that day, it wouldn't have been in violation of our open relationship, but the thought was just, I don't know, *unseemly.* "You think I'd sleep with *two women in one day?*"

"Maybe, I don't know. I'm just saying, I wouldn't care if you did. I wouldn't want to have sex, but I'd still come over and watch a movie and snuggle."

"Huh. And I thought *I* was open-minded."

Jordan grinned with pride. "But seriously—what's, um, going on down here?"

I took an existential sigh. I knew exactly what was going on down there, but it hadn't happened in so long, and it had been even longer since I'd talked about it that I didn't know if I could find the words to explain it to Jordan. And I didn't know if I wanted to. *But Jesus,* I thought, *Jordan shared her depression with me. Her most personal demon. How could I not be as vulnerable with her?*

I forced myself to begin, "I have this problem…I guess it's an odd form of anxiety."

"What's so odd about anxiety?" she coaxed.

"Well, mine's odd because I only get it during sex. That's it. Day to day, I'm hardly ever anxious."

"And when you get it, you can't get hard?"

"No, not exactly. As you can see, I get somewhat erect—just not very."

"Okay, but maybe if you'd let me keep going?"

"It's not that simple," I said. "Yeah, I could probably get a little harder if I let you go on. And there are things we can do—like watching porn and using toys—that will help. The problem is, once the anxiety comes with a woman, I start to get nervous before we even get into bed, during, after…and I get so in my head I can't even enjoy sex."

Jordan studied me like I was some psychological jigsaw puzzle. "So the anxiety *never* goes away?"

I wracked my brain for a way to admit this nicely, but had to say, "Sure, when a woman leaves."

Jordan reached for the bath towel and wrapped herself protectively in it. "Is that a hint?"

"No, not at all!" I insisted, fretting she might take offense. "In fact, I usually get anxious a few months into a relationship, so I think the fact that it's happening with you after a few weeks is a sign of how badly *I don't want you to leave.*"

Jordan smiled as if she'd found a huge corner piece. "So this isn't exactly ED, is it?"

I shook my head. "No, as matter of fact, I even tried Viagra once, and it didn't help at all. Just gave me a horrible headache."

"Interesting. Have you tried anything else, like Xanax?"

"Not for this. I was prescribed some for vertigo a couple years back, and it made me pass out. Somehow, I doubt being zoned out will help me get hard. Or harder, whatever."

"I don't know, the stuff works wonders for me. Sometimes it even helps with my depression—stops me from spinning out when I realize how unproductive spending days in the dark doing nothing is." Singsong, she added, *"Mother's little helper."*

I smiled at Jordan's attempt to bring some levity to the situation.

"No, I think the problem isn't in my little head, it's in my big one. I even came up with a name for my problem—I call it 'romantic anxiety.'"

She pursed her lips. "Good term. But if you don't mind me playing shrink here, I'd say there's a better name for it. Fear of intimacy."

I sat up and pulled my own towel over my lap. "So I've been told by more than one therapist."

"You don't think that's the issue here?" Jordan asked.

"Makes sense, I guess. But I've talked to shrinks about it for decades, and they didn't do shit to help."

"You've had this for *decades?*"

"Since I lost my virginity, anyway. Didn't seem to bother me when I was necking and begging girls for hand jobs."

Jordan chuckled. "How did you and Elizabeth deal with this?

"We didn't deal with it. That was part of the problem. I remember the first time I felt it with her—we'd been dating three months and I took her to Ojai for a weekend. It happened, and we had a short conversation about it. She said, 'That's a little scary,' and rolled over and went to sleep."

Jordan seemed too astonished for words. "You guys didn't talk about this in therapy?"

"Nope. We talked about every other problem we had but not this. I know, it's inexplicable. I just assumed I had a problem that couldn't be fixed."

"You must have gotten hard some way—you have two children."

"Of course. I don't have full disfunction, I just get sort of half-hard like this. And if I don't masturbate for a while, I build up sexual energy and can cum. But it doesn't make for a fulfilling sexual relationship."

"But you get hard with strangers?"

"The novelty helps," I admitted.

"Well, this sort of explains why you became a sugar daddy," Jordan said pointedly. "And if I recall from our first date, you told me the longest arrangement you've had lasted a few months."

I nodded. "Yeah, I guess it's no shocker they always end then—if I even get a hint of anxiety, I run for the hills. Although, in my defense, Allison and Tessa ended it before it could happen, not the other way around."

"But you probably would have left them eventually, right?" Jordan asked.

I nodded and choked up as I fought to say, "Which explains why I'm fifty-two and have never had a long, sexually fulfilling relationship in my life."

Jordan put a hand to her heart. "That's so sad."

"I know. I like to pretend I'm a prince living this fairy-tale existence, but the truth is, I feel like I'm the male version of Sleeping Beauty. It's like someone put a curse on me."

"Well, clearly *my* kiss didn't wake you," Jordan answered with a wry smile.

I saw past her joke—what woman wouldn't take it personally that she couldn't get a man more than half-hard?

"I'm sorry," I said. "*Now* look who's bringing drama into a no-strings-attached relationship."

Jordan rolled her eyes. "Please, my crazy sees your crazy and raises you *extra* crazy."

I looked at her. "What is it about you that makes me feel comfortable admitting all this shit? I mean, I think I've told you more about this than I told any shrink."

She shrugged. "Beats me. But I'm glad you did. Do you mind if I ask one more question?"

"Yes. But go ahead. Beat a man while he's down."

Jordan angled her head. She seemed to have discovered a crucial piece of that jigsaw puzzle and was searching for a place to put it. "Well, who was the witch that put this curse on you?"

Damn, this girl is emotionally intelligent. I swallowed and said, "Michelle, probably."

"Who's Michelle? And why just probably?"

"The girl I lost my virginity to," I answered. "And I say probably because it seems ridiculous to think having my heart broken at sixteen fucked me up for life."

"Well, everybody has their wounds," Jordan reasoned. "Plus, being disillusioned by your marriage, and from what you've told me about your family being so emotionally shut down—seems like the perfect storm. Besides, teenage heartbreak is pretty strong stuff. Hormones and all. What happened with you two?"

I squirmed. "Short, edited version. I met Michelle a week after I got my driver's license and fell madly in love. A few months later, she went

to summer boarding school and fell in love with another kid. I spent the
summer between ninth and tenth grade listening to sad Jackson Browne
and Neil Young ballads, swearing I'd never let myself feel *that* kind of
pain again!"

"That's interesting," Jordan said quietly.

"More like silly."

"No, you said, 'a few months.'"

"So?"

"So, I'm guessing you never had this anxiety with Michelle?"

"No, never."

"So maybe deep down that's some marker in your head. You feel
safe for a few months, then your fear of intimacy bubbles up in the form
of anxiety."

"Sound theory," I answered, impressed. "You'd think *one* of the
shrinks I've seen over the years would have figured that out."

Jordan squinted, again hunting for puzzle pieces. "Michelle was
when you were sixteen, and you were how old when you met Elizabeth?"

"Thirty-nine."

"Okay, well, you must have had *some* relationships in your twenties
and thirties?"

"I dated two or three girls. But none of them for more than a year or
so. The last one was a girl named Lisa. I was twenty-six."

"You didn't have *any relationship*s between twenty-six and thirty-
nine?" she asked with astonishment. "For thirteen years?"

Fuck, here it goes, I thought. I had tried to be honest with Jordan by
disclosing my marital mistakes, my history as a sugar daddy, and now,
my romantic anxiety. On our first date, I gave her the Cliffs Notes version
of my dating history, but now she was asking for James Joyce's *Ulysses*.
And this particular chapter might turn off any reader.

I inhaled for courage and answered, "No, the only women I saw
besides those couple and Elizabeth were escorts."

"You mean like the Heidi Fleiss girls?" Jordan asked.

I shook my head. Jordan referred to the famous "Hollywood Madam"
whose ring was broken up after her arrest in 1994, when I was thirty.

"No, I never used madams or escort services. The idea of some Russian girl coming to my house for an hour seemed too cold and a stop short of sex trafficking."

"Then how did you meet them? This was before Seeking Arrangement, right?"

"Yeah. My thing was these women who had websites. They advertised 'The Girlfriend Experience.' They'd screen you, then you'd pay them for a couple hours. Sometimes you'd have dinner with them, get to know them. I'm still friends with a couple of the women I met."

I looked to Jordan, wondering how all this information was washing over her, but she seemed unfazed.

"I've thought of building my own website," she said. "I mean, there has to be a better way than Seeking. I spend hours messaging men, negotiating, having meet-and-greet coffees. It's exhausting."

That's her reaction? I'd just admitted to spending nearly two decades avoiding relationships by sleeping with escorts I met online, and Jordan wasn't the slightest bit perturbed.

"Well, thank you for not judging me," I said. "Or for thinking I'm a sex addict."

"Judge you? David, you've had crippling anxiety for your whole life. The desire for affection, sex, touch, are basic human needs. If anything, this tells me that deep down, you were desperate for a relationship."

"Deep, deep, deep, *deep* down," I answered with a nervous chuckle.

Jordan grinned, and I sensed she was finally satisfied that she'd found every piece of the puzzle within me. "Thank you for sharing this with me," she said. "I assume you told Elizabeth about this?"

"A couple weeks after we met, yeah."

"And how did she react?"

"She appreciated the honesty," I said. "I promised her I was done with escorts. And I managed to stay monogamous to her for a couple of years. But the anxiety and the pressure of being unhappily married just got to me."

"Enter Seeking Arrangement," Jordan added.

I wanted to close my eyes with guilt and shame, but Jordan smiled at me with adoration.

"You know when you're vulnerable like this, your face actually changes."

"What do you mean?"

"You look, I don't know, more handsome…softer."

I groaned. "You had to say 'soft.'"

She laughed. "Sorry. But seriously. I like this soft David."

I forced an appreciative laugh. "Thank God for that. Because I feel like I've unzipped my soul and you're tinkering around in there."

"Still anxious, are you?"

"More than ever, sorry."

Jordan looked around the bed for her clothes. "Listen, I don't want to make you uncomfortable. Why don't I go home tonight? You think about it for a few days and tell me if you want to keep seeing me. I promise, I won't be the slightest bit offended if you want to end the arrangement."

I saw her sliding off the bed and quickly said, "I *do not* need a few days. I absolutely want to keep seeing you. Honestly, if I can't work through this with someone as amazing as you, I might as well become a damn monk."

"Well, we wouldn't want *that*," she laughed. "So what do we do to fix the problem?"

I glanced toward my bathroom. "I'm pretty sure I threw the Viagra away ages ago, but I guess I could get some, and we can try it out on our next date."

"Sounds like a plan," Jordan said gamely. "But maybe I should go home tonight anyway? Relieve the pressure a little?"

"Probably a good idea," I sighed begrudgingly. "There's only so much romantic anxiety a man can handle in one night."

MY AGITA LEFT THE house with Jordan that night, and the next morning Daddy Fix-It went into action. My doctor's office opened at 8:30 a.m., so by 8:32 I'd made an appointment. By 2:00 p.m., I was walking out of the pharmacy, a bottle of those famous little blue pills in my pocket, texting Jordan.

Hope you're having a nice day, I wrote, electing not to remind her of our dramatic evening. I was hoping we could have dinner Friday night?

Hiiii, she piped back. Friday is great. But can we keep it low-key? I can't remember the last time I celebrated Valentine's Day.

I stopped in my tracks right there on the street.

I had no fucking idea Friday was Valentine's Day.

I felt like *such an idiot*.

I mean, in my own defense, I hadn't celebrated it since I was married, but shouldn't I have seen some Hallmark ad for candy or flowers on Instagram? Had I seen one but been so subconsciously cynical about love that I'd blocked the night out of my mind?

My rare departure from replying within seconds must have given me away, because Jordan wrote, Did you know Friday is Valentine's Day when you asked me out?

I wracked my brain trying to find an excuse so Jordan wouldn't feel like an afterthought, but that damn radical honesty plagued my conscience.

I admit I had no idea, I wrote. But honestly, there's nobody I'd rather spend that night with than you.

Nice recovery! she teased.

I responded with an emoji of a shrugging man who had a lot more hair than I did. And probably more brains—because somehow, I'd tricked myself into choosing Valentine's Day, the most romantic night of the year, to try out Viagra as the fix for a lifetime of sexual and romantic anxiety.

Talk about pressure. If I couldn't get hard as rock on Friday night, I'd feel like a complete and utter failure as a man.

IN THE DAYS LEADING up to our Valentine's date, I decided the best strategy to assuage the pressure was to not talk about it at all, and Jordan took my cue. That Friday night, when I got dressed, I slipped one of the blue pills into my front jeans pocket, figuring I'd secretly pop it at some point in the evening. I did my best to keep the evening low-key. But of course, I also saw no point in celebrating Valentine's Day at all if I couldn't be a *little* romantic. I had the obligatory dozen red roses waiting for Jordan and cooked some steaks. And for dessert, I brought out red velvet cupcakes from the Sprinkles shop in Beverly Hills. Then we moved to the couch and tried to watch *Pretty Woman* for the third time.

Once again, it was only a matter of minutes before we were "buzzing" for each other and making out like teenagers. And once again, suddenly I found myself naked in her arms, post-coitally panting.

"I guess the Viagra worked," Jordan huffed as she pulled that giant Neapolitan-striped blanket over us.

I blinked several times. "Um, I didn't take it."

"What?"

I reached down to the floor, slipped the little blue pill from my jeans pocket and held it up. "I swear, I forgot I had it in here!"

"Oh, wow. And you were sooo hard."

I looked down. "I'm still hard!"

Jordan laughed. "And you didn't have any anxiety?"

"No! Not before, during, or after." I sat up for emphasis. "Jordan, I don't know if you understand how huge this for me. I've lived with this problem for as long as I can remember. I swear, I feel like the curse has lifted."

Jordan clapped her hands together as she sat up too. "I'm so happy for you."

"I guess your kiss is magical after all!"

"I don't know about that," she deflected with the humility of a saint. "I'm sure it has more to do with your being vulnerable and sharing it with someone."

I nodded at the irony. By being "Soft David," I'd gotten hard. And I understood Jordan's point—I'd certainly opened up to her about my problems in a deeper and more detailed way than I'd ever done with any woman or shrink, and probably even with myself.

"I hate to tempt fate," Jordan cautioned me. "But what if it comes back?"

"I'll cross that bridge when I come to it. Right now, the important thing is that *this gives me hope*. Just knowing it's even possible to get rid of it is life-changing for me."

"Maybe my kiss isn't so bad," she said. "But promise me you'll tell me if it comes back?"

"The moment it happens," I vowed. "We'll talk it out."

"Or find other ways around it," she flirted.

I took the hint, kissed her, and then pulled back an inch. "You do realize this will make me desperate to see you, right?"

"That's how I want you," Jordan answered. "Desperate for me."

AFTER JORDAN HAD HELPED me conquer my most humiliating neurosis, it was a given she was sleeping over.

"Need an Ambien?" I asked as I walked into the bathroom where Jordan was brushing her teeth over the sink.

She mumbled through Colgate, "I'm good."

I opened the mirrored cabinet, took out a pill bottle, twisted off that annoying childproof top, and took the Viagra pill out of my pocket. "Who needs Viagra? *You're* my medicine."

I dropped the pill into the bottle, slid it onto the shelf and closed the cabinet. Then I moved behind her, wrapped my arms about her waist, and kissed the nape of her neck.

Glancing in the mirror, I could see her close her eyes with pleasure, so I closed mine, too.

9

BEAUTY IN THE DETAILS

WITH JORDAN AND I GROWING closer with every date, I decided to introduce her to one of my most sacred places: my family's beach house in Malibu.

I took a Thursday off work, picked Jordan up, and drove down the Pacific Coast Highway and through the gates of Malibu Colony—"The Movie Star Colony" as it was called on maps peddled to tourists on Hollywood Boulevard. Our beach house was two stories of modern, pink-and-gray brushed concrete with inlaid glass bricks and a copper roof subtly shaped like a rising wave.

As I gave Jordan the tour, I explained why the house was so special. My parents had bought it when I was fourteen, and rarely a weekend went by when some or all of us weren't gathered there together. We celebrated every holiday from Mother's Day to Halloween there—I'd even met Elizabeth at one of our annual July Fourth barbeques, so the house had a hand in bringing my children into the world.

Wearing pink jean shorts and a gray sleeveless T-shirt tied in a knot behind her back, Jordan bent her tall frame over dozens of family pictures lined on a shelf crowded by crystal fish. After dutifully studying each picture and asking who each and every person was, she came to a photograph of me surfing on the North Shore of Hawaii, shirtless, on a wave so far over my head its crest didn't fit in the frame.

"Is that *you*?" she gasped.

"When I was twenty-two with muscles and hair."

"You're still hot," she smartly answered. "But look at that wave—you're a great surfer."

"Was," I corrected. "I pretty much gave it up cold turkey after I closed my surf shop."

"Where was the shop? Why did you close it?"

I chortled, amused by Jordan's inability to contain her curiosity.

"It was in Santa Monica. Somehow, I had the stupid idea owning a surf shop meant I'd spend more time surfing."

She leaned against the counter, crossing her arms with an expectant stare, waiting for more of the story.

I sidled next to her. "After a few years, I realized I wanted to do something more creative. I tried to sell the business but ended up closing it and lost a bundle my parents had invested. That was a little humiliating. Then I started writing and directing independent movies. I wasn't a genius but proved to myself that I could succeed in my father's business on my own. But, a few years ago, when my dad asked me to produce with him and my brother, Charles, I figured I was ready to join the family business."

Jordan gave me that same look as when I'd told her about my romantic anxiety—searching for puzzle pieces to assemble.

"What?" I chuckled nervously.

"You said you gave up surfing 'cold turkey.' Like you were addicted to it."

"I guess I was addicted to surfing. But I had a little awakening when I started writing. I realized I'd spent so many years on a fucking surfboard, staring out at the horizon, waiting for a wave, that I'd become anti-social. I'm still a little bit of an introvert, but I definitely stepped out of my shell when I stepped off surfboards."

"So interesting," Jordan said.

Not just interesting, but SO interesting, I thought. She made me feel *so* heard, *so* seen, *so* important.

"Sometimes I miss it," I went on. "I get out once in a while when I take the kids to places like Costa Rica or Mexico. But it's not worth going out here…"

I nodded toward the floor-to-ceiling glass windows. The sun was shining on the blue-green Pacific, but the waves were all but flat and windblown; it was such a crappy surf day even the "grommets," kids that usually crowded the break in front of our deck, were nowhere in sight.

But Jordan suddenly brightened. "Wait, do you think you could teach me how to surf?"

"Of course!" I said immediately. *How could she think I'd say no to anything she asked for?* "But I'm warning you, it's pretty fucking cold out there in February."

She waved that off gamely, so I took her by the hand and led her to our guest changing room where I kept a few old surfboards stacked in a corner. I opened a closet to dozens of wetsuits dangling on hangers and used my surfboard-salesman eye to choose a heavy, five-millimeter full suit for her.

"I am so down for this," Jordan said exuberantly as I held the suit open for her. She slipped out of her clothes and wiggled into the snug neoprene. I helped her zip up the back and pulled out one of my longboards—a blue Dewey Weber with a few dings.

Board tucked under my arm, I walked with Jordan out to the beach. As sunny as the day was, it was slightly chilly, and since the beach was a private one, it was the two of us alone on the sand.

I set the board down and gave Jordan some basic instructions. "Stand quickly, keep your balance…but the most important thing you have to do," I said pointedly, "is cover your head after your fall, like this." I put both arms over my head protectively. "That way, if your leash pulls the board back toward you, it won't bang you in the skull. The nose or fin can cut you anywhere else, but if your head is protected, you don't die."

Jordan laughed but got the point. "Injury okay, death bad."

I attached the leash to Jordan's ankle, then picked up the board and carried it toward the water.

"Holy shit!" Jordan yelped when foam washed over her feet.

I'd have said *I warned you* except Jordan's face was absolutely gleeful. I plopped the board in the water and helped her settle onto it on her stomach, then swam beside her as I guided it out to the breakers.

A minuscule wave approached, so I turned the board to face the shore and yelled, "Paddle, paddle!"

Jordan's arms dug into the water, and I thrust the board forward—she caught the wave, got to her knees, and promptly toppled under the surface.

"Shit," I yelled out—but she suddenly popped up, arms protecting her head, like I'd taught her.

I breast-stroked toward her. "You okay?"

"Yeah, but this is harder than I thought!"

She climbed back onto the board, and I pulled her back to the breakers.

"Any tips?" she asked with shivering lips.

"Nope, keep doing it, that's the secret. Get ready…"

I turned the board and gave her another shove. She rose to her knees, then one foot, then plop, went down again.

I swam to her as she came up, this time without holding her head and visibly frustrated.

"That hurt," she shouted, shivering. "You show me how to do it—I'll go in, grab my phone and take pictures."

"I'll go back in with you."

"Please? I'd really like to see you surf."

"Okay. One wave."

I helped Jordan remove the leash, then attached it to myself as she swam to the shore and ran up to the house.

I pulled myself onto the board, sat up and turned to look for a wave. The ones Jordan tried would hardly propel someone of my weight more than a few yards, so I let them roll under me and scanned the ocean for the slightest rise in sea level. But I knew this could take a while—surfable waves came in sets every five or ten minutes, even on a good day.

Suddenly a wave of loneliness washed over me. I felt like I was a ten-year-old boy dropped on a surfboard in the middle of a vast ocean with no land in sight. Around me was lapping water and stinging wind; no birds above me, no fish below.

And then it hit me. *I can't remember ever feeling lonely before.*

I gave myself a giant "huh."

I'd spent decades surfing alone, traveling alone, going to movies alone, golfing alone, and with my private pilot's license I would fly all around the country…alone. But somehow "lonely" had only been a word to me. I knew I must have felt it at least once in my life because I recognized the feeling. But how could I have made it to middle age with such a fundamental emotion so foreign to me?

But on the board there, I couldn't care less why I'd finally, suddenly woken up and felt this loneliness. Why I'd been shut to this emotion didn't seem as important as accepting I finally felt it. In fact, I was grateful for the discomfort. Just as I'd received a lesson in vulnerability from Jordan, now I was learning what it felt like to be less shut down to my emotions. Jordan wasn't some guru constantly dispensing sage advice, but being in a relationship with her was raising my emotional intelligence daily.

It occurred to me that although I never felt lonely in my marriage, I'd often felt like I was alone. Elizabeth and I had been so incompatible that it was hard for me to believe we stayed married for as long as we did. Elizabeth was a marathon runner, but I couldn't jog around the block without getting shin splints. Once I'd suggested she train me to. I offered to run a mile with her, then walk home while she jogged on. After a few days of that, I'd run two miles, et cetera, et cetera. But Elizabeth answered, "It would take months, and I don't really want to change my routine." I once suggested she learn golf and play with me, but she thought the sport was four hours wasted and loved to spend Sundays watching football. I, meanwhile, found the game unbelievably boring. Nobody was to blame in all of this; we just didn't take pleasure in each other's pastimes.

But there were other revealing differences between us. More than once, I asked Elizabeth to read a screenplay I'd written, only to watch weeks turn into months before she'd get to it. She explained that she read slowly, and probably had undiagnosed ADHD, so I offered to read the script aloud to her. "We'll sit on the couch for a couple hours, and you just listen," I suggested. But she refused, insisting she would read it. Eventually she did, and praised my writing, but the frustration ruined it for me, and I stopped asking her to read my work. Again, I can't blame Elizabeth. She did, after all, love coming to the set of films I produced, but it pointed to a deep incompatibility: I was a typically insecure artist, while she was a busy therapist and mother of two who either lacked the time or the understanding of how important it is to enthusiastically coddle creativity.

And then there was the fact that we'd argue about so many other things…what movies to see together, where to eat dinner…and our conversations were almost always about the children. The last half our marriage, our uncomfortable silences at restaurants gave me such anxiety that I would find any excuse to not go out.

Glancing back at the beach house, I saw Jordan sitting on the deck in her wetsuit, wrapped in a towel, cell phone in hand, waiting for me to do something picture worthy. As we waved, it struck me how different Jordan was from my ex-wife.

Elizabeth was never interested in learning to surf while we were married. But here was Jordan, so eager for me to teach her that she was risking frostbite and planting visions in my head of vacations to tropical spots. And though I hadn't asked Jordan to read a script, I was sure that as a struggling actor, it wouldn't take months of begging to receive her feedback. And Jordan and I never had a moment of uncomfortable silence—I could spend twenty-four hours a day with her and never run out of things to talk about.

Get back to shore already, I heard myself say.

In my peripheral vision I saw the ocean rising. The wave coming was one I'd usually ignore, but I wasn't going to let it pass when the antidote to my loneliness was waiting for me on the deck.

I paddled like a demon into the waist-high dribbler, effortlessly stood and rode it, bouncing at the end to milk it enough to reach the shallows. I jumped off, picked up the board, and paced toward the beach house. With every step I took toward Jordan, my loneliness eased, then disappeared.

"So that's how you do it!" Jordan yelled, filming me with her iPhone as she came down the steps to the sand.

"Ready to try again?" I asked.

"Nooo," she groaned. "But stand right there. You look ridiculously handsome."

Surfboard under my arm, I stopped and let her take my picture. I gave her what I think was the widest smile the skin on my face could handle.

AFTER A STEAMING HOT shower, Jordan and I dove under the covers in my bedroom. Free of anxiety, not even the lingering chill of the Pacific kept me from being hard. And though this was only the second time we had tested her kiss's ability to free me from my curse, I had absolutely no doubt it would never return.

Afterward, we huddled on a chaise under blankets on the deck and watched the sunset. The sun cast an orange hue on the beach, making the wet sand sparkle and shine like a billion tiny golden diamonds.

"You know I've seen thousands of sunsets here, but I've never seen the sun light up the sand like that before," I said. "I know it's cliché, but being with you really does make me see the beauty in the details."

Jordan laid her head on my chest and stared up at me. "I see why this place is so special to you. Thank you so much for sharing it with me."

"HOW'D THE FANCY EARPLUGS work?" I asked Jordan the next morning as I drove us back to town. (I was referring to the Bose noise-cancelling earplugs I'd given her before bed, an attempt to help her sleep after she had a restless night on our Valentine's Day sleepover.)

She sat cross-legged and barefoot in my passenger's seat, McDonald's coffee in hand. "Great! Only had to nudge you two or three times."

"*Only* two or three, huh? You're a saint."

"Hardly. You know what I think?"

"What do you think?"

"I think you use your snoring as an excuse to keep women from sleeping in your bed."

"Ya think!"

She chuckled and pulled an Egg McMuffin from the bag at her feet, unwrapped it, and handed it to me.

"Sorry we didn't have time for a real breakfast," I said.

"Got a busy day?" she asked.

"Sort of. After I drop you off, I'm going to see a new house I've been thinking of renting, then gotta pretend to work."

"You're gonna move? I love your little house."

"It's time. My lease was up over a year ago. And the kids loved the bunk bed when we first moved, but Eli needs his own room now. The other day, I found him changing in the closet so Chloe wouldn't see him naked."

"Hah! Well, tell me about this house you're seeing?"

"I'm really not all that excited about it."

"C'mon, details?"

"It's in Bel Air, a canyon north of Sunset, but still close to their school and mom's house. And it has a pool."

"Sounds ritzy!"

"It's no Beverly Hills, but definitely a step up. To be honest, I'm not even sure I can afford it. I'd be paying fifteen hundred a month more than I am now. And I hear pools are a bitch to maintain—probably cost me another grand a month to keep it heated."

"Gotcha," she said.

I smiled, thinking it was nice I could admit to her I wasn't the wealthiest of men.

"Well, you want me to come with you?" she asked. "Give a woman's opinion?

"Please! And it buys me an extra hour with you."

I drove us up the winding canyons of Bel Air to the address on Rosewood, parked...and just sat there. I'd seen pictures of the house online, but looking at it in real life, I was very unimpressed. The one-story, mid-century modern ranch house was painted bright white—only the roof was black, and it had just a few square windows facing the street. It reminded me of a rectangular-shaped chapel missing a steeple.

"I don't even want to go in," I muttered.

"Well, we're here," Jordan pointed out. "Might as well go inside?"

Unable to argue with her logic, I agreed, and we walked to the open front door where we were greeted by the broker, a woman in her fifties named Lisa. Behind her professional smile, pants suit, and heels, I got the sense that Lisa was no more excited to show the house than I was to see it—I assumed she wouldn't make much of a commission on a lease.

"The house is an open floor plan," she said droningly as she walked us into the living room. At least that's what I assumed it was because it was a long rectangle that stretched from one wall to the kitchen—there wasn't even a dining room. Every wall, even the ceilings, was a tired white—only the floors had a spec of color, a bland, sand-hued marble. The only interesting part of the house were the giant glass doors facing the backyard and pool but glancing through them revealed an equally unimpressive concrete yard surrounding an oval-shaped pool, right up against a canyon wall of overgrown jade bushes and untrimmed eucalyptus trees.

"There's three bedrooms and four baths," Lisa said as she showed us through the rest of the house.

Again, these bedrooms were small white boxes.

Itching to leave, I looked back at Jordan to see her paying far more attention than me—she'd open the bedroom closets, turn on the water faucets in the bathrooms to check the water pressure…

We rounded back to the living room, and I was about to thank the broker and tell her I didn't think the house was for me, when Jordan asked, "Can we look at the backyard?"

"Of course." Lisa opened the sliding doors, and we stepped outside. To my eyes, there wasn't much to see. The pool was filled with dead brown leaves and insects, and the previous tenants had left behind ratty, weatherworn teak patio furniture, one brown unraveling rattan chaise and a tin outdoor heater.

"Where does that dirt trail go?" Jordan asked, looking up at the canyon.

"It winds up to a little seating area," Lisa answered, then gestured at her feet. "I'd take you up there, but I'm in heels."

"Let's go up there?" Jordan suggested, wrapping her arm through mine.

How could I refuse that adorable display of affection?

We left Lisa behind and hiked up a dirt path lined by shoddy concrete retaining walls and came to a spot perched above the house.

"The place is a little small, don't you think?" I said. It was a comment more than a question.

Jordan shrugged. "Maybe. But if you slide all those doors open it will feel huge, like the backyard is part of the house."

I peered down—she had a point.

"Listen to that…" Jordan's voice fell to an awed hush.

I heard a few birds chirping. "The street's so quiet. You don't even hear any traffic."

"And this canyon is gorgeous," she said. "I see they have some lights there along the path pointing up the trees. I bet it's beautiful all lit up at night."

Now I noticed how verdant the surrounding hills were.

"Smell the rosemary?" Jordan asked.

I sniffed. Sure enough, there were rosemary plants everywhere, blooming purple buds.

"And there's so few houses above you, so nobody looks down into the backyard," Jordan pointed out. "And those ficus plants on either side of the house block the neighbors' view into the backyard. A girl could sit out naked by the pool all day."

I smiled. "You should give Lisa lessons on how to sell a house."

Jordan laughed. "Honestly, I think the place is perfect for you. You just need to use your imagination to see its potential."

Suddenly the house began to transform before my eyes, like a canvas being painted. I saw where to put my dining room table—close to the kitchen, atop the dinosaur rug. I saw my couch at the other end, with the Neapolitan blanket folded neatly on the corner, my television in front of it, playing *Pretty Woman*. I heard my children scream with joy as they and their friends swam in a clean pool on a warm day after school. I imagined a few close friends at an intimate dinner party. And, wiping the kids from the scene, I fantasized about Jordan floating naked on a raft in that pool.

"And the master bathroom has two sinks," Jordan's sweet voice interrupted my fantasy. "You do know if you ever want a woman to move in with you, she won't want to share a bathroom with your children."

I laughed, but realized her remark was pure genius, a subtle way of saying, *"Hey buddy, grow up a little. Make space in your life for a woman."*

❧

AFTER I DROPPED JORDAN BACK at her Venice place, I went to the office, where I made a deal to lease the house for two years, starting April first, five weeks away. Then I texted Jordan the news.

You closed the deal already?? she texted back.

Daddy Fix-It doesn't fuck around!

She sent me a few applause emojis along with a picture attachment. I opened it and saw it was a photo she'd taken of me, standing on the beach with the surfboard tucked in my armpit and that skin-stretching smile. But what caught my eye was Jordan's shadow on the surfboard. It was subtle, but if you looked closely, maybe zoomed in, you'd see it was a woman behind the camera.

On a whim, I decided to post the picture to Instagram. I captioned it: "Beauty is in the details."

10
SHITTY HOOKER

MY MESSAGE MUST HAVE been particularly subtle because the only person who commented was my mother.

Is she as pretty as her shadow? Margo messaged me.

Much prettier, I answered.

Whereupon, in typical Winkler fashion, she dropped it.

No "What's her name?" or "When do we meet her?" Not that I was exactly eager to divulge those details—especially not the "How did you meet?"—but I suppose a small part of me was disappointed my mother never acted like that typical nosy Jewish mother. I wanted to at least be given the opportunity to complain, "Mooom, stop prying!"

Regardless of who took notice, it was obvious Jordan was making a positive impact on my life. Every date we went on, something interesting happened, and I was learning and growing.

One morning at the office, I saw an opportunity to return the favor.

The night before, I'd reminded Jordan that she had never sent me her acting reel. She admitted she was embarrassed to give it to me until she had a chance to have it edited with more professional commercial work she'd done but gave me a link to her YouTube channel. There were only a half dozen fitness commercial videos on her page, but I was truly impressed with her talent.

Jordan had been true to her word from our first date and hadn't solicited me for career help, but armed with the knowledge she was talented, I felt inspired to offer her mentorship. I knew her limited résumé wasn't likely to impress casting directors or agents, so to get a foothold in Los Angeles, she'd need to present them with some new dramatic material. And, of course, Daddy Fix-It had a plan.

Good morning! I wrote to her from behind my desk. I was thinking you should make a short film. Something producers and directors would enjoy watching more than just a reel.

I attached a few samples of some short films I'd worked on.

She responded that she loved the idea, and then thanked me for being so supportive.

You make me feel like the luckiest girl on the planet, she wrote.

Then the girl vanished.

I CHECKED IN WITH Jordan at lunch, asked about her day, didn't hear back for a few hours so asked if she was okay, blah blah blah. Suffice to say, by 9:00 p.m., I was experiencing déjà vu.

Jordan was ghosting me again.

After what happened in New York, I wanted to give her the benefit of the doubt, but naturally, I was concerned she was fighting depression again.

At home alone on my couch, anxious with worry, I distracted myself by checking my messages on Seeking Arrangement. But then, glancing at my "favorites" section, I saw a little green light beside Jordan's profile indicating she was online.

Is there a reason you can't answer my texts but can find the time to be on Seeking Arrangement? I texted her.

I'M WORKING! she answered immediately in caps, Qwerty for "I'm pissed off at you!"

For the past eight hours?!

She came back at me without wasting time on grammar or punctuation, Sorry I have to make money to survive I hustled all day to find a guy to see and he's in the bedroom but I'm sitting here in the bathroom naked texting you.

I cringed, imagining Jordan sitting naked on a toilet, hunched over her cell phone with only a closed door between her and a man in her bed.

She "hustled" all day to find a guy to see?? This didn't sound like the sweet and classy woman I was dating: the woman who insisted on our first date that she didn't like to meet strangers in hotel rooms, and that she only used Seeking Arrangement as a source of extra cash. No, the word "hustle" made her sound a lot more like a straight-up Hollywood Boulevard streetwalker than a sugar baby. *And she has to "make money to survive?"* Why was she so desperate for money that she had to hustle "all day" to find someone to see tonight? I knew the allowance I gave her was on the modest side, but 4K, income-tax-free, is nothing to scoff at.

But when I thought about it, living in Los Angeles wasn't cheap. Jordan at one point mentioned her rent in New York was three thousand a month, and even if she was swapping apartments, she was still paying that. And then there were her medical expenses, her flights back and forth to New York, food—you name it. Maybe Jordan was being practical. After all, could she really count on me? How reliable is an arrangement with a man whose sexual anxiety might appear again on a moment's notice and sabotage our arrangement?

I felt guilty and cheap. Was I not giving her enough money to deserve the kind of attention she paid me? Was I being too controlling by expecting her to drop everything and text me when I demanded it? Yes, after talking and texting all day every day, her dropping off felt like she was disconnecting, but maybe I shouldn't be taking it as a rejection.

And then it hit me—if any of my friends heard I was upset my non-exclusive, twice-a-week sugar baby wasn't answering a text for a few hours, they'd think I was the crazy one. Why did I care so much, they'd ask? Or more importantly, why wasn't I jealous? *The woman you're dating is fucking another man right now, and all you're upset about is she hasn't answered a few texts?*

I struggled to explain this to myself, too. As crazy as I was for her, I simply didn't feel jealous. Maybe it was because I had compartmentalized women for so long, paying them to avoid getting attached to them. After all, Jordan was the first woman I'd met since my marriage that

I could consider being more than an arrangement. And even though we were blurring all kinds of lines between arrangement and relationship and were clearly becoming attached, I didn't see her fucking another client as a threat.

Whatever reason existed for my lack of jealousy, I still felt *furious*. Disrespected and rejected.

This morning she said I made her feel like the luckiest girl on the planet, I thought. *But tonight, I'm the last guy on earth she wants to talk to.*

"Hɪ...ʜᴏᴘᴇ ʏᴏᴜ ᴅᴏɴ'ᴛ ᴍɪɴᴅ I ordered for us already," Jordan croaked, standing as I walked toward the table at Gjelina, the restaurant in Venice where we'd dined a few times now.

"Great, what are we eating?" I gave her a hug and as I watched her take a seat, I could see the nervous energy in her movements.

"I got you the Moroccan baked eggs you like," she said. "Is that all right?"

"Of course, I love that you remembered."

Jordan smiled meekly. "I'm starving. All I had yesterday was two pieces of key lime pie leftover from I don't remember when."

"That's fruit, sort of," I joked.

"Hah," she laughed, less breathy than usual it seemed to me.

"Are you okay?" I asked.

She nodded. "But yesterday was rough."

"I'm sorry. Do you want to talk, or wait till we've got some food in your stomach?"

"No, I can talk."

Jordan lifted a cappuccino, and I noticed her nail polish was chipped and her cuticles looked like they'd nibbled at. *Was that unusual?* I wondered. I'd never been one to notice a woman's nails, but I'd also never seen Jordan pick at them.

"I'm so sorry I went AWOL on you," she said. "Again. What's this, the third time?"

I felt guilty saying, "New York and this is twice."

"You're forgetting my trip to the emergency room."

"ER visits don't count!"

Jordan laughed. "You're such an angel. But really, I should have answered your texts. I guess I got so caught up messaging people on the site, trying to find a guy to see—but that's no excuse, so I'm sorry, really. I fucked up. Full stop."

I smiled to accept the apology but let out a frustrated sigh. "Jordan, I don't understand. What was this about you having to hustle to survive?"

"What? Oh, that." Jordan rolled her eyes. "Yeah, I might have been a little bit of a drama queen. I get like that when I'm really upset—kind of lose control of my emotions. I was having a little panic attack there."

"I understand. But I'm honestly worried. I thought your turnstile-jumping days were behind you."

"So did I," she answered. "It's a little bit embarrassing, but over the last few months I got myself into a bit of a financial hole. I was doing really well on the site back in New York and had tons of money in the bank. So I figured I'd take December and January off, move out here. Turns out that wasn't the best idea."

"What do you mean?" I asked, trying to hide my irritation. *She met me, so how was moving here a bad idea?*

Jordan realized the misstep. "That's not what I meant. Honestly, you've been the only good thing that's happened to me here."

She reached across the table, palm up, so I slid my hand into hers, any rejection I'd felt by her ghosting being buzzed away by the electrical current flowing between us.

"And I don't know what it is with men in Los Angeles," Jordan continued. "Maybe it's because I don't have big fake tits and I'm not stick thin, but I can't find any other decent men to see. In New York, I make my rent in a night or two. Here I spend all day messaging, then they flake, or offer me like three hundred bucks."

"Geez. Is that what the guy you saw last night gave you?"

"No, I got him up to five hundred, but still, it was exhausting. He must have spent three hours talking on the couch before making a move."

She pulled her hand away and took sip of water. I shifted in my seat. I really hadn't heard Jordan sound so cynical.

"Don't get me wrong," she said. "I really love hustling—I'm not used to failing so miserably at it. Either the guys in Los Angeles don't like smart brunettes or I'm a shitty hooker."

I let out a gasp. *Did she call herself a shitty hooker?*

Jordan laughed. "Didn't mean to shock you. Listen, I love how you and I have turned our arrangement into something deeper, but with every other man, I'd just as soon be a straight-up escort, meet them in a hotel for an hour, have some fun, and get out of dodge."

"I…didn't know that," I stammered. From our first date, Jordan had pointed out the differences she perceived between sex work and sugaring.

"Does that bother you?" she asked.

I blinked to collect my thoughts. "Not really, I mean, I don't think there's anything ethically wrong with sex work. And I've had my share of five-hundred-dollar dates over the years. In fact, I'm kind of turned on by how shameless you are…I guess I'm just a little surprised."

"Oh, I'm full of surprises!" she stated with a proud laugh.

I found myself tallying up the surprises she'd dropped on me already. *Uber champagne spill, Ambien on dates, depression, plastic surgery bruises*…But oddly enough, none of them bothered me, maybe because she'd been so damn honest.

"And I'm concerned," I pressed. "I know I don't give you enough to live on, but isn't there anything you can do to cover the gap?"

"You mean like a real job?"

"I guess."

"Of course. I could always go back to physical training. But that was killing my body for peanuts. And then there's my depression. I've worked as a nanny and hostess, but I'd get fired for not showing up when it hit me—and working a boring nine to five *makes* me depressed."

"What about commercial modeling? Do you have an agent?"

Jordan shrugged. "I'm trying—my New York agency has a branch out here, but they haven't gotten me out on a single fucking audition. I think the ad execs here are probably the same men I meet on SA—they want the bimbo California look."

I took a beat to choose my words—this was the second time she'd said she wasn't the right "type" for LA men, and it didn't make any more sense now. "Jordan, I can't be the only decent man in town that wants to sleep with you."

"What can I say? This is my experience."

She glanced around the room. I got the sense she wanted the conversation ended, but the producer in me was just getting started.

"Don't you earn money for your Instagram posts?" I asked.

To this she laughed. "Trust me, unless you have a million followers, influencers are lucky if we get anything more than free clothes. Listen, I really appreciate the ideas, but the hole I'm in is deeper than you understand." With a grimace, she confessed, "I also have about thirty grand in credit card debt."

"Oooohhh," I said, the picture coming into focus. "School loans?"

"No, just bad decisions."

I laughed. "We're all guilty of that."

"And before you even think it," Jordan said. "I'm not asking you for more money. I'm very happy with our arrangement. If I could snap my fingers, I'd be paying you to date me."

"Oh, you'd be my sugar momma?"

"Exactly."

I felt myself relaxing as our food arrived. *At least she's not trying to hustle me out of more money,* I thought. In fact, I was mortified I'd been so obsessive demanding better communication from her—how could she pay attention to my ideas on how to start an acting career when she had such financial woes?

Jordan cut her lemon ricotta pancakes into dainty bites. "But wait until you hear the latest installment in the craziness that is the life of Jordan," she said.

"What do you mean?" I asked hesitantly—I didn't know if my heart could stand another surprise.

"Bobby, the guy I swapped apartments with, told me he's coming back to sell the Venice place and needs me out of there in a few days."

"In a few days?" My voice rose with alarm. "I thought you agreed to swap until the end of April?"

"We did, but we never signed any kind of agreement."

"Fuck him. I'm sure you have emails that would prove he agreed to this until the end of April."

"Yeah, but what am I going to do, sue him? You know how expensive lawyers are."

"Take him to fucking small claims court!"

Jordan smiled. "I appreciate you getting angry for me. But life is too short to deal with that kind of stress."

I stared at Jordan with admiration. *Why is she calmer about this than me?* "Okay, so we find you another place here on Airbnb?"

"It's not that simple. Since he's moving out of my place in Manhattan, I'll have to relist my place on Airbnb and find someone to replace him for a couple of months, which is almost impossible last minute. So I'd be paying rent on an empty place there *and* paying rent here."

"So this asshole is going to cost you…what?"

"If I spent the next two months here, at least twelve thousand bucks with all my other expenses."

"I see," I answered, the depth of her problem giving me pause.

"No," Jordan said with a deep sigh, "I think the best solution is I go back to New York for a while."

I matched her deep sigh. "I had a feeling you were about to say that."

"Just for a couple weeks," she quickly clarified. "I'll bank some money, come back, and find a new place here. I promise."

I glanced at my eggs, appetite lost. "Jordan, I understand your problem, but you just got back from there, and I didn't sign up for a long-distance relationship."

"I know. But I don't see any other way. And listen, our month is up next week, so don't send me my allowance."

"That's ridiculous," I scoffed. "What kind of man tightens his purse strings when a woman he cares about is stressed over money? Besides, then you'd have no reason to come back at all!"

"I'd come back for *you*, David."

That warmed my heart. Part of me wanted to end this whole discussion by throwing *more* money at it. I'd just signed an expensive lease on a house, but I wouldn't suffer if I wrote a check for say, ten or fifteen grand. But I wanted Jordan to know my generosity had limits. And maybe part of me wanted to know if she really would come back for me. The way she described it, she made four grand a *week* there, so if she was willing to come back for my paltry four a month, that spoke to her commitment.

"David, I feel terrible for disappointing you," she interrupted my thoughts. "If you want to stop seeing me, I wouldn't blame you one bit."

I immediately shook my head. "Not an option. I'm just…processing. I feel kind of powerless."

And I was worried she would think I was being controlling? I thought. *Hell, I'm so out of control I can't stop her from leaving.*

"Look at the bright side," Jordan said. "You can have a lot of fun while I'm out of town. All the hall passes you want!"

That made me break with laughter. "I swear, if you don't come back to Los Angeles soon, I'm flying to New York, kidnapping you, and hauling that perfect ass back."

Jordan grinned. "I don't doubt that."

11
NEGOTIATING LOVE

"WHAT THE FUCK IS with this rain?" I heard Jordan say as I drove her to the airport Friday night.

If I'm not careful, I thought, *I'm going to kill us.* Clutching the steering wheel with both hands, I leaned forward in my seat and squinted to see through the rain-blurred windshield. It was coming down so hard that the lane lines were drowned, and cars drifted menacingly toward me.

A minute later, I heard her again. "David, what's going on with you?"

This time I chanced a quick look. In her black Moscot glasses and green bomber jacket with her hair in a ponytail, Jordan seemed more worried about the tension inside the car than out.

"I'm trying not to crash," I insisted.

"I don't know…I'm leaving for a couple of weeks, so it seems to me we should be saying *something*…"

"I can listen."

Jordan went quiet, and I went back to paying attention to driving.

But she was right.

I didn't know what Jordan wanted to say, but *I* wanted to tell her, "Don't leave. I'm getting kind of attached to you!" But that seemed pointless now, so I was shutting down, calling upon Hard David to protect myself from disappointment.

We pulled up to the crowded LAX terminal and cars around us honked impatiently. Jordan scrambled out and hurried under the overhang as I pulled her suitcase from the back, dodging pellets of rain to bring it to her.

"Have a safe flight," I said as I gave her a hug and quick kiss on the lips.

"Drive carefully," she said, and then turned and rolled her suitcase into the terminal, glancing over her shoulder with a last wave.

Then I was back in my car, into the deluge again.

I WOKE THE NEXT morning glad to see beams of sunlight cutting through the cracks in my curtains and reached for my phone instinctively.

Landed! Jordan had texted while I slept. Can't believe how much I miss you already.

Bet I miss you more, I answered.

Bet you don't...

A video link appeared in the thread. I thumbed the "play" arrow and watched myself walking up the beach with my surfboard under my arm, waving at Jordan behind the camera.

At first, I didn't understand why she was sending me this random clip from our Malibu jaunt, but then I heard Jordan whisper off-camera, almost inaudibly, *"I love you, David."*

I stopped breathing.

Had I misheard?

I played it again.

"I love you, David."

My God, this is what Jordan wanted to say in the car last night.

Blissful chemicals that had been hidden in the corners of every cell of my body for decades released and raced through my bloodstream into my chest, warming and expanding my heart. It was as if hearing Jordan say the words had unlocked access to it, and what I found in there was my love for her! And not *just* love—mad, passionate, all-consuming love—the type of love that makes you wonder if you've ever been in love before.

I was struck with another epiphany. *I've wanted to tell Jordan this since our first date.* When I'd first seen her pictures, I said *she fits into my fairy tale.* And when we first had sex, I called it *magic.* But now I understood I had used these words to describe love because I was so damn emotionally stunted.

I love you, too, I typed—then paused before sending it. That "too" bothered me. It seemed to me the first time I tell someone I love them, it should be unqualified, unequivocal, undiluted.

I deleted it and wrote simply, I love you.

I pressed send and laid there, heavenly delirious.

My phone rang; I accepted, and Jordan's beautiful face popped up on my screen as she walked the streets of New York, boxing gloves over her shoulder.

"I'm so glad you caught that little gem," she said, beaming from ear to ear.

I stated the obvious. "Jordan, I cannot stop smiling."

"I can see! Me neither."

"Baby, this is un-fucking-believable. But you filmed this in Malibu over a week ago! How come you didn't tell me before? I mean, you wait until you've left to say you love me? That's nuts."

"Crazy, I know!" she agreed. "I guess I wasn't sure if you felt the same way. But the minute you drove away from the terminal last night, I felt like my heart was outside of my chest, and I knew I had to tell you."

"Well, mine feels like it's exploding. Honestly, I think I fell in love with you on our first date."

"And you're teasing *me* for waiting!"

"I'm an emotional moron, what can I say? I'm so good at hiding my feelings I hide them from *myself.*"

She paused her stride to emphasize, "You're not, David. You're the most sensitive, romantic man I've ever met. Honestly, the words came to me on the beach that day, but the feelings were always there for me, too."

I shook my head at the mystery. "Well, Jesus, what do we do about this?"

"What do you mean?"

"I mean you're three thousand miles away! You said you'd probably be back here in two weeks, but right now that seems like complete torture."

"I know."

"Fuck it, I'll book a flight and be there tonight."

Jordan laughed.

"What, you think I'm kidding?" I was already thumbing through my phone to find my American Airlines app.

"Baby, I'm dying to see you, but I came here to work and I'm already setting up people to see."

I looked up and saw her face scrunched with worry—perhaps that she might have insulted me. "Okay, why don't I come this weekend?"

"David, can we slow down here? I don't want to make any rash decisions."

"Rash decisions? What does that mean? Jordan, you told me you loved me. I would think you'd be dancing for joy at the idea of seeing me?"

She waved at someone beyond the camera. "David, I'm sorry, I'm at boxing class. Can we talk tonight?"

I felt my perma-smile vanish. "Okay..."

"I love you."

"I love you, too."

As we hung up, a lump in my throat swelled, sending pressure waves down to my chest. My breathing faltered. My eyes started to moisten. This horrible "uch, uch, uch" came out of my mouth, and then I started to wail and cry uncontrollably. I covered my face with my hands, humiliated by the thought of anyone seeing me like this.

Just then my phone rang. Hoping it was Jordan calling to explain what had just happened, I answered it without looking at caller ID.

"Yeh, yeh, yehsss?" I garbled, tears drenching my cheeks.

"David? Are you okay?" came Elizabeth's voice.

I sucked in enough air to say, "Ccccan I cccccall yuh you lllater?"

"Holy shit, *are you crying*?" Elizabeth asked. "What happened? I haven't heard you cry since Girl died."

She was referring to when I'd found my dog "Girl" dead on the floor from heart failure seven years before.

I steadied my voice to reassure her, "I'm okay, I'll explain later."

"Okay. But I'm here for you, whatever it is."

"Thanks, bye."

I ended the call, grabbed a pillow and covered my tearful face with it.

৯৫

"OH, BABY. I WISH I COULD hold and kiss you," Jordan soothed me as we FaceTimed again that afternoon.

Our screens mirrored each other's, both of us collapsed on our respective couches—hers, a worn, violet velour number that took up a third of the living space in her cramped Manhattan apartment. She had called me as soon as she got home from boxing class, sweat still matted down the tendrils of her hair.

"If ever I needed a hug from you, today is it," I admitted, Soft David face back in full bloom.

"I'm so sorry I made you cry."

"Don't be sorry," I said. "It felt great—like I was in touch with love and pain in the same moment."

"Okay, but I don't understand why? What did I do that hurt so much?"

"I've been meditating on that all morning," I answered. "And I think it's because the last time I felt anywhere near this kind of love was when I was sixteen…"

"With Michelle?"

I was impressed that Jordan remembered Michelle's name from our romantic anxiety-riddled conversation before Valentine's Day. "Right. Well, when you sounded less than excited about me coming, I felt rejected, and that reminded me how utterly, devastatingly heartbreaking love can be when it ends."

"Ohhhh. But why be afraid we'll end that way?"

I almost laughed but caught myself. "Jordan, you up and left for New York. You say you want to come back in two weeks, but come on, that's far from definite."

"Why does everything have to be so definite? I don't know about your life, but the universe laughs whenever I make plans."

"Huh?" I knitted my brow, unclear how my fear she wouldn't return from New York elicited a nebulous philosophical statement.

"Look," she said. "I don't know how to reassure you I'm coming back, other than to say I'm coming back—because I refuse to live my life without you."

"That's a good start."

She smiled, but gently. "You have to understand, this is all a little overwhelming for me. This relationship is once-in-a-lifetime material and scary as fuck. I need some time to process. You know, I didn't sign up for Seeking Arrangement because commitment was my strong suit."

Makes two of us, I thought, a touch surprised. I'd considered myself the one with commitment issues, but perhaps she had them as bad or worse than I did.

Jordan squinted. "And what's this Elizabeth said about you not crying since your dog died?"

"Hard to believe, huh? But true. Other than that, and a few tears of joy when my kids were born, I haven't cried since I was–"

"Let me guess," Jordan jumped in. "Sixteen?"

"Bingo," I said.

Jordan looked astounded. "You're always so emotional with me. But if Elizabeth never saw that side of you, I bet she was freaked. Did she even know we've been dating?"

"I've mentioned it a few times. But yeah, when I called her back, she was really worried."

"What did you tell her?"

"The truth. We've fallen in love, but you've moved back to New York."

"I'll be back in two weeks!"

"You're starting to sound like a contractor," I teased.

"Hah!"

The return of Jordan's breathy laugh relaxed me as always. "Hey, it's almost eight there," I said, glancing at the time on my phone. "No date tonight?"

"God no! After flying, if I don't get a full night's rest, I'm all but certain to get depressed. But I'll get to work tomorrow. I'm a hot commodity here, you know."

"You're preaching to the choir!"

Her smile dropped at one corner. "Is it weird we're talking about seeing other people?"

"Because we're in love now, you mean?"

"Uh huh."

I took quick emotional inventory and said, "I'm happy with our open relationship. But if this is your way of saying you want to be monogamous, let's talk."

"I'm not saying that *at all*," Jordan said demonstratively. "I really like my freedom. But I guess I want to be *emotionally monogamous*. I'm sure I'd be a jealous wreck if you went out on a real date."

"What's a real date?"

"You know, if you meet someone at the gym or a party."

I laughed at the idea. "First of all, I'm allergic to the gym and hate parties, so that's unlikely."

"You know what I mean," she said playfully. "And on normal apps like Bumble or Tinder."

Again, I laughed. Although I had those apps on my phone, I hadn't gone out with anybody from them in years. "Consider them deleted. And what about Seeking Arrangement?"

"Oh, I'm totally fine with us meeting people from there," Jordan insisted. "We're not going to get emotionally attached to people if there's money involved."

The irony was so rich I could barely keep a straight face. "Right, it's not like we would ever fall in love with anybody from SA."

"Hah! Trust me, we're outliers. The odds of this happening were astronomical."

"I know. I'm teasing."

Jordan grinned. "There really isn't a playbook for our kind of relationship, is there?"

I thought about her question. How did two people who had a history of compartmentalizing relationships, who didn't believe in monogamy, who were afraid of commitment—and who had trouble even recognizing and admitting to themselves and each other they were in love—negotiate a healthy, happy relationship?

"The playbook is the same as it's always been," I answered. "It's like what you said on our first date. If we're honest and transparent, everything is negotiable."

Jordan smiled. "We're very progressive, aren't we?"

"Very," I answered.

12
BROKEN FOOT

I TURNED FIFTY-THREE TWO days later, waking to my kids jumping on the bed and pulling me down to the playroom where they'd laid out dozens of three-by-five cards. On each one they'd written a word or two to describe me. I was Daddy Fix-It, Buddha (I wouldn't say I had a "dad bod" but the kids liked to tease me about the ten pounds camouflaging my abs), kind, funny, and so on.

"And best in bed," Jordan added when I relayed the story on FaceTime later that morning—she was in her apartment, feet up on her velour couch.

"*Happy birthday to you, happy birthday to you, happy birthday, dear David!*" she sang.

At my desk in my office, I applauded. "Damn, how can the day get any better after hearing you sing?"

"Shut up," she flushed. "So what are you and the kids going to do tonight to celebrate?"

"Taking them to Benihana, of course."

"I want to go!" she pretended to whine.

"We'll go to one when I get there," I promised. The day before, we had agreed I'd visit her in New York on March 13, eleven days and a lifetime from now.

"My treat!" she insisted.

I laughed, amused by the idea that my girlfriend would pay for dinner out of the allowance I gave her. "And what are you up to tonight?" I asked. "Got a date?"

"Are you sure you want to hear this?"

"I promise to tell you if I get even the slightest bit jealous," I vowed. "But think of this as a test of how progressive we really are. I mean, if we can't even talk about it, we shouldn't be doing it, right?"

"God, I love you how think. But do me a favor—spare me the graphic details about *your* dates. All I want to know is who you see and when."

"As you wish."

Jordan took a breath. "His name is Christopher. He lives in LA but has a court case here. We had the *longest* lunch yesterday. I finally got it out of him that he pays a grand every date, but then he said he doesn't like it to feel transactional and didn't invite me to his hotel. But he asked me to dinner tonight and sent me the money already."

"Sounds like a gentleman," I commented.

"Yeah, and a super nice guy. Oh! And I almost forgot—he was on crutches!"

"What?"

"His foot was in a cast. He said he broke it tripping over a desk or something yesterday morning."

"And he hobbled to lunch with you? The guy must have a high threshold for pain."

"You'd never know it from looking at him. He's like a six-foot-tall Pillsbury Doughboy with brown hair."

Her description sprang to life in my head. "I need to see a picture of *this* guy."

"Let me pull up a link to his firm's website for you." Her screen paused while she navigated away, and gentle taps sounded through the speaker.

"Did your pre-date google, did you?" I asked.

"Girl can't be too careful."

My phone vibrated, and I clicked on the link to the firm's page and selected the "Attorneys" tab. Christopher's picture was front and center—

he was managing partner of the business litigation firm. With his double chin and pleasant smile, he was indeed "doughy."

"I have him in my contacts as Christopher Lawyer," Jordan said as she reappeared onscreen. "But maybe I should call him Doughboy?"

"No, call him Broken Foot," I suggested. "Like Kevin Costner's Native American name was Dances with Wolves in that movie."

"Because they'd seen him playing with a wolf!"

In a very culturally insensitive Native American voice, I pronounced, "I am Broken Foot."

Between a cascade of laughs, Jordan gasped, "I'm not going to be able to keep a straight face when I see him."

I GOT THE REPORT on Jordan's date the next morning, when she texted me, How was Benihana, honey?

Never disappoints, I answered. But how was your night with Broken Foot?

LOL. Just leaving his suite now.

Lucky guy got a sleepover on the first date! I pointed out.

Only because I didn't want to deal with a forty-minute ride back to Manhattan at 1 a.m. And there wasn't cuddling, that's for sure. The chemistry with this guy is nothing like what we have.

That does not sound fun, I wrote back. You're not going to see him again, are you?

A girl's gotta eat, she answered.

That made no sense whatsoever. Jordan had repeatedly insisted she fought off suitors in New York, but here she was forcing herself to have another date with a man who she had no chemistry with. Couldn't she go back on Seeking Arrangement and find someone she liked better? Oh, and Broken Foot was from Los Angeles, the place Jordan said had no decent men besides me, so that was confusing. *But Jordan is an adult,* I told myself. *She can make her own decisions.* Besides, I had my own adult plans.

I'D MATCHED WITH HELENA, a thirty-nine-year-old redhead on Seeking about a month prior, and if it weren't for my preoccupation with Jordan, would probably have already met her. We'd chatted and had a few phone calls, and Helena met most of my qualifications for that oh-so-rare genuine connection. She was an avid reader of historical fiction (intelligent), she'd worked as a makeup artist on adult films and saw no shame in befriending porn stars (open-minded), and she seemed to be taking to sugaring for the best of reasons—recently divorced from a man with whom she'd owned an animal rescue that went bankrupt, Helena hoped to find a man who could help her with her legal bills.

"I was thinking we could finally meet!" I told Helena when I called her from my office that afternoon.

"It's about time," the soft-spoken, eloquent woman answered. "What were you thinking?"

I'd been honest with Helena about my relationship with Jordan, and that I was seeking little more than a casual arrangement, but ever the gentleman, I suggested we meet for a drink or dinner to get to know each other. To my surprise, Helena had other ideas. She thought of herself as a modern-day courtesan, akin to those of Paris in the court of Louis the Fifteenth, and there was no need to wine and dine her.

"Let's use our creativity and have some fun with this," she said. "I'll come to your house, and when you're done with me, send me away."

I laughed at Helena's eccentricity—she reminded me of a more refined Colette of Sanctum—and let my imagination run.

"Why don't you come to my house at four?" I suggested, then paused for dramatic effect. "In a blindfold."

Just as it was occurring to me a woman might feel unsafe showing up at a stranger's door blindfolded, Helena cooed, "Oh, that sounds lovely."

"Should we discuss the arrangement?" I asked.

"Surprise me," she astonished me once again.

Damn, I love my life, I thought as I texted my assistant to cancel my afternoon meetings and rushed back to the Westwood house.

I showered, put on a white T-shirt and faded jeans, drew my bedroom curtains, and tuned a sexy Spotify playlist on the house speakers.

The doorbell rang, and I walked to the front door and slowly opened it. Helena stood there in a cream-colored silk dress with lace edges, her long rose hair tucked under a brown satin blindfold, her pouty, naturally pink lips alternating between nervous quivers and smiles of anticipation.

"Hello?" she whispered.

I took her hand and put my mouth to her ear. "Why don't we talk after?"

Her breath skipped a beat, which I took for a yes.

I led her inside, closed the door behind me with my free hand, and gently escorted her through the foyer.

"Stairs here," I thought to advise her, and we took one step at a time.

"Last one," I said, then guided her into the bedroom and stopped at the edge of the bed.

"The bed is behind you. Sit please."

Helena followed my direction, and I let go of her hand to reach into the bedside cabinet drawer for a condom. When I turned, she'd shed her green flats, and her feet dangled off the bed as she blindly slipped her panties from beneath her skirt.

I stood over her to kiss her and felt her chest heave breaths into my mouth. Then I pulled back, bent my knees to the floor, parted her legs, and licked the inside of her thighs.

Helena laid back on the bed with a sigh and came to an orgasm so quickly I thought she might be faking it—I certainly couldn't give my talents credit for such an overwhelming response.

But then she came again and again.

I was awed—I'd dated women who were capable of multiple orgasms, but this woman had a gift. I lifted my dampened face without an attempt to wipe it, slid open the condom, and placed it on myself. Helena felt my pelvis move toward hers, reached down and guided me inside her.

"Oh, my God," I gasped as she shuddered against me and came yet again.

HELENA LAY BESIDE ME in my sweat and bodily fluid-soaked bed, naked limbs crossed, both of us satiated, our breathing settling. I carefully lifted her blindfold and was rewarded with her beautiful brown eyes blinking up at me.

"Well, that's a relief," she sighed as the blinks creased into a smile. "I'd have been depressed if you turned out to be less handsome than your pictures."

"Glad I didn't disappoint. Meeting me blind was pretty brave of you. But I don't suggest you make a habit of it—I've heard there are some unsavory characters on the site."

"I don't know, there was something about the way we talked that made me trust you. Now, I'm annoyed you're not single."

"Why so?"

"Because you're the first person I've met on or off the site I think is even remotely relationship-material."

You might not have thought that if you'd met me before Jordan, I wanted to say, but contained myself—pillow talk about my relationship felt like crossing the line that separated physical from emotional monogamy.

Perhaps sensing I was holding back, Helena sat up and looked for her dress. "I guess I'll go, but I'd love to see you again."

"I hope so," I answered, then reached across the bed to the end table, where I'd left a plain white envelope with seven crisp hundred-dollar bills inside. "And I hope this doesn't disappoint you."

She flushed as she accepted it and placed it into her dress pocket without counting it. "Are you kidding? Whatever it is, I should be paying *you.*"

I laughed as I pulled on my jeans. "I'm sure it will only be a matter of time before someone takes you off the market."

"I don't know, I'm a little damaged goods," she said shyly.

"Why do you say that?"

"Well," she lamented, "I usually don't spill it on a first date, but I feel like I could tell you anything."

"I'd like to think I'm not too judgmental," I said, but felt some alarm.

"It was a total misunderstanding. My ex-husband hadn't gotten the proper license for our rescue and the city closed us down. They said we had too many animals for the space. Unfortunately, the press twisted it to sound like we were hoarding animals, so the city attorney brought charges against us."

That didn't sound as bad as whatever my imagination was concocting. "Really? Well, you sound more like a saint than a criminal to me."

She smiled. "You're sweet. Anyway, do me a favor and don't google me?"

I felt like young George Washington standing before his father with an ax. "Come on, you know that's the first thing I'm going to do when you're gone."

She laughed. "Okay, well, I hope you still want to see me again after."

I walked her to her maroon BMW coupe, gave her a hug, and watched her drive away, then rushed back inside to find my phone.

I'd barely finished typing *Helena, animal rescue* before the algorithm brought up a news article…

Woman Charged with Animal Cruelty in Hoarding of 42 Dogs.

I scanned the article and saw pictures of dogs suffering from malnutrition in dirty cages, some with open, festering wounds. The police described Helena's house as "disturbing," and neighbors complained about the reek for months. Helena and her husband had been not only been arrested and charged with three counts of animal cruelty, but they'd gone to trial and had been convicted!

And this was the woman who was just in my bed?

I was stunned. I'd always considered myself the Rare Gentleman, the man who made women feel safe, the man they could trust, and my house and home were an extension of that self-image. But never in my wildest imagination had I stopped to think I might need to worry a woman would bring danger into the house. Was I being dramatic? Probably—I didn't think Helena was a real threat to *me*. Was she going to show up at my house and boil a rabbit? No. But in that moment, I felt exposed and full of self-doubt for having been so naïve and trusting.

"Holy shit," Jordan said when we spoke on the phone the next morning. As she had requested, I spared her the graphic details about sex with Helena, but how could I not share how it had ended?

"Crazy, isn't it?" I groaned. "I'm usually so careful about googling someone before we meet. I don't know, I dropped the ball."

"I wouldn't be too hard on yourself. But you might want to block her number, just in case."

I nodded and tried to see the humor in the situation. "We sure can pick them, can't we? My date turns out to be a convicted felon, yours is a hobbling lawyer."

"Ugh, don't remind me. Broken Foot invited me to see some play tonight, but I'm on the struggle bus. It's below zero here, and I think I'm coming down with the flu."

I decided not to make Jordan feel worse by telling her I was sitting on the Malibu house deck, taking a break from building sandcastles with my children in eighty-six-degree sunny weather. "Oh, no, can I Postmates you some soup?"

"That's sweet, but he wants dinner first, too. God, the last thing I want to do is put on clothes and pretend to feel sexy with this guy."

I didn't know what advice to give Jordan. For all our teasing, Broken Foot was treating her like a queen.

"Do you want a pep talk?" I asked her.

"To cancel? Or to go?"

"Whatever makes you happy."

Jordan forced a laugh. "I do love you. Never mind—my bank account is the answer."

❧

BUT THE NEXT DAY, I started to question if Jordan's bank balance was worth her seeing Broken Foot.

I'd finished lunch with the kids when I checked my phone and saw I'd missed a FaceTime call from Jordan, so I excused myself to my bedroom and called her back. She picked up, lying on her side in bed—pale, her nose flared red. She was clearly ill. Tucked into her chest was a gray stuffed bunny.

"Who's that little fella?" I asked.

"That's Harvey!" she answered with sniffle. "He travels everywhere I go."

"How come I've never met him before?"

Jordan shrugged. "You only slept at my place in Venice once. He must have been hiding. He's shy."

I laughed. "Well, nice to meet you, Harvey. How's your mom doing today?"

"Mom is in hell," Jordan said.

"Then I want to go to hell," I answered.

She tried to laugh but hacked a cough. "My temperature is through the roof. I was shaking and sweating through this four-hour play. It's fucking *four* hours long."

"Did Broken Foot even notice?"

"Yeah, he could see I was suffering and let me go home instead of back to his hotel. But he extended his trip here to see me for the weekend and already sent me two grand, and I'm not going to be able to get out of bed."

"I'm sure he'll understand."

"Probably. He is getting a little obsessed with me. He keeps talking about taking me to Hawaii and Paris, and he said he could see having children with me."

"Jesus," I said. *Here I've been afraid to have pillow talk with a woman, and Jordan's dates are planning a life with her?* "What did you tell him?"

"I told him I didn't think I could handle being a full-time mom with my depression, but he said he'd hire a team of nannies to help around the clock."

"As if that's the key to raising children," I opined. "And wait, you told me you didn't think you wanted kids?"

"I'm conflicted, what can I say? One minute I think I'll be the best mother in the world, but after about an hour with my sister's kids I'm ready to shoot myself. Besides, picture me in a depressive episode with a baby on my hip. Chaos."

She laughed but I didn't. "Jordan, this is getting out of hand. Seems to me it would be better not to lead Broken Foot on. Tell him the truth—you're already in a relationship."

"No. It would totally ruin his fantasy. Not everybody is as open-minded as you, David."

I couldn't argue with that. I couldn't explain why I was built the way I was. But something needled me—I didn't like that she was lying to this unfortunate, earnest man. Why couldn't she be as honest with him as she was with me?

"But something has to change," Jordan lamented. "I feel like my soul is on the line every time I see him."

I blinked. *Her soul is on the line?* I found it amusing when Jordan joked about being a "shitty hooker" and "a girl has to eat," but suddenly she was existentially conflicted?

"Just ignore me," Jordan added. "I'm probably coming down with depression. You really have no idea how disgusting it is to be in this head."

My mouth fell open and I felt like I might cry out of empathy for her. "Baby, I'm so sorry you're suffering."

"Thank you," she forced out. "But I need to disconnect from the world, so I'm going to bed, okay?"

"Okay. I'm here if you need me."

Her face disappeared on my screen, and I sat there a moment, feeling frustratingly helpless. Just two days ago, I'd seen our dating other people as some fun test of how progressive we were. But now it felt like that test had failed miserably.

Jordan is breaking, I thought to myself. *And I've got to fix her.*

13
THE GRAND GESTURE

"THE POOR GIRL," SIGHED my friend Megan as she absently stirred a dirty martini.

"Yeah. She's a bit of a hot mess right now." I strained my voice over loud bar chatter.

It was two nights later, and Megan and I sat at the bar at the Chateau Marmont hotel in West Hollywood. Known for its rich Hollywood lore (every actor and musician from Jim Morrison to Johnny Depp had partied here, and John Belushi famously overdosed in one of its rooms), Marmont was a bit too hip for my introverted soul. But Megan made it her second home, and I was so eager to talk about what was going on with Jordan that I obliged her.

"And where's Jordan tonight?" Megan asked. "Is she feeling any better?"

"Laying low in her apartment," I answered. "And no, she's suffering. It's really frustrating for me, Megan. I feel useless, like nothing I say or do helps her *at all.*"

"I understand, really, I do," she said.

I smiled appreciatively at Megan and thought if anybody in the bar were people-watching us, they'd draw the most inaccurate conclusion from that smile. After all, Megan was twenty-six with long black hair and ruby lips. She sported tight black jeans and a snug wife-beater tee. One look at her, and it was obvious she was a struggling actress. And sitting next to a man in his fifties in the film producer attire of jeans and a sport coat? *He's fucking her*, anybody would think. But I didn't care what people might think; I knew the truth—Megan and I were just close friends, so close I shared all my secrets with her, and she shared hers with me.

"Megan, I'm so fucking in love with this woman," I said as I stabbed an olive and sucked the vermouth soaked into its core. "But I have this sinking suspicion she and I are not going to walk into the sunset together. I feel like I'm that sap in the movies who falls in love with his hooker, and you know that never ends well."

"That's not true," Megan scoffed.

I grinned, knowing we were about to begin one of our classic film trivia competitions. It was funny—with most people I didn't like to talk about movies, mainly because I hated the perennial Hollywood chatter. But Megan's love for the movies was so pure, and her admiration for their history so deep, when she and I spoke of them it was like we had a language of our own. (This game was how our friendship had started—we'd met at a film screening a few years back.)

"*Moulin Rouge*…Nicole Kidman dies," I began. "*Leaving Las Vegas*… Nic Cage dies. Tragedies, both of them."

Megan squinted, opening an Internet Movie Database page in her mind. "*Breakfast at Tiffany's*!" she called out.

"Okay, so there's one," I allowed. "But what about *McCabe & Mrs. Miller*? Julie Christy gets gunned down. And *Les Mis*! Anne Hathaway got a damn Best Actress Oscar for dying in that one."

Megan pretended to frown—she loved the game as much as I did. "*Pretty Woman*! Richard Gere climbs up a fire escape and kisses Julia Roberts."

I couldn't help feeling a bit of amusement at Megan's mention of Jordan's favorite movie, the one we kept trying to watch together—but then I remembered some little-known film trivia.

"Ah, but did you know the original ending of *Pretty Woman* was *very* dark? Julia Roberts's character was a dope fiend who ends up thrown out of the guy's limo, back to the street."

Megan looked like I'd burst her cinematic bubble. "Fuck, that's dark."

"That's Hollywood," I said. "Disney bought the script and that was all she wrote."

"Okay, you win this one," Megan surrendered, holding up her martini glass. She shifted on her stool to face me. "All right, I understand why you're worried about Jordan. Depression's rough. But from everything you've said, it sounds like she's as madly in love with you as you are with her, and you're going to see her in New York in a week, so why the doom and gloom?"

"Think about it," I said. "When she left, she said she'd be back in a couple weeks. Now *I'm* going to visit *her*. And what happens after that? We have a wonderful weekend, I fall deeper in love, then it's another few weeks before she comes back? Meanwhile, she's got rich guys like Broken Foot throwing money at her..."

Megan interrupted me with a chuckle. "That nickname, I'm sorry."

"I know, it's silly. But seriously, I feel like Jordan and I are one conversation away from breaking up. She'll say she can't handle a relationship now or something."

"Well, you're a producer—if a writer was pitching this story to you, what would you tell him to change so it had a happy ending?"

I traced the wet ring my martini glass left on its napkin, pensive. "I'd tell the writer to have the hero make a grand gesture. Something romantic and thoughtful that proves how much he loves the woman."

"I love a good grand gesture," Megan gushed. "Remember *Notting Hill*—Hugh Grant running through London to stop Julia Roberts from leaving?"

I rose my pitch and batted my eyes like Julia Roberts. "I'm just a girl, standing in front of a boy, asking him to love her."

Megan cackled at my impression.

I sobered and went on, "I need to do something that shows her how important she is to me. Something that will help her out of this survival mode. I'd really have no problem with her being an escort if it made her happy, but honestly, I think it's half the reason she's depressed."

Megan sat up straight as if to demonstrate respect as she ventured, "Could you afford to give her more money? Buy her out, so to speak."

Quickly, she added, "I'm not saying you should—I know plenty of women, myself included, who could live happily off what you give Jordan—but I'm just wondering, is all."

"I'd have to give her ten grand a month or something, so the answer is no. I'm not that rich. And to be honest, even if I could wave a wand and make all her money problems go away, I'm not sure I would. As much as I love her, I want to be in a relationship with someone who is capable of helping herself."

"That's fair."

"But I do want to help her in some way. Give her a goal, or a plan, and of course, give her a good reason to come back to Los Angeles."

As I said this, I found myself brightening with a memory. "Wait a minute, I have an idea."

"Tell me."

"Well, Jordan once told me she wanted to take yoga teacher training. I think it was on our first date. I bet that can't cost more than five grand. I could afford to give her that."

"That would be a great grand gesture," Megan agreed. "It would show her how thoughtful you are, how you're thinking of her career…"

Megan and I withdrew our phones from our pockets like guns from their holsters and started firing at Google.

"Here's one down in San Diego," I read aloud. "Two hours south of here. Six weeks intensive, starting in three weeks, thirty-five hundred dollars."

"Perfect! How could she refuse?"

"I'm telling you…this girl is very unpredictable."

"Okay, well, what if she says no?"

I shuddered to think about it. "Then I guess I gots to know."

"Gots to know?"

I smiled and knew I had Megan on this film reference. "*Dirty Harry*," I said. "Clint Eastwood breaks up a robbery and chases down a thug. He holds his .357 Magnum over the guy and dares him to run. Says he can't remember if he shot all his bullets or not."

Megan suddenly beamed with recollection and did her best Clint Eastwood imitation. "Do ya feel lucky?" she grumbled.

I went on, "The thug gives up, but as he's being hauled off, he asks Clint, 'Hey man, I gots to know?' So Clint aims the gun, pulls his trigger... click, he was out of bullets."

Megan moaned. "The guy gambled on fate and now he's a sucker."

"Right. Well, if Jordan says no to my grand gesture, I'll gots to know *I'm* a sucker. She probably never intended to come back to Los Angeles."

"No, David, she'd be the fool for giving you up," Megan insisted. "Okay, so when will you tell her about the training?"

"I don't know. Maybe tomorrow? Maybe when I get to New York? I'll sleep on it."

Megan sighed. "The suspense is going to kill me."

⁂

IT KILLED ME TOO.

Driving home from Chateau, I knew there wasn't a chance in hell I'd wait till I got to New York to present the yoga teacher training to Jordan. I was far too excited about my plan. It was close to 2:00 a.m. New York time, so I tamped down my enthusiasm, figuring any grand gesture worth its salt could be slept on for *one night*.

But a funny thing happened. I'd plopped myself on the couch and flicked on CNN, only to see these ominous news reports—weather forecasters were reporting that a massive blizzard was fast approaching the East Coast. Already calling it "The Great North American Blizzard of 2019," they predicted ten to thirteen feet of snow would blanket New York over the next week. Airports from Nantucket to Atlanta were expected to shut down, and airlines were already canceling flights, basically telling anybody who expected to travel on the right side of America in the next week to get a brain.

Ten feet of snow? Airport closures? Jordan was only hours from getting snowed-in in New York with Broken Foot!

I imagined the two of them holed up in his suite at the Plaza or Ritz Carlton, in robes, eating room service and drinking champagne, watching *Dateline* on television, making occasional forays to the bedroom. I tried to stop myself from imagining what they'd do in bed, but not because

I was jealous. I *was* threatened by Broken Foot's money—given a few more weeks and tens of thousands of dollars, Jordan might find dating him palatable.

I felt like a knight called to action—I needed to save Jordan from Broken Foot and her depression. And I couldn't wait till the morning; I wouldn't even be able to sleep now.

Please be awake, I thought as I took a screenshot of my weather app showing nothing but sunny weather icons in Los Angeles for the next week and texted it to Jordan.

I hear it's supposed to dump in New York, I wrote beneath it. Why don't I cancel my trip and you come here instead?

I pressed send and looked to the cottage plaster on my ceiling. *Am I being obsessive, impulsive, dramatic?* But really, I didn't care. I was madly in love and unwilling to let such things as clocks or time zones or imaginary peoples' opinions of my behavior stop this glorious madness.

My phone vibrated.

Get me outta here! Jordan wrote.

Thank God! I thought. (No small thing, considering the only thing keeping me from being an atheist was humility.)

I'll book you on a flight first thing tomorrow morning, but I think it should be one way.

Ha-ha, why?

Because I want to give you this, I answered, attaching a link to the San Diego course.

She must have speed-read it because she FaceTimed me immediately.

"Are you serious?" Jordan asked, sitting up in her bed with her computer on her lap, her nose still red from wiping it, and of course, Harvey nested beside her.

"Yeah, I want to invest in your future," I said.

"Baby, this is my dream!"

Jordan stood on the bed and did a happy dance. I laughed—I'd thought the suggestion would cheer her up, but it seemed to have snuffed out her depression altogether.

"I'm so glad you were awake," I said as she plopped down again and pressed her face close to the camera.

"I wasn't! I usually keep my ringer off, but I must have fallen asleep and forgot."

"Kismet!" I insisted.

"I'm gonna kiss you, all right!" she twisted the word with a laugh. "You know, with my social media following, any yoga studio would hire me. And a friend of mine owns a wellness center in Fiji and always says if I get certified, he'll let me organize yoga retreats."

"I'll come and surf while you teach!"

"Deal!"

"But wait," Jordan said, suddenly worried. "This course has to be ridiculously expensive. Are you sure you can afford it?"

"I wouldn't offer it if I couldn't," I said. "Question is, can you?"

Jordan paused, which I took to mean she understood what I was implying.

"I know what you mean," she answered. "The course is supposed to be physically exhausting, and I won't be able to use depression as an excuse. And I wouldn't have much time to see people and make money. But I think if I lower the price on my place here, it will rent out quickly. And it's not like I'll need more than a bed in a cheap place in San Diego. I probably won't even spend much time there—I'd want to come up and see you every weekend and nights you don't have the kids."

I couldn't believe how fast she'd come up with such a detailed plan.

"Window or aisle?" I asked. "I'll book your ticket as soon as we hang up."

"Window, always!"

"See, we're perfect for each other, I'm an aisle guy!"

We both laughed, then I straightened my face. "Listen, I know you owe Broken Foot a few dates…"

"To Hell with Broken Foot! I'll send him the two grand back."

Now I was *impressed*. Jordan could have easily told me she wanted to come to Los Angeles in a week or two and see Broken Foot a few more times. Instead, she was leaping to accept my offer and giving up money. I wasn't certain how much of this success was due to the genius of my grand gesture, her love for me, or just desire to escape the coming storm—but I was so damn happy all I could say was, "Better get off the phone and start packing, honey."

"Holy shit, you're right!" Jordan echoed my glee. "David after the week I've had, I can't tell you how incredible you are. I love you so much. You're my best friend, my angel."

We said our "I love you's" and hung up.

I promptly booked Jordan a one-way flight to Los Angeles and called Megan.

"God damn," Megan gasped after I shared the news. "Let's hear it for the grand gesture!"

"Guess we gots to know!" I answered. "Gots to know."

14

THE HALVES OF MY HEART

JORDAN AND I SPENT A blissful week in Los Angeles before she moved down to San Diego, where I rented her a bedroom in a condominium a few blocks away from the yoga studio. And that Monday, the day she started teacher training, I moved into the new house on Rosewood.

As excited as my kids were about getting their own rooms and a pool, they were understandably nervous about leaving the house they'd been in since my divorce, so I did my best to make it quick and painless. I hired a moving service, and four of the burliest Russian men I'd ever seen showed up and wrapped, boxed, and moved everything in a single day.

My maid, Elvia, spent two days helping me unpack. A forty-four-year-old Latina, Elvia spoke even less English than I did Spanish—which was basically none—so we communicated mostly by text, sometimes even when we were in the same room! Elvia helped me unwrap every glass and dish, put our clothes into their dressers and drawers, hang my art and family pictures on the walls, and arrange and rearrange furniture.

Elvia had been working for me for over ten years. She cleaned a few days at my house and a few days at Elizabeth's house, so she'd seen me married, divorced, and dating, but because of the language barrier, our relationship remained more professional than what you might expect after a decade. But that night, as she passed me the last stack of flattened boxes to squish into the recycling bin, she smiled at me and seemed to have a little tear in the corner of her eye.

"What's the matter, Elvia?" I asked.

Elvia shook her head and smiled. "Nada. You are happy."

I was glad to see she was crying because she was moved rather than upset by something, and even more impressed that she'd somehow noticed a change in me.

"I'm pretty happy these days, yeah," I said with a sheepish grin.

"Her name?" Elvia asked.

Now I was surprised. Sure, I knew Jordan was making my life immensely happy lately, but it wasn't like there was a physical trace of her in the house. So how did Elvia know? Woman's intuition? Did I have some silly smile perpetually pasted on my face?

"Jordan," I admitted. "Her name is Jordan."

ON TUESDAY AFTERNOON, I PICKED the kids up from school and brought them to Rosewood. They rushed to their rooms. Eli was thrilled the bunk bed was all his now, and Chloe was overjoyed to discover how feminine her new room was—I'd found her a giant shag rug with pink, fuchsia, yellow, and turquoise geometric circles, a whimsically arched bookcase for her stuffed animal collection, and a slender white metal bed with a giant heart designed into its frame. Then we donned our bathing suits and dove into the pool.

"It's like we're in Hawaii!" Eli announced when he came up for air.

I swept him into my arms and swelled a bit with pride. The landlord had installed that pool heater and over the past two days, I'd dipped a foot into the water hourly to test the temperature until I raised it to eighty-nine degrees. Not eighty-eight—which felt chilly—and not ninety—which made the pool feel like a hot tub. It would be a month before I realized this nearly doubled my utility bill, but swimming with Eli and Chloe ensured I'd never regret the cost.

OVER THE NEXT FEW weeks, on weekends or weekdays when I didn't have the kids, I'd send an Uber to bring Jordan up from San Diego. Teacher training went from seven thirty in the morning until three thirty in the afternoon, where Jordan would sit in an un-air-conditioned studio on a hardwood floor, with nothing but a yoga mat and small pillow. She'd often arrive at Rosewood exhausted, hunched over, neck, shoulders, and back in pain from eight hours of practicing yoga poses.

Her protesting body inspired me to surprise her by booking a private massage therapist to set up shop in my bedroom.

"I feel like a different person," Jordan said as she emerged two inches taller, so I added it to our blossoming routine and made it a weekly engagement.

In the evenings, we worked together on the couch, I with my scripts while she studied from her training manual.

"We learned all about Ayurveda medicine today," Jordan would interject. "It's really good for my dosha type to have routine and structure—even if I fucking loathe it."

What Jordan loathed even more than routine was waking up for her morning class. No iPhone alarm was loud enough to rouse her from her dreams, so I'd be her alarm clock. On days when she was in San Diego, I'd text, call, FaceTime, WhatsApp, and Facebook message her—I even had to ring her roommate a couple times to knock on Jordan's door— and she'd frantically rush to class. The yoga studio was mercifully near a McDonald's, and she and I shared a love for Egg McMuffins, so she'd make a pit stop. On days when Jordan slept at Rosewood, I'd rouse her with espresso, fruit, and sunny-side-up eggs, but because the drive back down to San Diego often began before dawn, getting her out of bed and into an Uber was quite a feat.

IF THE SUN WAS OUT, and it always seemed to be when Jordan was at the house, she and I spent most of our afternoons by the pool, lounging on the cheap wicker chaises the previous tenants had left behind. And Jordan made good on that sly promise she'd given when we first toured the house—she was often naked, covered in coconut oil or a Hawaiian Tropic tanning lotion containing zero SPF protection.

I maintained our paradise religiously—no easy task when you live in a canyon surrounded by trees. The pool man came one day a week, but it only took a single gust of wind to instantly fill the pool with brown leaves, seeds, and insects. I bought a solar-powered robot that skimmed the surface of the pool, and another that roamed the bottom sucking up debris, but if Jordan wanted to take a dip, I'd still rake the surface with a ten-foot pole net. *God forbid my love swims in a pool with a few leaves in it!*

But in truth, I took pride in being her pool boy. Despite coming from an estate in Beverly Hills with an Olympic-sized pool, Rosewood—and the beautiful woman swimming naked in its tiny, oval pond—made me feel like I'd reached the pinnacle of success. Rosewood had become my own royal castle.

∂℘

THREE WEEKS INTO JORDAN'S training, she called me to say class had let out early, and she was on her way up in an Uber. I was about to step into a meeting, so I shared the alarm code to the house and told her where I kept an extra key. As soon as my meeting was over, I rushed home to find Jordan floating naked on a raft in the pool, reading a magazine, her skin growing tanner as summer approached.

I quietly shed all my clothes and jumped into the water, the splash surprising her. She gleefully screamed, slipped off the raft, and swam into my arms. I kissed her and guided her to the shallow end of the pool, where we started to have sex. Her back was against the wall, her arms around me, and my face was buried as I gently bit where her neck and shoulders met.

"Excuse me–" A baritone voice startled both of us.

I looked up to find two officers in private security uniforms standing at the open glass sliding doors.

Jordan quickly folded her arms across her breasts, speechlessly embarrassed.

"What's going on?" I asked the officers.

"We got an alarm call for the house," said the older of the two men.

"I didn't hear anything," I insisted.

"It was a silent alarm," he explained.

The screenwriter in me instantly saw a plot hole here. "But my girlfriend turned off the alarm almost an hour ago, so if she didn't do it right, why did it take so long for you to come?"

The officer shrugged. "I'm sorry, you'll have to ask maintenance that question. In the meantime, can I have your password?"

"Malibu," I said.

"Thank you, sir. We'll show ourselves out."

"Please."

The officers turned and headed back into the house, and I glanced at Jordan. We instantly collapsed into each other's arms with laughter.

"Oh. My. God," she uttered, face flush. "That might have been the most embarrassing moment of my life."

That coitus interruptus hadn't embarrassed me as much as it had Jordan—after all, I'd had sex in front of a crowd of strangers at Sanctum. And to be honest, it might have been one of the most ego-boosting moments of my life. *How many fifty-three-year-old men are lucky enough to get caught having sex with the love of their life in a pool?*

But I did take steps to ensure it didn't happen again. The alarm company serviceman came out a few days later and discovered the batteries on the window sensors needed replacing, and the next time Jordan came to visit, I had a surprise waiting for her.

"Awwww," was all she could say when she saw the house key on the tray between the plate of eggs and the espresso.

A little nervous—I'd only given a key to one other woman in my life, and that had ended in divorce—I rambled, "It opens both the top and bottom locks on the side door...which seems pointless. If you're not safe enough with one lock, why have two but on the same key? And nothing drives me more nuts than when someone locks the top lock from the inside, and I have to use the same key *twice* to get into the door."

Then, as she'd done so many mornings over the past few weeks, Jordan hurried through breakfast and climbed into an Uber.

After she left, I went through my bed, scanning to make sure we hadn't left evidence the kids might stumble upon that made it obvious a woman had been there.

Since my divorce, I often felt like I lived two different lives—one was a bachelor of epic proportion, the other "super dad." And until a few weeks ago, I never had a problem transitioning between these two happy personas. The kids left; a woman came. But now, whenever Jordan left in an Uber, it felt like half of my heart was leaving with her.

And I knew it was time to introduce the two halves of my heart to each other.

⁂

"HAVE YOU DECIDED WHAT you'll do after yoga training?" I asked Jordan one evening as she studied on the couch beside me.

She took off her glasses and rubbed her eyes, which I took as a bad sign. I'd asked her this a few times lately, but she sounded philosophically opposed to looking more than a few days down the road. But tonight, Jordan surprised me.

"I'm *pretty sure* I want to stay in Los Angeles," she said. "I've been sort of poking around Craigslist for apartments."

I laughed, knowing that "pretty" was as sure as I was going to get.

"That's good," I said, pouring on the nonchalance. "Because knowing you're not rushing back to New York makes me a lot more comfortable introducing you to the kids this weekend."

Jordan clasped two giddy palms together. "This weekend? Are you serious?"

"Yup, I even told Elizabeth it was going to happen."

"Holy shit. What did she say?"

"It was an interesting conversation," I said, trying to sound upbeat so she didn't take the rest to mean Elizabeth didn't approve. "She said she trusts my judgment but wondered if the kids should meet *anyone* before we knew that person was someone who we wanted to spend the rest of our lives with. She asked me if I thought you were 'The One.'"

"Oooo, *The One...*" Jordan pretended to be frightened. "And what did you say?"

"I said I thought I could spend the rest of my life with you, but you couldn't really be 'The One' if our kids didn't love you."

Jordan laughed gamely, "No pressure or anything."

⁂

WE FIGURED THROWING A very small pool party would be a relatively pressure-free way of introducing Jordan to the kids, so I called my friend Kendra. A forty-year-old producer and screenwriter, Kendra had once pitched me a book called *The Sugar Baby Club* about college students turning to the lifestyle. For obvious reasons, I'd taken to the project, and in our meetings felt comfortable telling Kendra why. Her fascination with *my* stories had created a trusted rapport, but more importantly, Kendra was dating a man with three kids.

"Count us in!" she said after I explained the significance of the party. "Peter is an excellent cook, and we can grill up a feast."

"Excellent, see you Sunday at noon," I said.

But after we hung up, I realized there was a small problem with this plan—I didn't have a grill. In fact, I was completely unprepared to have a party. All I owned was a bachelor set of four plates, glasses and silverware, maybe six beach towels, and the teak table the previous renters had left behind was in even worse shape than the rattan chaises.

"Go to Target!" Jordan suggested. "I don't know what it is about that place, but I can get lost in there for hours."

I loved her down-to-earth sensibilities but pointed out Amazon would deliver anything in two days.

"You can't buy furniture online," Jordan smirked. "You need to *touch it* and *sit on it* and see if it feels right."

"Well, you're going to be down in San Diego, and I have a busy week, so maybe we should push the pool party a week?"

"I'd rather die than delay meeting your kids," Jordan answered.

So, on Amazon, I ordered a propane grill, grilling tool set, plates, glasses, silverware, beach towels, and patio umbrellas, and enough pool toys to keep the kids busy for days—a mega inflatable pink swan, floating basketball hoop, masks, and snorkels. But the pièce de résistance was a ten-piece wicker patio sectional—couch, chairs, and coffee table—which had great pictures and reviews and seemed like a steal for $500.

The sectional arrived in giant boxes on Friday morning, and I cursed myself for not having ordered the "with expert assembly" option. Putting it together was such a chore, I ended up taking the day off from work.

I'd finished when Jordan arrived, backpack of clothes for the weekend over her shoulder.

"What do you think?" I asked, hoping she wouldn't see what I saw. The wicker was plastic, the cushions cheap nylon, and it was half the size the pictures on Amazon had led me to believe.

Jordan tried not to laugh. "Did you ever see the movie *Spinal Tap*?"

"Oh, God," I said, knowing the mockumentary about a hapless heavy metal band well. She was referring to the scene where a stage designed to look like Stonehenge had been accidentally built in inches instead of feet, so the band hired little people to dance around them.

"You were right," I conceded. "You're always right, damn it."

But we planned our Sunday more carefully. That morning, we filled the pool with a hundred water balloons, then I went to pick the kids up from their mom's house. Jordan thought it would be odd if the kids walked in to find a strange woman already in the house, so she killed time by going to get her nails done. When she came back, she rang the doorbell instead of using her key.

I led her into the backyard, where Peter, Kendra, and all five kids were already in the pool tossing water balloons at each other.

"Everybody, this is my *friend*, Jordan," I so specifically announced.

The gang shouted, "Hi, Jordan..." and she waved back and called out, "I want to play!"

Jordan changed into a bathing suit—a one-piece she'd carefully chosen to hide her curves—then she and I jumped in the pool. The kids took to her like a magnet, Chloe clinging to her shoulders at every opportunity, Eli showing her how to play water basketball, and, of course, insisting she be a shark who chased them through the pool. Peter,

Kendra, and I got out to grill, but Jordan stayed in the water for hours. At dinner, as we crowded onto the *Spinal Tap* sectional, Eli and Chloe insisted Jordan sit between them, talking her ears off. And, after dessert, Jordan helped all five kids build a fort in the living room, using pillows and blankets from every room.

As Peter helped me clean the kitchen, Kendra wandered in with a glass of white wine and said, "Well, this couldn't have gone better."

But it did.

After the sun went down and everybody was leaving, Jordan prepared to go back to San Diego. But Eli and Chloe tugged each of her arms, begging her to stay for a little while longer and help me put them to bed. "Of course!" Jordan answered. The kids donned their pajamas, and I stood in the hallway between their rooms, silently watching as Jordan tucked Chloe in. Sitting on Chloe's bed, Jordan suddenly noticed a small gray bunny among her stuffed animal collection.

"Hey, I have one just like him," Jordan announced.

"His name is Harvey," Chloe said.

"So is mine, look!"

Jordan ran back to my bedroom, grabbed her Harvey from her suitcase, and brought it in to show Chloe.

"They're twins!" Chloe cried out.

I couldn't write this shit. It was the sort of magical coincidence that made an agnostic believe in God.

Then, Jordan moved to Eli's room, passing me with a knowing smile. I smiled back and dialed up an Uber on my phone.

"Will you lay with me and snuggle?" I heard Eli ask.

I looked up, surprised. He'd asked that of his mother or me every night since he could put a sentence together. But he'd never asked anyone else. Jordan looked at me, respectfully, and I nodded. She pulled her feet off the floor and nestled beside him atop the covers.

I felt more happy, more whole than I ever thought I could be. My two hearts had merged, and never again would I have to transition between them.

If Jordan isn't the one, I thought, *there never will be one.* She was the one, my soul mate, my twin flame, the love of my life, you name it.

15

THE GRADUATION SURPRISE

MY ALARM CLOCK CAREER ended on May 12, Jordan's last day of teacher training. A few weeks prior, I'd surprised her by planning a graduation gift trip to the Four Seasons resort in Punta Mita, Mexico. That morning, I'd drive down to San Diego to pick Jordan up for her final yoga examination, then we'd catch our flight the next morning.

For Jordan's final, she was to teach yoga to a pupil and have her technique critiqued by her instructors, so naturally I'd offered to be her guinea pig. I got to the studio after lunch, where she met me in the reception, gave me a quick kiss, then ushered me into the studio. The class was already in session, so we crept to her mat and watched the other trainees lead their guests through routines. When Jordan was called on, we went to the front, where she guided me through a series of poses for about fifteen minutes. I'd practiced enough yoga over the years and followed along easily, tinged with pride that I'd managed to remain flexible at fifty-three.

After the instruction, we guinea pigs sat against the wall as Jordan and her classmates communed in a circle of candles, gave short speeches expressing their gratitude, and exchanged small gifts and farewells. Although Jordan had been too busy studying and swimming by my pool in her free time to make close friends with her peers, the tears of relief and exhaustion she shared with them gave me a sense they'd all been through a physically and emotionally challenging six weeks.

"I'm so fucking proud of you," I declared as we walked out of the studio.

"Thank you so much for this experience," Jordan answered, then winced. "God, my body is a wreck."

"Four days in Mexico, sandy beaches, and warm water will heal all your wounds."

"I might have a margarita or five," she quipped.

"You know, I've never even seen you tipsy."

"Oh, I'm a lot of fun, you'll see."

I laughed as we reached my car and I opened the passenger door for her.

"Hey, can we make a stop down the street?" Jordan asked. "I need to get some prescriptions refilled."

"No problem," I answered.

᙭

"I CAN FILL THE Prozac and Wellbutrin," said the CVS pharmacist, a thin Persian man, as he tapped away at his computer, glancing at the hardcopies of Jordan's prescriptions on his counter. "But the Vyvanse is a Schedule II Controlled Substance, and since your prescribing doctor is in New York, you'll have to get it filled there."

Idling beside Jordan, I didn't recognize the drug but thought nothing of it—I could barely recall the generic names for my cholesterol and blood pressure meds.

"Since when?" Jordan frowned. "I've definitely had Vyvanse refilled out of state before."

"Technically, the law changed in January, but they gave us a few months to get our computer system up to speed."

"Can't you make an exception?" she asked politely. "We're going to Mexico tomorrow morning, and I don't know how I'll get it filled tonight."

"I'm sorry, it's illegal."

Jordan shifted on her feet. "Can I speak with a manager?"

"I manage the pharmacy," he answered almost apologetically. "Trust me, even if I wanted to give it to you, the computer won't even let me print the label. Do you still want the other medications?"

Jordan nodded reluctantly, and he slipped the prescription back to her, then she turned to me. "I can't believe I waited until the last minute to get my refills."

"How were you supposed to know the law had changed?" I commiserated.

She took out her phone and started texting. "Let me see if my doctor can get around this. I literally don't have a single Vyvanse left."

"What is Vyvanse, anyway?" I asked.

"It's an amphetamine like Adderall, nothing near as stimulating. It's the only drug approved by the FDA for my eating disorder."

I blinked in utter astonishment. "You have an eating disorder?"

Jordan didn't look up from her phone. "It's not a big deal, I swear. Let me try to find my doctor and call a few other pharmacies, and I'll explain in the car."

I stood there, feeling a pit in my stomach growing and filling with questions.

❧

"MY PSYCHIATRIST SAYS THERE'S nothing she can do," Jordan bemoaned while reading a text in my passenger seat. "I'll either have to go to New York or see a doctor here—neither of which is going to happen before tomorrow morning."

She slid her phone between her thighs and sighed with minor frustration.

I, on the other hand, was majorly frustrated.

"Jordan, help me understand this," I asked.

"I used to binge eat—that's all."

That's all? I thought. Jordan's lack of shame or embarrassment was evident, but I didn't find that very reassuring. I wondered if she was one of those women who binged and "purged" by sticking their fingers down their throats after meals.

"I'm not bulimic," Jordan clarified before I could ask. "That's *really* hard on a woman's body and much more addictive than just binging. I met girls in rehab who were literally starving themselves to death because they couldn't keep food in their systems."

She went to rehab? Hold on. How do I talk to her about this without shaming her? Calmly, I asked, "When were you in rehab?"

But as usual, Jordan saw right through me. "Look, David. This really isn't a problem in my life anymore. A few years ago, I spent a few weeks in this inpatient place in Arizona. The doctor prescribed Vyvanse. Overnight, my cravings went away, and they sent me home. I've been fine since. Maybe once in a while, when I'm severely depressed, I'll binge, but that's about it."

I nodded, soothed by the realization that nothing I'd seen since we met indicated Jordan had an unhealthy relationship with food.

"And my problem with food isn't really food," Jordan continued.

"What do you mean?" I asked.

"I mean, it's all about my depression. It's really common for people with depression to self-medicate with food. Eating releases those *happy endorphins!*"

I laughed at her high pitch but understood—who didn't get a rush from a phenomenal meal?

"It's so hard to imagine you binging," I said with a shake of my head. "I mean, *look at you.*"

Jordan smiled at the compliment. "I think that's why I got away with it for so many years. I started binging when I was, like, ten. My folks were workaholics, so they were never home for dinner. I learned to cook at a ridiculous age and became obsessed with cooking shows. Desserts were my specialty, of course. If I was depressed, forget it—I'd make a double serving so I could take it into my room after and binge."

"And your parents *never* noticed?"

"No, because like you said, I looked great. I was competing in talent shows, singing and dancing, working it off. Only when I got to college did it start to show. Dorm life added a few pounds."

I laughed and recalled my own dorm nights filled with pizza and beer.

"But when I got to New York, all hell broke loose," she continued. "I was working as a hostess at this amazing restaurant and shot up thirty pounds—here, I'll show you."

Jordan pulled her phone from her lap, scrolled through her photos—way, way back—and held one up.

"Wow,'" I said, glancing from the road and seeing a picture of her that was almost unrecognizable; Jordan was a good forty pounds heavier.

"Still love me?" she asked with a testy grin.

"More than ever," I said in complete sincerity. "You're very brave for showing me that."

"Maybe now you understand why I dream of liposuction," she said. "I want to get rid of this *last little bit…*"

Watching her pinch only an inch of skin made me shake my head in wonder.

"I went to rehab right after taking this picture," she explained. "Started taking Vyvanse and voila! Without dealing with constant cravings, I was able to work it off with exercise."

"Voila indeed!" I echoed.

But I heard a voice inside me, a little troubled, asking, *but why am I learning this now, two months into the relationship?*

"Jordan, let me ask you something," I said, trying to sound non-accusatory. "Why haven't you shared this with me before? We've been so open with each other, after all."

Her face went soft with regret. "It wasn't a conscious decision. I guess maybe deep down I was afraid of scaring you away?"

"That's impossible," I answered.

"You're sweet," Jordan gushed. "But really, don't you ever wonder if I'm too much drama for you? After all, I have an eating disorder, depression, body dysmorphia…hell, I can't even get my shit together to refill my prescriptions on time. Meanwhile, you're Daddy Fix-It."

I rolled my eyes and regretted I'd ever told her the nickname. But at the same time, a fix to her present problem *did* come to mind. "You know, we could always go to a pharmacy in Mexico," I suggested.

"I've never been to Mexico, but somehow I doubt they accept American prescriptions."

"I doubt you'd even need to have a prescription. Last time I went down there, I got a sinus infection and went to a pharmacy for antibiotics. Every drug you could imagine was over the counter."

"Huh," Jordan said, a sudden bounce in her tone. "I guess it couldn't hurt to try."

"Either that, or we could postpone our trip a few days," I said. "Really, your health is far more important than a vacation."

"Don't be silly," she said. "I can go without it a few days. The worst thing that will happen is I might be irritable and eat too many chips and guacamole."

I laughed. "Nowhere better than Mexico for that."

16
HAPPY PLACES

WE TOOK A RIDICULOUSLY early flight the next morning, the idea being we'd get to the Four Seasons before noon and spend as much time in the sun as possible.

That morning, I paid close attention to Jordan's moods, wondering if she'd downplayed her eating disorder. But she wasn't even irritable—our plane hadn't yet taken off before she was excitedly chatting about her hopes we might try to teach her to surf again in the warm Mexican waters

After a noneventful plane ride, we whizzed through customs and were greeted by the Four Seasons resort handlers, then led to our black Cadillac SUV.

"Señor, Señorita..." said our driver, a handsome young man with the best teeth in Mexico, as he handed us a plate of rolled-up towels, moistened with aloe vera.

Jordan and I wiped our faces with them, even though we were anything but hot and sweaty—the weather was perfectly comfortable—eighty, sunny, and only enough humidity to remind us we were in the tropics.

"Muchas gracias," I said.

He naturally assumed that meant I spoke Spanish and rattled off a few sentences in his native tongue.

"Sorry, I really don't—no hablo Español."

"No problema! My name is Roberto. Welcome. Would you like some bottled water?"

"Thank you, yes," I answered. "And if you don't mind, we'd like to stop at a pharmacy on the way to the hotel?"

"Farmacia, no problema!"

He gave us a thumbs-up and drove us into the small town of Punta Mita, a one-street fishing village that kept its charm despite being overrun with restaurants and gift shops.

We parked in front of a small pharmacy next to a surf shop where our driver jumped out, opened the doors for us, then escorted us inside. He had a quick conversation with a young woman behind the counter—she wore a white lab coat but seemed more clerk than pharmacist. Above her head were shelves stacked with every drug imaginable, sorted by labels in English: PAIN, BIRTH CONTROL, SLEEP, ANXIETY, ANTIDEPRESSANTS.

"Buenas tardes!" The clerk greeted us like a cheerful salesperson. "Que te traigo? Vicodin? Xanax? Ambien? Viagra?"

I elbowed Jordan, as if to say, *Don't need Viagra, do we?*

She winked, then turned to the clerk. "Do you have Vyvanse?"

"Vyvanse?" the clerk asked, confusion on her face.

"Amphetamines?" Jordan tried.

"Ah, Amfetimina! Solamente Ritalin," the clerk said, and pulled a box of pills from under the counter.

I'd heard of Ritalin and asked Jordan, "They give that to kids with ADD, right?"

Jordan nodded as she studied the box. "Yeah, it's even less stimulating than Adderall. I've been trying to get my shrink to up me to Adderall, but she won't. I don't know what she's afraid of—me getting too much shit done?"

I laughed and Jordan pointed to the Ritalin. "I'll get this," she said. "I'll research it online tonight and make sure to take a dose comparable to my Vyvanse after breakfast tomorrow. Combined with a diet pill, it should work exactly the same."

I scrunched my face. "You want to take both? Is that safe? I mean, why not just eat a lot down here?"

Jordan smirked. "David, I've been managing my medications since I was a teenager. Trust me, the worst thing that will happen if I take too much of this is I'll want to dance for hours on end."

I chuckled. "Okay, but if you pull me onto a dance floor, don't say I didn't warn you."

"Algo mas?" the clerk chimed in.

Jordan searched the aisles and pointed toward a shelf labeled DIET, and asked, "Por favor, Qsymia?"

"Si," the clerk said and handed her another box.

"What's Qsymia?" I asked.

"It's a diet pill I used to take all the time," Jordan answered. "I can't find it in the States anymore for some reason."

I took out my wallet. "I like the name. Sounds like 'kiss a me.'"

"It's LIKE HEAVEN," JORDAN gasped reverently while a concierge drove us by golf cart through the Four Seasons resort, winding along a path of tropical gardens set against the blue Bahia de Banderas to a series of low-lying traditional Mexican casitas dotted among the four-hundred-acre grounds.

"My happy place," I sighed, restraining myself from telling Jordan *yet again* how much it meant to me to be sharing this special corner of Mexico with her. I'd probably told her three times in the last two days how I'd frequented the resort either to surf or be with my family. We'd shared Thanksgivings, spring breaks, and even celebrated my nephew's bar mitzvah at The Four Seasons.

"I may have gone overboard on the room," I conceded as our concierge parked in front of a casita and led us inside.

"A little? This is un-fucking-believable," Jordan exclaimed as we entered and saw, through massive glass sliding doors, nothing but sand and a private plunge pool between our room and the ocean.

"Have a wonderful vacation, Mr. and Mrs. Winkler," said the concierge as he directed a bellman inside with our luggage.

Jordan and I exchanged a smile as if to agree it would be more fun to enjoy the fantasy that we were married than correct him.

"What do you say we don't even unpack?" I asked Jordan as the door closed behind the bellman. "Just find our swimsuits and jump in the ocean."

"That beach is so private, I doubt anybody would notice if we didn't even wear them."

I chortled at the image. "Let's not get kicked out of the hotel on the first day."

We rummaged through our luggage, and Jordan slipped out of her clothes and into a nearly sheer, formfitting white one-piece swimsuit.

"Twenty bucks at you know where," she boasted.

I gawked, wondering how something purchased at Target could accentuate her curves so seamlessly.

Holding hands, we ran down the soft sand to a small cove sheltered from the waves by an offshore reef. We dove into the water—I guessed it was only a few degrees cooler than I kept my pool, but somehow it felt even more welcoming—and swam, floating up to each other and kissing for minutes on end.

We dried off with towels that had appeared mysteriously on the sand, settled onto our wide canopied daybed, and watched the sun lower in a blaze of tropical color. Then we scampered back into our casita, slid the giant hacienda shutter doors closed, made love, and fell into one of those deep naps only found on vacation.

I woke up two hours later and kissed Jordan's shoulder.

"Baby," I whispered, "should we get up and have dinner?"

She stirred. "I'm so happy here in bed."

"I'm fine ordering room service," I offered.

"You don't have to babysit me, sweetheart. Go."

Jordan rolled over and went back to sleep so I threw on some jeans and a T-shirt, hung the "No molestar" sign outside the door, and walked the winding paths to a restaurant that sat on a torch-lit beach. Loath to feel like a loser sitting all alone at a table, I took a seat at the bar and ordered grilled lobster.

When the massive entrée arrived dripping in melted butter, I took a few pictures of the dish and texted them to Jordan. Even if she wasn't beside me, I wanted her to enjoy every bite of the meal as much as I did.

Then I hurried back to the room and found Jordan sleeping so soundly I didn't dare wake her. I closed the hacienda shutters so morning light wouldn't wake us early, slipped out of my clothes, and climbed into bed, spooning contentedly up to her.

"WE HAVE TO REMEMBER to call our mothers at some point," I said as Jordan and I walked to the brunch buffet set up in the hotel's main restaurant, a giant, unwalled palapa of dried, thatched palm fronds.

"That's right, it's Mother's Day!" she answered. "Thank God *you* remembered."

As Jordan and I moved down the line, I couldn't help but watch what she spooned onto her plate. Although we had sushi after our trip to CVS, a quick egg sandwich in the airport, and a healthy dose of chips and guacamole on the beach the day before, I'd yet to see any sign of Jordan binging. But I also knew it had been close to forty-eight hours since her last dose of Vyvanse, so I found myself relieved when she settled on huevos rancheros and fresh fruit, and even avoided raiding the table stacked with Mexican pastries.

And as we ate, it occurred to me I hadn't even noticed Jordan become irritable.

"Are you sure you even need those?" I asked as she took the two boxes of meds from her purse and opened them.

"Baby, you worry too much," Jordan said with a loving smile, then downed a Ritalin tablet and Qsymia pill with orange juice.

A WALL OF CLOUDS had appeared, and wind whipped the ocean, but the air was still warm, so I reclined on a chaise lounge in the sand in front of our casita, reading a book. Ten feet away, Jordan sat on the day bed, wearing a blue and white tie-dyed bikini and a straw hat, swiping through pictures on her phone.

"Why bring me all the way to Mexico but not sit with me?" she called out.

I sensed she was annoyed but decided to take her needing me as a compliment and moved my stuff to the daybed.

"Better?" I asked.

She nodded but didn't smile. "By the way, what the hell happened to you last night?"

"What?"

"How could leave me in the room on our first night here?"

"I tried to wake you," I reminded her. "You said you weren't hungry and that I should go by myself."

"I don't remember saying that. And then you send me fucking pictures of the lobster, like you're rubbing in what I'm missing."

"I'm sorry, I thought you'd find it sweet I was sharing the meal with you."

She hardly received that and immediately demanded, "Well, who did you eat with?"

"Nobody. I sat alone at the bar."

"You didn't meet some girl there?"

I would have laughed if I wasn't so offended. "Come on, you think I would try to get laid while we're on a trip together?"

Jordan blinked, as if she realized how ridiculous she sounded. "I'm sorry, I guess my abandonment issues were triggered."

What abandonment issues? I thought. I shook it off and finally addressed the elephant in our palapa. "Honey, is it possible you're having a reaction to the stuff you took this morning?"

She took a centering breath. "Maybe you're right. Ritalin is a stimulant, and most diet pills have caffeine in them. I'm sorry. I should move and burn some energy. Why don't we go see what's going on at the main pool?"

"Sure."

Jordan slipped a sundress over her bikini, and we strolled down the beach. Arriving at the massive infinity pool, we were surprised to see we were the only guests there.

"Maybe the weather chased everybody inside," I guessed. "They usually gather here to watch the sunset."

"This is perfect," Jordan said cheerfully. "I need to post from down here, so why don't you shoot some pictures of me? I can do some yoga poses without people staring at me."

I pulled my phone out of my swim trunks. "Nothing would make me happier."

Jordan slipped her sundress up and over her bikini, and we waded into the pool. She dunked her head and emerged with dripping hair she swept back stylishly before climbing onto the infinity ledge.

"Since nobody's here, might as well get a little sexy," she suggested as she stood, raised her hands to the sky, palms together, and turned so her ass stuck out provocatively.

I happily shot picture after picture as she moved through a few other yoga poses, adding a sexy touch to each, acting more Bettie Page pinup than yogi—pressing her breasts together to enhance her already ample cleavage, licking her lips, pulling her bikini bottom to the side so more cheek showed.

Astonished at this overtly sexual side, I glanced behind me and caught the pool waiters and staff staring—then quickly looking away.

"Got enough?" Jordan called out.

"Never!" I admitted.

She cackled, dove into the water, and swam toward me, pressing me against the side of the pool.

"Let's get a piña colada," she said between kisses.

I hesitated. "Maybe we shouldn't add alcohol to what you already took today?"

Jordan scoffed, "That was like six hours ago. It's out of my system by now."

"Probably, but—"

Before I could finish, Jordan spun from my arms and climbed out of the water, found her dress and slipped it on as she headed to the poolside bar.

I gathered our belongings and followed.

"Hola! Dos piña coladas, por favor," Jordan sang to the waiter as she perched on a stool.

"Buenos dias," the bartender answered and turned to mix them.

I sat beside Jordan as she took a quick glance at a plastic menu on the bar top.

"Also," she called out to the bartender, "Baja tacos and a tuna ceviche tostada!"

"Bueno!" he answered.

Jordan suddenly hiccupped so loud she sounded like a frog.

Amused, I asked, "Where did that come from?"

"Hell if I know," she said, then hiccupped again.

"Hold your breath," I suggested.

She gulped air, held it for twenty seconds, then hiccupped again as she released it.

"Agua?" I called out to the bartender, but he was already putting the piña coladas before us.

"Get out your camera again," Jordan commanded.

"Why?"

"Just trust me, video this!"

I obliged as she lifted her drink and stood off the stool.

"Okay, so this is how you get rid of hiccups," Jordan said to the camera. "You drink backward!"

She leaned forward so she was facing the ground and sipped from the side of the glass furthest from her face until there was nothing left but coconut froth, then quickly stood up and held her breath for a beat, listening to her body. "See! No hiccups!"

She raised her arms in victory as another hiccup came belting out.

I nearly dropped my phone with laughter.

The bartender brought over two bottled waters, and as Jordan sipped at them, eventually the hiccups disappeared. I was just happy whatever medication reaction she was having was turning into a laughing matter.

But as our food showed up and we ate, I noticed Jordan kept pulling out her phone from her dress pocket, checking for messages, and tapping out one or two. Each time her face seemed to grow sullener.

"Is everything okay?" I finally asked.

"Fine," she said dismissively. "I have to pee."

She and her phone headed toward the restroom cabanas.

Nibbling at chips, I glanced at my phone—it felt like five minutes since Jordan had gone to the restroom. After two more glances, it had been fifteen minutes.

Are you okay in there? I texted her.

She didn't respond, so I worriedly signed for the check and walked to the restrooms. As soon as I rounded the corner, I found Jordan standing outside the ladies' room, hunched over her phone, tears dripping from her eyes.

I stopped and lowered to her level. "Baby, what's going on?"

She looked up at me, her head shaking, eyes darting like a scared animal. "Something's wrong with my mother!"

"Oh, no, what happened?"

She rattled, high-pitched, "I don't know. I called and texted her a few times today, but she never answered, and she always answers me within minutes—no matter where she is."

"She's probably celebrating Mother's Day," I assured her.

Jordan shook her trembling head. "David, she could be having a heart attack and is lying on the floor in the kitchen, and nobody would even know!"

I heard the fear in her voice, but not the logic. "Honey, I'm sure if anything happened to her, your father would have called."

"He's never around; he's never around," she cried, more tears streaming down her face.

"Okay, well, let's call him," I said. "Or your sister or brother…"

"YOU DON'T UNDERSTAND!" Jordan exploded. She crooked an accusatory finger at my chest. "MY MOTHER LOVES ME! SHE WOULD NEVER NOT ANSWER ME!"

I reeled as she darted away, hunched over her phone.

"Jordan, wait!" I called out, running after her as she tore down the dimly lit path back to the casita. Finally, I caught up to her.

"Jordan, honey," I pled. "I think you're having a bad reaction to the drugs—"

"DON'T COME NEAR ME!" she hissed and spun toward me. "YOU HAVE NO FUCKING CLUE HOW I FEEL! I CAN'T LIVE IN THIS BODY ANYMORE!"

She clawed at her chest as if she was trying to peel off her own skin. "I HATE THESE SAGGY TITS!" she cried out. "MY HAIR IS THINNING! I NEED FUCKING LIPOSUCTION! HOW CAN YOU EVEN LOOK AT ME? THE ONLY PERSON WHO REALLY LOVES ME IS MY MOTHER!"

Gasping for breath, she unleashed low and pitiful moans unlike any noise I'd ever heard.

"Jordan," I whispered softly, "please come back to the room. I'll call the hotel doctor."

Her eyes locked on me with a measure of clarity, as if the mention of a doctor instantly sobered her. "I'll be fine. I need to lie down."

I took a sharp breath, almost more frightened by how abruptly she'd calmed down than by how she had exploded.

"Promise me you won't call a doctor?" she pled, her voice shaking. "I don't want to go to some fucking Mexican hospital and have my stomach pumped."

I nodded, that being as much promise as I dared to make.

"I'm so lost," Jordan croaked, throat dry from yelling. "Where's the room?"

"Follow me."

I offered her my hand, but she clasped hers together, so I dropped mine and walked slowly back to the casita. She followed a few steps behind; I'd look back occasionally only to find her staring at her moving feet.

"Just book us back to Los Angeles tomorrow," I heard Jordan grumble as we reached our casita.

"Huh?" I stammered as I opened the door.

"THIS PLACE IS HELL!" she barked, then pushed past me, made a turn into the bathroom, and slammed the door shut.

Stunned, I closed the door to the casita and wandered into the bedroom. *My happy place is hell now? How fucking ungrateful!*

I sat on the bed and reminded myself, *Jordan's high, sick, I don't know what. Don't take anything she says personally.*

I listened as noises came from the bathroom—Jordan running water, a glass clink as it was placed down, the toilet flushing. My mind raced, trying to piece together what the fuck had just happened. Had Jordan downplayed her reliance on Vyvanse and was having severe withdrawals? If so, Ritalin hadn't been a good replacement. Or was Jordan having a toxic reaction to mixing it with a diet pill and alcohol? And she was also on a high daily dose of antidepressants, so God only knew what kind of cocktail was wreaking havoc in her nervous system. In the last two hours, she had been all over the emotional map—cranky, joyful, sexual, paranoid, accusatory, enraged with self-hatred. Was that cocktail causing a psychotic break with reality?

My thoughts were interrupted as Jordan emerged from the bathroom, wearing a hotel robe. Avoiding my eyes, she crawled into bed and turned on her side so her back faced me.

"Are you okay?" I whispered.

"Exhausted," she moaned.

I stared at her terry-clothed back and tried to think of a game plan. *Should I call the hotel doctor?* Jordan seemed calm now, so if the doctor came to the room, what would I say happened? Jordan had been pretty fucking clear she didn't want me to call for help, so she could easily deny it, and we'd come across as two rich Americans ruining a good vacation with some booze-fueled argument. And she didn't appear to be having some overdose seizure or urgently needing her stomach pumped. *And Jordan in a foreign hospital*…now that was a frightening thought. On the other hand, how did I know she wasn't going to get worse? I couldn't do *nothing*.

I glanced at Jordan. She seemed to have fallen asleep—her eyes were shut, and she was breathing steadily. But I needed to be prepared—if she started heaving, or if she stopped breathing, I'd need to pick up that phone. And fast. *And if I do end up needing to call someone, surely they would need to know everything she has taken.*

I quietly got up from the bed and went into the bathroom. I immediately noticed Jordan's toiletry bag on the counter beside the sink, unzipped.

That freaked me out. *Did she take MORE drugs? Ambien to get to sleep, maybe?*

I looked inside the bag—sure enough, right at the top was a prescription bottle, label up: 10-milligram zolpidem tabs, generic for Ambien.

Fuck, I thought. Ambien, Ritalin, some diet pill named Qysmia...

And then I had another *fuck*—because I saw that the name on the Ambien bottle was David Winkler.

What the hell is my Ambien doing in Jordan's toiletry bag?

I'd shared my Ambien with her before, that I knew. Hell, I'd even refilled my prescription once for her to combat my snoring—those fancy earplugs I'd given her worked some nights, others I'd snore so loudly she needed to either move to the couch or go to my medicine cabinet. But I also knew Jordan hadn't asked if she could bring the bottle on our trip. If she had, I'm sure I would have agreed.

But she hadn't asked, and I started to wonder how often she had been siphoning my Ambien. Had Jordan been taking my Ambien *recreationally?* She'd told me she only took Ambien on our first date to calm her nerves, and I'd never before had reason to suspect otherwise. But now...

What other drugs of mine might Jordan have taken without asking?

I put the Ambien bottle down beside the sink and opened Jordan's toiletry bag. I had a moment of guilt at the thought I was betraying her privacy, but that lasted about as long as it took to read my name on another bottle in the bag. I pulled it out: 0.5 milligrams of alprazolam, generic for Xanax.

I recalled Jordan saying more than once that Xanax—"Mother's little helper!" she liked to joke—helped her with post-depression anxiety. I could remember her even asking once or twice if she could have one of my pills, and I'd agreed. But looking in the near-empty bottle, I could tell she'd taken many more than she'd asked to borrow.

Up until this moment at the sink, I'd thought Jordan might have just made a stupid mistake in taking the Ritalin and Qsymia, but now it was becoming clear she had a worse problem than poor judgment.

A drug problem.

I wasn't sure the exact nature of Jordan's problem—was she addicted to amphetamines, Ambien, Xanax? All three? Or was there a term for someone who self-medicated with a host of drugs? "Generalized Medication Addiction," maybe? But the evidence was right in front of me. And with a few blinks, I realized it might have been behind me, too. I thought of Jordan missing our second date because she'd gone to the emergency room with "dehydration." Was I crazy, or had that been code for an overdose? Had I missed other red flags of her drug use?

And the more pressing question remained: what exactly did Jordan take today? That cocktail in her system might now consist of Ambien, Xanax, antidepressants, Ritalin, and Qsymia. *And what the hell is Qsymia, anyway?*

I pulled my phone out of my pocket and googled. Qsymia was the Spanish name for a drug called phentermine. That rang a bell, so I clicked through a few articles, stopping when I read, *FDA Orders Phen Fen Off Market After Drug Linked to Heart Failure.*

My heart felt like it was failing.

Not only did I have to worry about Jordan having a drug problem, now I had to worry about her dying in her sleep. Goosebumps sprouting up on every pore of every limb, I turned and left the bathroom, went to Jordan's side of the bed, and kneeled so I was looking directly at her face.

She was fast asleep, breathing evenly, but I vowed *I* wasn't going to go to sleep that night. I would stay up all night and watch her. I sat down beside her and put my hand on her, so if she stopped breathing, I'd feel it.

Stay strong and watch over the woman you love. Nothing else matters.

17
THE PICTURE OF HEALTH AND WELLNESS

THE HEAT OF SUNLIGHT streaming in through the seams of the hacienda shutters settled on my eyelids and stirred me.

How the hell did I fall asleep?

I sat up and looked at Jordan, still under the covers in her robe. I could hear wisps of breath coming from her mouth, so I knew she was alive, at least. My open laptop was between us, and I guessed I had succumbed to sleep sometime a few hours ago, after spending most of the night googling all the drugs Jordan had ingested and booking us flights home.

Jordan shifted groggily beside me, and I mustered up a stoic whisper. "Are you okay?"

She rolled to face me and blinked her eyes open. "Yeah, I just have the mother of all hangovers."

I closed my eyes and exhaled a breath I couldn't remember taking. *Thank God*, I sighed, relieved she wasn't slurring her words or showing some other sign of permanent neurological damage.

"What time is it?" she groaned.

I looked down at the time on the menu bar of my computer. "Just past nine. We should order room service soon, or we won't have time to eat before the airport."

"Huh?" Jordan said, authentically confused. "We don't leave till Wednesday."

"You don't remember telling me you wanted to go home today?" I asked.

"Why would I do *that*?"

I stared at Jordan, stunned as I realized she probably didn't remember the most horrible night of my life. *Be gentle*, I told myself as I asked, "Jordan, what's the last thing you remember us doing last night?"

"We were in the pool," she said, then let her mouth gape. "Everything after that is a blank...oh, God, what the hell did I do?"

"I'M HORRIFIED...TOTALLY ASHAMED OF myself," Jordan said quietly and pulled her knees to her chest as we sat on our casita patio, both of us in hats and sunglasses to protect from the sun's vengeful return.

I stared at her, tired of talking after having spent half an hour walking her through our night. I knew I ought to say something reassuring, but honestly, I felt like it took all my emotional strength not to break down and cry. *Christ, I need some reassurance*, I thought. *Last night was the darkest night of my life.*

"I'm so sorry, David," Jordan went on. "So, so sorry."

She lowered her eyes, as if she understood she would need more than apologies to fix the damage done.

I pointed to her phone, sitting on the table. "Has your mom texted you this morning?"

Jordan nodded. "And called and emailed...she was out to dinner later than usual. I fucked up her Mother's Day, too."

"The things you were saying..." I stopped mid-sentence, seeing no point in going into any *more* detail. "Is there something between you and your mother I don't know about?"

"Not at all! Honestly, I think it was the drugs and alcohol—if it were Father's Day, I'd probably have flipped out about my dad. And did I really tear at my own skin?"

"Have a look."

Jordan pulled her robe aside and studied the red welts on her chest. "Jesus. Thank God I bite my nails."

I took off my sunglasses and rubbed my eyes. "Can we talk about the drugs?" I asked gingerly.

"Of course. What do you want to know?"

Where do I begin? I thought. "Well, what do you think you took when we got back to the room? Xanax? Ambien? Both?"

"I wish I knew. But from what you told me about how panicked I was, I'm glad I took *something* to calm me down."

"Jordan, I'm not ready to start looking at the bright side here," I sighed. "I'd like to know how much of everything you've been taking. I know I've let you take some of my stuff, but that was before I knew you had a..."

I trailed off—I wanted Jordan to admit the obvious, not me.

"I have a drug problem," she stated.

She's not arguing, that's something. "Can you be more specific?

Jordan nodded and removed her own sunglasses. "I think Xanax is the worst problem. I take the Ambien to sleep, but I go days without it fine. Hell, I'm usually so tired after yoga I collapse. But in the last four or five weeks with the stress of teacher training, I started taking your Xanax every day. Last week I tried to stop taking it, I swear, but I literally couldn't go without it. I'd get anxious and shake."

"So this is a new problem?" I asked.

"Yeah. Why are you asking that?"

"I don't know. I guess I'm wondering because I remember little details now, like you going to the ER on the night of our second date."

"I was sick, David."

She seemed irritated, but I just stared at her.

"Okay," she said, backing down. "Under the circumstances, I don't blame you for doubting me. But I swear on my life, this is as shocking to me as it is you. I mean, have you ever seen me *act high?* We spend so much time together, don't you think you'd have noticed?"

"I like to think so," I answered.

My obvious doubt brought tears to her eyes. "David, I promise I haven't been hiding some drug problem from you for the last few months. I fucked up this weekend, full stop. I was so damn stupid—I should never have tried to make my own Vyvanse."

She wiped her face with her robe sleeve. "You realize this is all related to my depression, right? I'm so fucking tired of fighting this dragon I was born with."

My sympathy for her was clouded by déjà vu—only two days ago Jordan had blamed depression for her eating disorder. On top of that, I felt a sense of responsibility. *Should I not have shared my prescription medications with her?*

"I guess I didn't help, did I?" I admitted. "Giving you my stuff."

Jordan shook her head. "Everybody in the world gives their girlfriends or boyfriends or family their medicine, David. I took advantage of your trust. Again, I'm sorry. I wish I knew a way to share with you how guilty I feel."

"I'd rather focus on what we need to do about this," I answered. "You tell me, is this something you need to go to rehab for?"

"No, rehab would be overkill. I just need to taper off the Xanax."

"Carefully," I cautioned. "I did some reading about benzodiazepines last night. It's supposed to be one of the hardest addictions to quit. People get seizures if they go cold turkey."

"Really? Will you share those links with me?"

"Of course. But I think we should talk to a doctor about this."

"Absolutely—as soon as we get home."

That didn't seem soon enough to me, and it reminded me we had a plane to catch in a few hours. "What time is it?" I asked, nodding at her phone.

She tapped on her screen. "Ten fifteen. But did I *really* tell you I wanted to leave today?"

"Yeah, you said this place was hell."

Jordan blinked. "Actually, I remember that now. David, I was talking about *this place*..."

She tapped her head to indicate the hell was in her brain.

And with that simple gesture, the stoic composure I'd been trying to maintain abandoned me—I started to sob, tears pouring out of my ducts like they were faucets.

"Baby?" Jordan quickly got up and moved onto my lap, wrapping her arms around me.

I closed my eyes but that did nothing to stop my crying. "I was so fucking scared, Jordan…"

She started to weep with me as she pulled my head to her chest. "It's okay, I'm okay…"

I shook my head because I couldn't explain how I felt—it wasn't lingering fear from last night. My chest was filled with Jordan's guilt, her shame, her humiliation, her fear. I was sobbing with as much empathy for Jordan's feelings as my own.

"I'm so sorry I did this to us," Jordan said through her own sniffles. "My soft, soft David."

A teary laugh tumbled out of me.

"What?" Jordan said tepidly.

"I don't know, something about you calling me that right now was funny."

I pulled my face from her chest and saw her smiling.

"You know, this is the first time I've ever seen you cry," she said.

"Is it?" I asked, not because I doubted her, but because it amazed me. It amazed me she was the first woman I felt comfortable crying in front of, and it amazed me how good it felt to share such depth of emotion with her.

"It's beautiful," Jordan assured me. "I love you so much."

"I love you."

Jordan put one hand on each of my cheeks like she was praying with my face.

"Come with me," she whispered as she patiently withdrew.

I could have stayed in that kiss forever but opened my eyes to find her getting up and reaching for my hand.

I stood and let her lead me into the casita, past the bed and into the bathroom. She let go of our grip at the counter, where she picked up the boxes of Qsymia and Ritalin. I silently stood and watched her take the pills from their plastic packaging, dump them into the toilet bowl, and flush.

"Thank you," I whispered.

JORDAN AND I ORDERED ROOM service and discussed our next steps. Since going cold turkey off Xanax was dangerous, I'd hold onto the Xanax and give it to her only as needed. I called my old psychiatrist, who I'd seen when depressed (a.k.a. married) and told him the situation. He confirmed a taper was the best course of action, and although he wasn't seeing new patients, referred us to a colleague—a specialist in both drug addiction and depression, Doctor Browning.

Browning's first available consultation wasn't until the following week, so after lengthy discussion, we decided to stay in Mexico as originally planned and try to salvage the trip.

To my surprise, Jordan only asked me for a Xanax once in the next three days—when our plane encountered some turbulence. I didn't know if that was a sign her drug problem was as small as she believed it to be, or if she was showing incredible willpower. Or maybe she was just so relaxed by spending two days lounging in the sun, getting couples massages in the spa, feasting on those lobsters together, and floating along the peaceful lazy river on rafts, tethered to each other by our outstretched hands.

Really, the *only* thing Jordan did to make me raise a proverbial eyebrow at her mental state happened when we were in the back of the Uber, driving to Rosewood. Scrolling through Instagram on our phones, I noticed she'd posted a picture of herself I took on our last afternoon dip into the ocean. Jordan wore that fabulously sheer white swimsuit and playfully splashed water at the camera. Her caption read, *Hasta La Vista, Mexico!* but her hashtags were *#health* and *#wellness*.

Though we'd managed to salvage the trip, after Sunday night, it was hard for me to believe Jordan would have the nerve to post about her health and wellness.

18
THE QUEST FOR TMS

"WHAT A NIGHTMARE FOR *both* of you," I heard Megan lament over my Mercedes speaker.

It was the afternoon after we returned from Mexico, and I was driving to pick the kids up from school, having dropped Jordan off at an Airbnb, a small guesthouse close to Rosewood where she'd stay while we looked for a more permanent spot for her to rent.

I hadn't seen Megan since our drink at the Chateau Marmont and tried to sum up the Mexico ordeal in a way I knew her cinephile mind would appreciate.

"It was very *Betty Blue*." I said, thinking of the tragic French film about a writer who falls in love with a stunning woman who has a psychotic break of epic proportions.

"At least Jordan didn't gouge her eyes out like Betty does," Megan sighed.

"Okay, maybe Mexico wasn't as tragic as that, but damn, it was quite a plot twist."

"So you're going to get her a psychiatrist ASAP?"

"Already have an appointment next Monday," I reported. "Beyond helping her kick Xanax, we're hoping the guy can finally help Jordan with her depression."

Megan paused for so long I thought we'd been disconnected.

"Did I lose you?" I called out.

"Sorry, I was just…" she paused with obvious tension. "Listen, I've never told you about my own depression."

"No, you haven't. Why not?"

"Well, because the way I treated it is a little embarrassing. There's such a stigma attached to it that I never tell anyone."

"What, did you have shock therapy?"

"Sort of. I had this treatment called transcranial magnetic stimulation."

"I've never heard of it."

"Probably because it's a relatively new experimental treatment," Megan explained. "TMS was only approved to treat depression a few years ago—they're also using it on vets with PTSD."

"Interesting. I'm sure Jordan knows about it but tell me."

"It's really nothing like shock therapy. I would sit in what looked like a dentist's chair with this small device trained at my head. It shoots gentle magnetic waves at specific parts in your brain. It was so painless I'd take naps."

I laughed. "Sounds like my kind of therapy."

"It worked in a huge way," Megan said. "Before TMS I could barely get out of bed and go to auditions, but I've felt great ever since."

My eyebrows shot up at how perfectly her description mirrored Jordan's debilitating symptoms. "When did you get this done?"

"A few years ago. I went three times a week for a couple of months, and that was pretty much all I needed. Once in a while now, I'll feel a little down, so I go in for a session. Now, I can't say my depression was as bad as Jordan's—I never even took antidepressants—but I've heard TMS works even on the worst cases."

"That's amazing. Do you mind if I tell her about this conversation? I don't have to use your name."

"Please, have her call me if she wants, or we can all have coffee and I'll tell her everything about it. Honestly, I feel bad for not telling you about this sooner. I should have known you wouldn't judge me."

"I don't blame you really; it *does* sound like something out of *One Flew Over the Cuckoo's Nest*."

And then, naturally, Megan followed up with a quote from the movie, "*I must be crazy to be in a loony bin like this.*"

I laughed, then called Jordan.

But that's when *a really* crazy thing happened. To begin with, she'd never even heard of TMS.

"How is it possible none of my psychiatrists ever mentioned this?" Jordan said, googling while I drove. "Hold on. You won't believe the first thing to come up when I googled TMS, Los Angeles. Dr. Browning's website! He specializes in TMS!"

"And we already have an appointment with him? If that isn't the stars aligning, I don't know what is!"

My whole body tingled with goosebumps. Forget crazy—this coincidence was downright magical, right up there with Jordan having a Harvey bunny just like Chloe. And I felt such hope, thinking maybe, just maybe I'd found something that could help fix Jordan's depression. I patted myself on my back, feeling like I was a knight on a quest. *Have I found the magic elixir that will, once and for all, cure my fair princess of her curse, just as she kissed mine away?*

❧

"LOOK AT THE NAMES of these rolls!" Jordan gushed as she read the menu at the strip mall sushi restaurant we walked to after her consultation with Doctor Browning. "There's the Sexy Dancer Roll, the Show Me the Money Roll—and look, the Sugar Daddy Roll!"

"I'm definitely trying that one," I answered, squirming in my seat. Having sat patiently in the doctor's waiting room for ninety minutes, the suspense was eating at me. "Details, please!"

Jordan chuffed like some star pupil who had aced a test. "Doctor Browning said I'm the perfect candidate for TMS. And this guy deals with people who make my mental health look like a walk in the park— he said he's helped people with a history of suicide attempts, bipolar disorder, and even schizophrenics. He said it was eighty percent likely I'd get completely off antidepressants."

"That would be incredible," I answered, then tried to gently broach the Xanax issue. "Did you tell him about Mexico?"

"Of course. He said it's common for people to self-medicate when their depression is treatment resistant. And we were smart to taper off."

That was validating—though Jordan had only asked for a few tabs of Xanax since the flight home, it was good to hear that giving her mine had been a healthy decision.

"He gave me a new taper schedule and called in a prescription for a little more Xanax, so I should be off it in a few weeks," she added. "Oh, and he said if I want TMS, I have to get clean of benzos anyway. There's something in the chemical makeup that interferes with the treatment. He also called in my Vyvanse, but thinks once I'm not fucking depressed, I'll be better equipped to deal with my cravings for food, too."

"TMS can do all that?" I asked, trying to sound impressed despite the voice of caution creeping up on me. *If it sounds too good to be true...*

Jordan, as always, saw through me with a smile. "If TMS does *half* of what he says, it would be a total godsend. I mean, it's such an amazing alternative therapy—it literally reroutes your neural pathways."

"So when could you start?" I asked.

"As soon as I get off my shitty New York Medicaid," she said, her face falling a bit for the first time since we left the office. "His assistant said only the best policies like Blue Shield and Anthem cover TMS."

"How much would it be out of pocket?"

Jordan laughed. "Don't even think of it—he said it usually takes four or five hour-long sessions a week for six weeks, so about thirty grand."

"Ouch," I said. I knew I couldn't afford to pay that myself. And though I had an incredibly wealthy family, I couldn't exactly ask them to pay thirty thousand dollars to help the girlfriend they hadn't even met yet.

"Well, it shouldn't be too hard to get you new insurance," I said.

She looked at me like I was the one who might need a few neural pathways rerouted. "Getting insurance is no cakewalk."

"Forget cheap Medicaid," I suggested. "We'll get you the best insurance. I have Blue Cross through my company, I think it's seven hundred a month. I'll pay that for you."

"Thank you, baby," Jordan said. "But I spent some time researching plans, and it's not so simple. Open enrollment is only September through February, so the only way I can get insurance is if I have a 'qualifying event' like a baby or a new job or move to a new city."

I didn't need to remind Jordan the baby thing wasn't a possibility with me but joked, "We could say my company hired you, but I don't know how I'd explain your job duties to business affairs…"

"Hah!" That elicited her breathy laugh. "Well, I have *pretty much* moved to California but proving that is another story."

"Why is that?"

"Every plan I checked out says I'd have to give a California driver's license or ID, plus some other documentation like utility bills in my name."

"That's an easy fix," I answered. "You can use Rosewood as an address."

Jordan raised a coy brow. "Is this your way of asking me to move in with you?"

"I admit I fantasize about you living with me one day, but it's a little soon, don't you think? You only met the kids like a month ago."

"Hogwash!" Jordan teased. "But I'll definitely take you up on the offer to use the house address. That should be easy enough, right?"

ADDING JORDAN'S NAME TO the utility bills *was* easy—I had an extra phone line installed at Rosewood under her name, and, to make it all the more believable, bought her a phone that we installed in the living room. And going to the DMV went smoothly—humorously so.

After we waited in line for *only* ninety minutes, Jordan presented her application and utility bills to the clerk, then moved to another line to have her picture taken.

"Please, don't smile," said the second clerk as Jordan settled in front of the camera.

"Okay," Jordan answered and wiped her hand over her face like she was removing a mask. But the minute the clerk clicked his computer to take the picture, another grin sprouted.

"I'll have to take that again," moaned the clerk.

"I'm so sorry," Jordan giggled apologetically.

"Is it illegal to smile in California?" I wondered aloud. I loved that she simply couldn't force herself not to smile—under all her depression lived the happiest soul waiting to be set free.

"Regulations," the clerk muttered.

Jordan clenched her jaw shut but still her cheeks spread into a narrow but sublime smile.

The clerk glanced at the line of people growing annoyed behind us and took the picture.

"I'll print out your temporary card," he sighed. "The ID will come in the mail in six to eight weeks."

But no quest is complete without facing a few dragons, and on the road to get TMS, we met our match in Blue Shield customer service. Essentially, once Jordan sent in her California ID and utility bills to the insurance behemoth, she was met with a wall of bureaucracy designed to keep her from getting insured. First, Blue Shield rejected her application outright via email but gave no explanation. To appeal, she would have to go through a division called "The Underwriting Department."

"Sounds like some nefarious company in a science fiction movie," I said to her one day after watching her patiently spend all afternoon on the phone, being shuffled from one unhelpful customer rep to another.

"It's maddening," Jordan vented. "Now they're telling me I can't even reach the underwriting department by phone, only email."

"Be patient," I urged. "If you think about it, we're gaming the system."

"What do you mean?"

"Well, you haven't moved in yet, so we're sort of committing fraud."

She laughed. "True. Well, it's not fucking fair people with mental health issues have to fight to get treatment, but I'll stay positive."

Unfortunately, staying positive wasn't enough.

Jordan finally heard from the underwriting department that there had been a clerical error in some paperwork from her New York Medicaid. It took weeks of calls and emails before she cleared that up—and then, when she reapplied, Blue Shield emailed and said they couldn't accept her temporary California ID, and there were no further appeals allowed.

Jordan and I were incredibly frustrated. Yes, we understood the insurance company rules were there to prevent people from doing *exactly* what we were doing. But it simply didn't seem fair Jordan had to try to game the system. Why should any human being struggle to get the medical care they so desperately need, when they need it?

Although Jordan and I hadn't beat the dragon or found the magical elixir yet, going on the quest and fighting together had brought us closer. It went a long way towards healing the psychic wounds of Mexico. And in some small way, my own neural pathways had been rewired. I'd always known I was born lucky to have a family with deep pockets and the generosity to open them whenever one of us was sick, whether insurance covered the treatment or not. But going through this with Jordan, I learned a new level of compassion for people who might not be as fortunate.

And though it would be two months before Jordan could even reapply for insurance, I had no doubt this wasn't the end of the quest for TMS.

As Jordan said on that day in June, "I'm getting this therapy, even if it kills me."

19
ROLE PLAYING

"So...I WAS THINKING I SHOULD go to New York and work a little," Jordan panted as we trekked up Devil's Backbone, a steep and winding trail in Malibu Canyon.

I stomped along beside her, proud my ass—twenty years her senior—could keep pace with her much prettier one.

Obviously, I knew "work" was code for seeing other men.

I thought a moment. Jordan had committed to getting her mind and body in shape whether she got TMS or not, and over the past several weeks, we'd gone on hikes and taken yoga classes together. Even so, it seemed early to be reintroducing "soul-killing" work.

I took her hand and wiped a sweaty tendril from her brow. "Are you sure you wouldn't rather put yoga teacher training to good use?"

Her tone was chipper and agreeable. "I definitely think teaching a few times a week would be great for me to stay healthy and meet some new friends."

"Did you ever call Kim?" I asked. I'd given Jordan the number of an old friend who taught yoga in Santa Monica and offered to make introductions with her studio manager.

"Damn, I keep forgetting," Jordan sighed. "But really, teachers only make like seventy bucks a class and that won't go far in paying off my credit cards."

"Gotcha," I said instead of nagging her as we reached a shady spot beneath a giant oak tree.

Jordan sipped from her water bottle. "I really do enjoy the escorting, you know. It was Broken Foot I couldn't stand. But when I find the right people, I love playing the porn star role. I go all out, curlers in my hair, bronzer on my skin, hairless, lingerie, show up ready to fuck."

"Why don't I get that?" I pretended to complain. "I love our afternoons by the pool, but I haven't seen you in lingerie since our first few dates."

"Because we were something deeper from the first minute," she said with an impish grin. "But I know—overt sexuality turns you on. I'll step up my game and be naughtier with you."

I smiled and took my own sip from the bottle.

"It's time we have some fun again," Jordan went on, reaching up to a tree limb. With both arms, she pulled herself up and hung with her ankles a foot off the ground, her shoulder muscles sinewy, beads of sweat glistening in the sun.

Watching her, I had to admit I'd been impressed by her growing strength, and how she'd addressed the drug issue. Doctor Browning now had Jordan on only the lightest dose of Ativan, a mild benzodiazepine she could take if she felt any lingering anxiety.

"Well, who would you see in New York?" I asked, warming to the idea.

"This guy Paul has been texting me a lot lately, asking when I'm coming back to New York."

"And he's not soul-killing like Broken Foot?" I asked.

"No, he's a smart and funny Jew like you."

I laughed. "Okay, and I assume you're fine with me seeing someone while you're there?"

She dropped off the tree branch gracefully. "Totally. Just wear a condom and change the sheets on your bed afterward."

I was speechless by how casual she was about all this, but it was hard to argue she wasn't ready to go back to work.

❧

"HOLY FUCK, THIS HUMIDITY!" Jordan gasped on FaceTime as she pounded the pavement in Manhattan a week later. "Oh, and I'm walking in the wrong direction. Two months away and I'm a tourist!"

"How was the afternoon with Paul?" I asked from behind my office desk.

"Couldn't have gone better—he wants to see me again tomorrow!"

I smiled, any worries she'd find Paul soul-killing erased.

"It's such a rush," Jordan professed, "checking into a hotel at 2:30 and walking out at 4:05 with $1,500 in my purse."

"I want that job!"

Jordan chuckled, then grit her teeth. "I made a video in the hotel, but I'm afraid it might offend you."

I frowned. "You made a sex tape with Paul?"

"God no!"

"Phew. Then why would it offend me?"

"I'll shut up and send it. Call me back after you watch it."

We hung up and I waited, beyond curious. Jordan had never been one to send me explicit photos, just the occasional nude here and there. Her text came in, and it was a video selfie she'd taken of her writhing on a giant hotel bed in a lace lingerie bodysuit, letting hundred-dollar bills rain from her hands to the white linens.

Offended? Hell, I'm turned on.

"I'm into this game," I said when I called back a minute later. "If seeing cash makes you this hot, why I don't give you four thousand in hundred dollar bills every month, instead of transferring it over Venmo?"

"That sounds fun—I need to earn my allowance!" she said lasciviously.

We laughed together, but as soon as we hung up, I walked out of my office, down to the Bank of America on my corner, withdrew twenty hundred-dollar bills, and texted Jordan a picture of the cash fanned out in my hand.

That may be the hottest picture you've ever sent me! she gushed back. But don't tease me when I know some of those Benjamins are going to someone else.

I tapped back the laughing emoji character, knowing Jordan was referring to the date I had coming up in a few hours with Colette, the queen of sexual games and role play herself.

Since being introduced to Colette at Sanctum back in February, she and I had met for coffee several times. Colette's apartment was in a high-rise on the Wilshire Corridor, only a short walk from my house in Westwood, but since she didn't have a car, she'd ask me to pick her up at the curb, drive her to Starbucks, then to the liquor store to buy her beloved American cigarettes. Then we'd park ourselves in my backyard with espressos where she could chain-smoke while we shared our respective lifestyle and relationship tales.

And flirt, of course.

"You're a little vanilla, but I do wonder what it would be like to fuck you," Colette would say between drags. "But I'm in a monogamous relationship."

"With a married man!" I'd point out.

"I told you love is legal insanity!"

This tease had gone on for months, only slowing down when I moved into Rosewood and started spending so much time with Jordan. But it clearly was not for lack of desire. There was something about Colette—her ability to talk about her animalistic sexual appetite without shame, and, of course, her beauty—that drew me to her like a moth to a flame. Even if I wasn't interested in her violent rape fantasies, I'd always wondered what the kinkiest woman at Sanctum could teach me about sex.

Then, coincidentally enough, only a few days after Jordan brought up seeing Paul in New York, Colette called to catch up. In the last two months, she revealed, her secret paramour's wife had discovered some very explicit texts and pictures of him and Colette on his phone and threatened to go public and divorce him. He'd blocked Colette out of his life, and she was over pining for him. As she put it to me in her French accent, "I'm done being monogamous to a ghost!"

Colette also shared that she'd overstayed her six-month tourist visa, so both the INS and her rich parents were demanding she return to France; she'd been cut off financially, and she was surviving on (what else?) Starbucks and Marlboros.

"And how is your Jordan woman?" Colette asked.

"Things are good," I told her. "She's in New York, so I have a hall pass."

"Is that so? Well, from what you've told me about that site you're on, I'm sure you're overwhelmed with options…but maybe it's time I try being one of your sugar babies?"

"Are you sure?" I asked her. "I don't want to take advantage of your situation."

"You Americans and your selective morality. Yes, I'm sure!"

COLETTE AND I PERCHED ON the edge of my pool, legs dangling into the shallow end.

"This Jordan woman knows you're here with me?" Colette asked, naturally topless like any European woman would be, her pert breasts and small, brown nipples already tanned, and, of course, a Marlboro dangling from her lips.

"Yeah, our deal is we can sleep with other people as long as there's money involved. And as long as it's not organic—like meeting at the gym or a party."

Colette cackled. "David, *we* met at a party!"

"I know, I know. Jordan and I discussed it, and she agreed Sanctum is basically live action Seeking Arrangement. Most of the girls there are on it."

Colette smiled suggestively, put her cigarette out on the concrete, then slid into the pool and swam to the giant pink swan floating in the shallow end. She pulled herself onto it and sat with her back against its neck for support.

I dropped into the water and waded to the edge of the raft. Gingerly, I slid Colette's legs apart, wrapped my arms around her wet thighs and started kissing my way to her vagina; she reached out and pushed my head down. My fingers pulled her suit bottoms aside, and I started to lick her.

Still holding my head, Colette shuddered and jolted to a loud orgasm. Then she leaned forward and kissed me harder than any woman had ever kissed me. I felt like her mouth and tongue weren't just trying to connect but rather devour mine.

Pulling away for breath, I whispered, "Come to the stairs."

We slid off the swan together, embraced, and she gasped at feeling how hard I was against her pelvis. She kissed me again and pushed me back against the edge of the pool; I felt her hand stroking me through my shorts and went to slide them off.

"Wait," Colette said, "I should tell you something."

"Okay…?"

"I had sex with someone else this morning."

"Oh." Long pause. "This morning?"

"Does that bother you?"

I blinked, conflicted—being the second man to have sex with her that day felt distasteful and unhealthy, especially since at the rate we were moving, I'd have been surprised if I had the willpower to run inside and dig up a condom. But at the same time, I appreciated how honest she was being, and my attraction to her was so strong I was still erect.

"I'm not judging you, but I'd prefer to wait," I answered. "My girlfriend's away for a few days still, so maybe we can hang out another time?"

She smiled, not offended in the least. "Tomorrow works."

Colette and I toweled off and went inside the house. As she slipped on a long, black T-shirt dress, I picked up a plain white envelope I'd left on an end table by the living room couch.

"This is for you," I said, as I placed seven hundred dollars into her purse. We hadn't discussed the money before our date, but from experience, I guessed it wouldn't disappoint her.

But Colette gave me an odd look. "We didn't even fuck."

"I don't pay for penetration, Colette," I answered. "The money is for your company and the experience."

"Wow, you really are understanding. And I doubt there's many men who would be so generous."

Colette picked up her purse, took the envelope, and offered it back to me. "I want to see you again, but I don't want this."

"What do you mean?" I asked.

She smiled as if she had a secret she'd been holding onto since we first met. "You really don't understand? David, I don't really need to be a sugar baby. Yeah, my father is furious with me for overstaying my visa, but he'd never cut me off. My mother would cut his balls off if he let me suffer!"

I laughed with a stutter. "So this has been a game?"

"I was role playing. I wanted to know what it felt like to be paid for sex without becoming a hooker."

"Holy shit."

Colette grinned. "I told you when we met, the best sex comes when your mind is turned on."

"Well, you just fucked my mind!"

I started to take the envelope back, then realized I had a dilemma on my hands. "There's just one problem, Colette," I said. "If you don't take the money, I'm breaking the deal I have with my girlfriend."

"I'm sure Jordan will understand."

"I am *not* risking it."

Colette smiled like she was doing me a favor and put the envelope into her purse. "Pick me up again tomorrow afternoon?"

ARE YOU ALONE?

Jordan's text popped up on my phone as I was about to plug it into its charging station that night.

She left hours ago, I wrote back as I sat down and against my pillow.

Seeing her again?

Tomorrow, while you're with Paul.

He cancelled. His son came to town or something.

I'm sorry, you gonna find someone else?

I doubt it. Think I'd rather go to Colorado earlier than spend the next few days here hustling. And I'm kind of depressed. Even been binging a little.

I silently cursed myself for letting Jordan go to New York as I wrote, Is there anything I can do to help?

The phone was silent a moment, then she wrote, Why do you want to have sex with someone other than me?

That seemed like an odd question, considering she'd had sex with Paul that afternoon, so I dialed her on FaceTime.

She picked up, and I could see she was on her bed in her Manhattan apartment, wearing old sweats.

"Talk to me, honey," I said.

Her face was so red and puffy from crying that her cheeks pressed against her glasses. "I guess I don't understand why you're so insatiable?"

"I'm insatiable?" I stammered.

"You're fifty-three years old. I thought by now you'd have had enough of fucking random women."

Feeling defensive, I leaned forward. "First of all, I think I have a healthy libido. You and I have sex, what, three times a week? And Colette's the only woman I've seen besides you in months."

"But you *want to*."

"How's that a problem? Every man *wants* to have sex with a variety of women. I'm just honest about it. *We're* honest about it. I mean, you were glowing about being with Paul today."

"For work!" she snapped. "Don't you dare compare my having sex with clients to what you do! I give you my all. Not another ounce of emotional or romantic energy goes to anybody else!"

"Come on, that's semantics. You didn't enjoy fucking him?"

"I enjoy playing a role and making money!"

"Really, that's all? Be honest—did you have an orgasm or two this afternoon?"

"What does that have to do with anything?"

"I'm just saying, you're sounding pretty hypocritical suddenly."

"I don't think so. I signed up for the promise of monogamy."

I reeled, confusion and betrayal filling my chest. "The promise of monogamy? When the hell did you ever tell me that? Have you forgotten every conversation, every negotiation we've had? I think once you said we could 'work' toward it, but that's it, and don't forget it was *your* idea to go to New York!"

"Because I knew you wanted me to go so you could see someone!"

"You're rewriting history, Jordan."

"No, you're flipping the switch on me, claiming I said things I didn't say, and it's maddening!" she yelled, but her tired voice was more of a croak.

I'm flipping a switch?! I thought as I took a breath to calm myself, then found myself reminded of how Jordan hadn't been able to remember any of the irrational things she said while under the influence of the Mexico cocktail.

"Jordan, what medications have you taken today?" I asked.

She stared daggers at me. "Not even an Ambien with Paul. So fuck off! You don't deserve my heart! You can box up my clothes and ship them here!"

Jordan reached down to the screen and ended the call.

I laughed—she'd made so little sense, I couldn't even take this seriously.

I redialed, and she surprised me by answering.

We didn't speak for second, just stared at each other.

Then she broke into an embarrassed smile. "I'm so sorry."

"What just happened?" I asked.

After a pregnant pause, she whispered, "Jealousy happened."

"Oh. That's a first."

"Scare you?"

"A *little*," I lied.

"I know it makes no sense considering my day," she said. "But when I came home, I found myself looking at Colette's Instagram and thought, 'How could he want to be with this sketchy young French chick?' Next thing I know I'm a cauldron of jealousy and crying, trying to keep it in so I wouldn't ruin your afternoon."

"Jordan, if I'd known, I wouldn't have seen her. We didn't even f—"

"I don't want to know the details," she interrupted. "You did nothing wrong. If anything, you should take this as a compliment—shows how much I love you."

"That's one way of looking at it, I guess."

"I'm sorry I said you didn't deserve my heart."

"People say things when they're upset," I reasoned. "And I guess jealousy is a primal emotion, like happiness or anger—it's how you handle it that matters."

Jordan allowed tears to drip onto her glasses. "Thank you for understanding. I guess I've gotten super attached to you since meeting your kids. And the idea that you'd share yourself with someone makes me feel like I'm not enough for you. But I know it's not your responsibility to make me feel whole."

"Honey, I'm so sorry this triggered you," I said. "You know nothing is more important to me than making you happy."

Jordan nodded. "I should get some sleep. Are you still going to see Colette again tomorrow?"

"You're joking right?"

"I'm over it, I promise," she said with clear conviction. "I don't want you to abstain from any kind of behavior just because my emotions spiral. I like how we've set things up. Seriously, get laid tomorrow, I'm begging you."

"Honey, I love you, but there isn't enough tea in China."

She laughed. "Love you too. Goodnight."

We got off the phone, and I called Colette and told her why I needed to cancel.

"Okay," Colette said, more amused than disappointed. "But this Jordan woman sounds like she has multiple personalities. Porn star girlfriend by day, jealous lover by night."

"Yeah, it sounds a little crazy," I admitted. "But as you always say, love is legal insanity."

20

NICE COUNTRY JEWISH BOY

Two weeks later, I walked through the Denver Airport with a black overnight bag slung over my shoulder.

The trip had been a last-minute change of plans—after Jordan left New York to spend the July Fourth holiday with her family, she decided she'd need a car in Los Angeles. So she invited me to fly to her home state, meet her folks, then drive west with her in the car she'd left behind in Denver after moving to New York.

Jordan pulled up to the curb in a red Volkswagen Beetle as I walked out of the terminal. The car wore its age. The paint bubbled from oxidation, its tires had no tread, and a narrow spider crack split the middle of its windshield. But the Bug had such character—my first impression was that it was magical, flaws and all.

Kind of like Jordan, I recall thinking.

"You're really here!" Jordan yelled as I climbed into the passenger side, and we hugged tightly between the seats.

"I missed the fuck out of you," I whined amiably before I pulled my door shut and tossed my small duffel into the back seat.

Jordan stepped on the gas pedal—the engine revved, but the car didn't budge. She stamped on the pedal a few times before we lurched forward.

"The old girl's been sitting in my father's garage for seven or eight years now," Jordan winced.

"Hope she makes it to Los Angeles," I said and knocked on its dashboard in lieu of wood. Then I unzipped my overnight kit and pulled out a plastic shopping bag. "I picked up a few small things for your folks at LAX."

I pulled out the gifts—at the airport it occurred to me I shouldn't show up to meet Jordan's parents empty-handed, but I also didn't want them to think I was trying to buy their approval with an expensive scarf or sweater. So, instead of something from the duty-free shops, I bought a coffee mug, T-shirt, and baseball cap, all printed with a neon view of the Southern California sunset, complete with the Hollywood sign in the background. Dreadfully touristy things, I knew, but maybe in some way I wanted to see if her parents had a sense of humor.

"Oh, Lord," Jordan chortled. "Just what my mom needs. The woman is a damn hoarder."

I laughed and assumed her indictment of her mother was just nerves. After all, Jordan's mother was downright intimidating...she's a criminal attorney who handles murder cases!

"Seriously," Jordan went on, "every shelf in my parents' house is cluttered with junk she 'had to buy' at a swap meet, garage sale, or Target."

"Now I know where *you* get your love for that store," I teased.

"Oh, she's much more addicted than I am. I like to distract myself by shopping. She'll buy shit—rugs, lamps, a lot of decorative, kitschy crap—and swears she'll return them if they don't fit the house. But she never takes anything back! It's like once she lets something in her house, she becomes attached to it."

Again, giving her mother the benefit of the doubt, I said, "Well, I can't wait to see the house you grew up in."

"*That's* not gonna happen," Jordan stated emphatically.

Too emphatically, I thought. "You *are* kidding about the hoarding, aren't you?"

"Sort of. I mean the place is ridiculously cluttered, but at the same time there's not an ounce of dirt or dust."

"She's an anal-retentive hoarder?"

Jordan didn't laugh. "Do you know she gave me shit for having to move her hair appointment to have breakfast with us tomorrow? I know she's had this standing appointment every Saturday for over twenty years, but *please*, you'd think she'd be more enthusiastic to meet you."

"So your mom's a creature of habit," I reasoned. "Why didn't we meet for lunch?"

"Because my dad told her he *absolutely* has to work tomorrow. Even though it's Saturday."

"They do sound a little inflexible. But honestly, I could have stayed another night and met them later."

"I want to get on the road," Jordan groaned. "This trip has been exhausting. My old bedroom is now my mother's office, so I've been sleeping on the couch or spending the night at my sister's place. And that's mayhem—her kids are complete brats. Nothing like *your* angels. And the constant questions! Everybody's either probing me about what I'm doing with my life or telling me what they think I *should* be doing. My mother is under the delusion one day I'll move back here and go to law school!"

"Doesn't she know you just graduated yoga teacher training?"

"Of course—and about Browning and TMS. She's well aware my depression makes everything a struggle. But sometimes she lets it slip that she thinks I'm just impulsive and immature."

I bit my bottom lip and pondered the possible harsh verdicts of Francis. "I bet your mom thinks I'm some sleezy Hollywood producer who took her daughter to Mexico and corrupted her."

"Hah! If only they knew how we met," Jordan said, then frowned. "Wait, how *did* we meet again?"

"Facebook recommended we be friends, remember?"

"That's right," she said with a finger snap.

"Would Francis flip out if she knew we met on the site?"

"Probably—although she's always told me to date someone with money."

"That's a tad hypocritical," I said, adding that "tad" only to be polite.

"She's crazy conservative. So is my dad. He's a dull accountant. A workaholic, inattentive to my mom and uncommunicative—I'd be shocked if he says more than two words the whole meal."

"Well, my dad isn't much more communicative, so I won't take that personally. What did your parents think of Ray?"

Jordan looked irritated by the mention of her ex, the alcoholic who broke up with her over text. "He and my mom were thick as thieves until he dumped me. Then he kept texting and calling her so that pissed her off."

"Seems stalkerish," I said. "Why would he do that?"

"Because he woke up and realized he'd made a huge mistake. He kept trying to get me back, but I wouldn't give him an ounce of energy. So he'd reach out to her and pretend he was being friendly. 'How's our girl doing?' he'd say, but she saw right through how manipulative he was."

Jordan rolled her eyes. "You do know she's been watching everything you do on Instagram for months, right?"

"For months?" I asked, surprised. I'd recently noticed Jordan's mother followed me, but I had no clue when she started.

"Oh, my mom is a total snoop. She tells me things about you that I don't even wanna know!"

"Like what?!"

"She made some comment the other day that some of the girls you follow look like porn stars."

I frowned—now I felt judged. "Right. I almost forgot they're republicans. Do they know you voted for Hillary?"

Jordan gave me a death stare. "Yes, but God help me if we talk politics tomorrow. I cannot handle an argument about Donald Trump over breakfast."

I laughed, knowing I tended to climb up on my soapbox. "Probably a good idea. You know, I used to have republican friends. But this asshole has caused such a divide I can't even follow them on Instagram."

"Oh, so you'll unfollow people who are republican but not porn stars?"

"Okay, okay! I'll go through my social media and delete any woman who's hot. God forbid Francis doesn't approve."

Jordan smiled. "Thank you. And really, my parents aren't monsters. I'm clearly anxious about you meeting them."

"Tell me about it. Fifty-three and I feel like I'm sixteen again, standing at your front door on prom night in a rented tux, hoping your father doesn't answer the door."

Jordan laughed. "My mother wears the pants."

"I guessed that."

"How could my mother not like you?" Jordan asked, then teased me in a comically bad Yiddish accent, "You're such a nice Jewish boy."

❧

BRIGHT AND EARLY THE next morning, we met Francis and her husband at Jackson's Corner, a restaurant nested between the orchards and vineyards west of Denver. They were standing at the table at an outside patio when we arrived, and it became quickly apparent Jordan's parents were far from monsters.

Francis enveloped me in the most enthusiastic, welcoming hug. She sported brown hair sprayed and shaped into a perfect, curly bob (*she either found another appointment or slept standing up!* I recall thinking), and her smile stretched the confines of her narrow mouth. And though John only shook my hand, his smile was almost goofily wide.

"We're so excited to bring you here," Francis said as we sat. "Jordan told me you love cinnamon rolls, and Jackson's is famous for them!"

"She told you that?" I said, glancing in mock horror at Jordan. I *was* in fact a connoisseur of sorts, but it was embarrassing her parents would know this of a man my age before we even met.

"But they always run out of them early—that's why we insisted on breakfast," Francis added.

More thoughtful than inflexible, it seemed to me.

Then, no sooner had our waitress walked over with coffee and taken our breakfast orders than John started to chat amiably.

"Been to Denver before?"

"Only once, I used to fly a private plane and landed in Denver for a few hours to refuel."

"Hear you're a good golfer? Got a handicap?"

"I love the game but haven't kept score in years."

"Smart. I'm a hacker, but there's that quote: golf is a good walk spoiled if you take it seriously."

My glance at Jordan found her mystified that her father was talking. And he wasn't done.

"I've seen a few of the movies you've produced. Loved *Creed* and *The Mechanic*. And I saw on IMDB that you directed a film called *Finding Graceland*. I'm a *big* Elvis fan. And I noticed you recently directed a television pilot about the film industry in the 1960s and 70s? Believe it or not, I used to be a hippie."

"What!" Jordan demanded and slapped the table with her palms.

"Even marched on the first Earth Day in 1970," John boasted.

Jordan whipped her head between her father and me with her jaw agape. I realized that she had never seen me interact with strangers— despite my introverted soul, one doesn't survive *The Industry* without learning how to turn on the charm.

"I can't believe I didn't know this. What happened?" she asked her father.

"Your mother happened. She was in law school, and I was a philosophy major. So I cut my hair, transferred. Almost fifty years and four kids later, here we are, still married while half our friends got divorced."

Maybe he's not so inattentive, either? I mused as the waitress brought over those cinnamon rolls and coffee.

"Top five!" I pronounced after my first bite.

"What's number one?" Francis asked.

"Hard to say. Maybe the Main Street Café in Aspen or Tulsa's Savoy Bakery? But I must say, I'm not a snob—I do love Cinnabon."

Francis laughed and insisted Jackson's was also famous for its grits and gravy, so we ordered them. And as we ate, she came clean on the snooping concern.

"I saw on Instagram that you posted a picture celebrating the Fourth of July in Malibu with your ex-wife and children," Francis noted. "Says a lot about both of you that you're amicable."

Guess I can't really blame Jordan's mom for monitoring me, I decided. After all, if Chloe were ever to date a man twenty years her senior,

I'd probably hover over his social media like a hawk. I even found myself wondering if Francis had really told her daughter that the girls I followed looked like porn stars. It was hard to imagine this prim and proper woman even uttering the word "porn." And, coming only days after Jordan flipped a switch over Colette, perhaps Jordan might have been projecting her lingering jealousy onto her mother.

As our plates were cleared, Francis said, "We're very excited to see what Jordan does with her yoga. That was a very thoughtful gift you gave her. You're a very *grounding* influence on her."

Her emphasis on "grounding" seemed significant to me. She was subtly acknowledging she didn't see me as that sleazy Hollywood producer. We locked eyes for a moment and an understanding passed between us—one that made me think Francis might indeed know about Mexico. She might not have all the sordid details, but she was versed enough in her daughter's illness to know she could be a bit of a hurricane.

Then Francis released me from her stare and brought up the one subject Jordan had asked me not to, saying, "So tell me, what do you think of the job our president has done in his first two years in office?"

Out of the corner of my eye, I caught Jordan signaling our waiter, "Check please?!"

What was I to do? *There has to be something about Donald Trump adults can agree on.* And then I realized the thing Francis and John and I had most in common was that we were parents.

"Policy aside," I said, "it's really hard for me to explain to my kids why the most powerful man in the world acts like a schoolyard bully. He's cruel; he insults people left and right, and lies every time he opens his mouth."

Francis gave a judicious nod. "He's certainly not the first dishonest politician. I remember when Bill Clinton went on television and told America he'd never had sex with Monica Lewinsky."

"Clinton absolutely deserved impeachment," I agreed. "He'd have been better off just telling us it was none of our business. But at least he eventually came clean and asked his wife and the country to forgive him."

John chuckled, so I sensed I'd found what hippie was left in him, but Francis studied me.

"Come on, you're a trial attorney," I appealed to her. "Doesn't it make all the difference to a man's sentence when he throws himself at the mercy of the court?"

Francis suddenly burst out laughing. "You're so right—Donald Trump will *never* admit he's made a mistake."

"I rest my case!" I announced.

Jordan smiled at me like I'd given her a clock-beating death-row reprieve.

The check came—John saw it coming first and had his credit card out before I could object—so I promised to treat them when they came to visit Los Angeles.

"Speaking of, I brought a few things for you," I said, lifting the shopping bag from under my chair.

John and Francis laughed as I handed them the silly gifts, and really that was all I'd hoped for.

"We have some things for you, too," Francis said. "In the back of John's car. I know you just moved, and Jordan said you didn't have much in the way of cookware, so I pulled some extra things from my kitchen."

Jordan and I followed her parents to the parking lot where John opened the back of his SUV, loaded with knickknacks, more than a few of them with Target price tags still on their boxes. A new blender (because she knew Jordan liked to make organic juice smoothies), a juicer (because Jordan mentioned I had orange trees planted on the side of my house), plastic serving trays decorated with palm tree motifs, and a giant matching set of Calphalon pots and pans.

A hoarder? I thought as we transferred those and more to the trunk and back seat of Jordan's Bug. *The woman is cleaning out her closet for me!*

But all jokes aside, there was a moment between Francis and me I'll never forget.

Jordan had taken the last of her mom's gifts to the VW, and John was already in the SUV. Francis closed the back of their vehicle and gave me a final hug.

"Take care of your new home," Francis said to me, but I swear I heard her saying so much more.

Take care of my daughter, I heard her saying. *Because I know she's a part of that home now.*

"I will," I promised Francis.

❧

JORDAN AND I DROVE OUT of Colorado and into Utah at a leisurely pace, mainly because the floor beneath our feet rattled uncontrollably whenever we pushed sixty-five miles per hour.

While Jordan drove the first leg, I plugged my phone into the dashboard stereo with a special wire she bought—the car was so old it didn't even have Bluetooth.

"In honor of your roots, I thought we'd start out with some of this," I said as I pushed 'play.'

As the first twangs of Randy Travis's classic, "Forever and Ever, Amen" played on the car's tinny speakers, Jordan glanced at me, stunned. "I didn't know you liked country music?"

"Are you kidding? I've been listening to country since before you were born."

I sang along with Randy. Jordan joined in, her honeyed voice drowning out my embarrassingly tone-deaf one.

Then she stopped and pulled her phone from her jeans pocket and read a text. "It's official, my mother says you're marvelous. Guess she really likes nice Jewish boys!"

I laughed. "I'm not a nice Jewish boy," I said. "I'm a nice *country* Jewish boy."

21

THE SNOW WHITE OF BEL AIR

THE FIRST ORDER OF business upon our return to Los Angeles was a makeover for the Volkswagen. The Bug got a new windshield, fresh tires, a paint touch-up, and its fuel line replaced. And that incessant rattle turned out to be the easiest fix—"Just a few loose screws on a dust plate," according to the mechanic.

Then we parked the Bug at Rosewood. The spot was temporary, of course. Although Jordan and I openly fantasized about her moving in, we were still on the hunt for a sublet to give my kids time to adjust to her.

Not that they were having any problems adjusting.

I'd pick the kids up from summer camp, and the first thing out of their mouths would be, "Where's Jordan?" As we wound up the canyon to Rosewood, the three of us strained against our seatbelts to compete to see who'd spot her Bug in the driveway first.

"Hug Bug!" the winner would call out. The car had received its nickname after Jordan told them about a game she played as a kid called "Slug Bug." Jordan and her older brothers would try and spot a VW Beetle first. The victor would yell "slug bug" and get to hit someone in the shoulder. We tried it, and it took all of one slug from Eli to Chloe before she burst into tears, so Jordan lovingly amended the game. From then on, whenever my kids spotted a bug, they yelled "hug bug," and we hugged it out.

Walking from the garage to the side door that led to the kitchen, goose bumps would form on my arms as I spotted Jordan's sweaty Adidas cross-trainers drying out from her daily walks up and down the canyon.

"Jojo!" Chloe would squeal as the kids pushed past me to find Jordan baking lasagna or taking over Taco Tuesday. Our chef wouldn't just bend her five-foot-eight frame for a hug—she'd get down on both knees, at the kids' eye level. "Do you have math homework I can help you with?" Jordan would ask Eli, and he'd get excited about doing it with her. (Probably because she had the patience of Job, while I honestly hated that one parental job.)

We'd abandoned the pretense Jordan was "just a friend" ("Duh!" Eli said when we told the kids), so Jordan slept over more nights than not. Occasionally we'd rent her an Airbnb, then I'd beg her not to go to it. And though I wasn't a fan of letting the kids sleep in my bed, Jordan would melt at their pleas.

"Everybody in daddy's shirts," she would announce, and they'd dig through my dresser for one of my extra soft, worn cotton tee shirts, then huddle under the covers as Jordan read them a bedtime story.

Watching Jordan work her magic with my children, I felt as if I were living in an altered version of the Cinderella fairy tale. I saw Jordan as the kindest stepmother-to-be, her Bug her magical carriage, her sneakers golden slippers. And I saw myself as a prince forever being woken to his heart by Jordan's true love's kiss.

※

JORDAN ESSENTIALLY JOINED THE royal Winkler Family clan on July 25, when she accompanied me to my younger brother's fiftieth birthday party. (You know you're getting old when your *younger* brother turns fifty!)

The night really was enchanting, if very different from my introduction to Jordan's parents.

"The difference between your family and mine..." I cautioned Jordan as we pulled up to the valet at Wolfgang Puck's Asian/French fusion restaurant, Chinois, "...is your parents asked a thousand questions of me. They wanted to know everything about the man who's dating their daughter. But I'll bet nobody in my family asks you much about yourself tonight. It's not that they're rude or they don't care, they sort of don't talk about anything below the surface."

"Not getting the third degree would be a relief," Jordan assured me.

Given that in one fell swoop, Jordan met not only my parents, but my brothers, their wives, all my nieces and nephews, and most of our close family friends, I wouldn't have blamed her if she needed one of those Xanax she quit, but if Jordan was nervous, I'd never have guessed. She even met Elizabeth. I recall watching them chat politely and thanking the God I wasn't sure existed for my charmed life.

Dinner was disrupted only by the most subtly remarkable event. At dessert, while my brother was being toasted, Chloe, sitting in Elizabeth's lap, grew restless. Silently, Chloe slipped away from Elizabeth, crossed to the opposite side of the table where Jordan and I sat, and climbed onto her lap!

I could see everyone in my family exchanging shocked glances. *Who is this woman? Why is Chloe leaving her mother's lap to sit in this stranger's lap? Elizabeth must be humiliated!*

I glanced at Elizabeth, but she was smiling with such grace and acceptance, as if to say, "If Chloe is happy, it's all good."

And in that moment, I remembered the many times I'd looked at pictures of Jordan, even before we'd met, and thought to myself, *I can't explain it, she just fits.*

And I realized my instincts had been dead on. Jordan fit, all right— with my children, into my family, and most of all, into my heart.

"I THINK THE STARS are lining up here," I said to Jordan one night as we sat on the couch, laptops propped up. "Someone I know on Facebook wants to sublet her place for two months—two bedrooms, twenty-eight hundred a month in Beverly Hills."

"I'd rather get liposuction and a fat transfer," she said cheekily as she pushed aside her computer, on which I could see the page for Realself.

com, a website where people posted reviews of plastic surgeons and cosmetic procedures.

"You don't need lipo!" I whined. "But I'm happy to pay for the apartment."

"You're killing my dream," she joked, then studied the post. "You're right, this place looks too good to be true."

"It's like a castle," I said, hopeful. We'd spent days looking at Airbnb, Zillow, and Craigslist, but the only places available month-to-month were either outrageously expensive or executive suites, hotel rooms with a microwave.

"But seriously, are you sure you can afford this?" Jordan asked. "Maybe I should suck it up and get a room in a shared place like I had in San Diego? It's not like I'll spend many nights there."

"I love your modesty," I said. "But this place is a few blocks from my office—I could walk there during lunch for quickies."

Jordan chuckled and scrolled through the pictures of the apartment. She glanced at my friend's profile tab. Renee was a fortyish, freckled brunette.

"How do you know this woman?" Jordan eyed me suspiciously.

"No, I did not sleep with her," I headed her off. I'd gone through my Instagram and unfollowed basically every attractive woman except for my ex-wife, but I used Facebook so rarely these days I hadn't even thought to comb through it. "We matched on Tinder right after Elizabeth and I split. We chatted but never met."

Jordan brightened, as if to demonstrate she wasn't jealous. "Not that it would matter—I just don't like thinking that if we go see the apartment, I'd be talking to someone you slept with and not know the deal."

A Shakespeare line came to mind: *The lady doth protest too much.*

"Why *didn't* you go out with her?" Jordan pried.

"Honestly, I hate to sound superficial, but there was something strange about her pictures."

Jordan's visage turned to intrigue. "Do tell!"

I grinned. *What couple isn't privately catty together?*

"Look," I said, reaching out to click through some of Renee's photos. "In every picture, every selfie, every group photo, she's always in the exact same pose, turned forty-five degrees to the right."

Jordan squinted. "Damn, you're right. She probably studied the celebrity red carpet poses. But a girl has to know her angles."

"In every single picture? I don't know, it just instinctively creeped me out a little, like she was fake or hiding something."

"Like what?"

"I don't know, a hideous scar or lazy eye maybe?"

Jordan laughed. "Well, message her, and we'll see what her secret is when we see the apartment."

❧

THE NEXT AFTERNOON, JORDAN and I walked from my car to Renee's apartment building, a Spanish-style complex of only eight units surrounding a small courtyard on Crescent Drive.

Jordan looked about, content. "Such a quaint street."

"Hey, the Hotel Beverly Wilshire is only a few blocks north of here," I realized. "Where they shot *Pretty Woman*."

Jordan attempted not to look *too* impressed her favorite film was filmed so close by. "My own apartment in Beverly Hills. Guess I'm doing *something* right."

We both laughed and walked to Renee's door, painted a glossy black to match the windowpanes that stood out against the building's pleasant, beige plaster.

"Wonder if she'll answer at a forty-five-degree angle?" I whispered as I knocked.

You're terrible but I love it, Jordan's look said.

"Hello! Come on in!" Renee said as she opened the door, and right away I understood the only thing Renee was hiding when we matched on Tinder was some wrinkles. Like many people, Renee used photos from about ten years ago. And, Jordan had been right; the woman knew her angles.

"I don't mean to rush, but I have a client meeting in ten minutes," Renee apologized as she closed the door behind us.

"No problem," Jordan said. "What is it you do?"

"I'm an interior decorator."

"I can see," Jordan complimented her. "The place is so cute. I love shabby chic."

Renee led us through the living room, which sported arched ceilings, hardwood floors, shelves lined with books on interior design, and tables loaded with fabrics—but one thing jumped out at me.

"You have no couch?" I pointed out. This was very important because Jordan and I spent almost as much time snuggling on couches as we did lying by the pool.

"Oh, sorry, yes," Renee answered. "I have a really nice custom one being delivered next week."

We peeked our heads into the narrow kitchen, which was small but had the most charming nook, then Renee led us upstairs and into the master bedroom. The sun-bleached room had French doors that opened to a balcony, and a king-sized bed with white linen sheets.

Jordan and I exchanged smiles—the apartment looked even more lovely than it had in the pictures.

"So your post said it's available in three weeks?" I asked Renee.

"Yeah, I'm leaving August first. I spend every summer visiting my family in Wyoming."

"Really?" Jordan said. "I'm from Denver."

"No shit! Do you know the Srethen family?"

"Of course! Ken Srethen was in my class."

The girls lobbed names back and forth, and I stood there, feeling stupid for not knowing Wyoming and Colorado shared a border.

"We should get together when I'm back in town!" Renee said to Jordan.

"Absolutely! Maybe we can organize a Midwestern friend reunion."

They went on, pulling out their phones to exchange numbers and Instagrams, and I happily stood back and gave silent thanks to how those stars had indeed lined up. Not only had they bestowed upon us the perfect apartment, but they also delivered what looked like would be Jordan's first female friend in Los Angeles!

But then came that "ugh."

﹩

It was a week after we met Renee, and Jordan and I were walking through The Container Store—she'd decided she would set up the apartment living room as a studio to make yoga videos for Instagram and YouTube, so we were shopping for O-ring lights and a tripod.

"This apartment is going to be so good for me," Jordan said as we walked through the aisles. "Maybe I should start my own health and fitness website!"

"That's easy enough!" I answered. "I think we paid a couple grand for a graphic designer for our company website. Find one you like, and I'll pay for it."

Her eyes widened. "Thank you! I'd need to shoot some new pictures first. I found some amazing Los Angeles photographers on Instagram, but that won't cost anything—most of them are free if you let them use the pictures for their books."

"What better backdrop than the beach house!" I suggested. "What else do you dream of doing?"

"I don't know, learn to play guitar?"

"Done! Find a teacher on Google. And I have two guitars in mothballs in my garage."

"Do you play?" she asked.

"Three chords, terribly."

"I'm sure you're better than you say," she said with a laugh, then took out her buzzing phone from her shorts pocket.

"Ugh?!" Jordan said as she read a text on her phone.

"What?" I asked, stopping and turning back to her.

"Renee texted me, but it was obviously meant for someone else," Jordan said and read aloud, "*Ugh. I checked Jordan out on Facebook. She's twenty years younger than him.*"

"You're fucking kidding me," I hissed. Maybe I shouldn't have been so annoyed, but I never noticed people staring at us when we were out in public, and this was the first time I knew of anybody that had made it an issue or point of gossip.

"Hang on," Jordan said. "She just said, 'Sorry, this was about another Jordan.'"

"Now she's insulting our intelligence!"

Jordan finally lowered her phone. "You know, when you first told me about her, I did some research on her."

I wasn't terribly surprised Jordan might have been more jealous than she let on and had snooped on Renee's Facebook. "What did you find?"

"Well, she claims to be an interior decorator, but she has no website and has no client reviews on Yelp or LinkedIn. And she can't be doing well if she needs to rent out her goddamn apartment for two months! That's why it's so cheap—she's desperate for money."

Jordan's face quivered with indignant fury, so I decided to diffuse the situation. "Look, I'm insulted too, but maybe we should laugh this off? The woman probably hated seeing the guy who wouldn't ask her out show up with a beautiful, younger woman."

"No, your instincts about her were right—that bitch is definitely hiding something."

"Jordan, I only meant she had a physical deformity, but if you're that offended by this, we can back out of the apartment—she hasn't even asked for the first month's rent yet. Just text Renee a 'fuck you.'"

"We could spend another month looking and never find a place like hers."

"I know, but maybe that's better than renting a place with negative energy attached?"

Jordan tapped at her phone and saw Renee hadn't texted her anything else. "I need to think about this."

"Good idea."

Jordan and I walked around the mall for a bit, discussing the situation. As annoyed as I was, Jordan seemed to have a black cloud hovering over her head. But we came to the conclusion it was in our best interest to forget Renee's gaffe, if not forgive it.

"I'm going to pretend I never saw the text and take the place," Jordan ultimately announced. "But I'll tell you this: Renee's dead to me personally."

But the severity of that "ugh" revealed itself a week later as I was walking out of the chiropractor's office. (My lower back had been bothering me recently, no doubt from all my pool cleaning, and when the doctor adjusted me, it sounded like popcorn bursting in a microwave.)

Jordan's text lit up my screen, Your girlfriend has lost her damn mind!

I speed-dialed her. "What's going on, honey?"

Jordan spoke fast, pumped with adrenalin, "I was driving to get my lashes done in Beverly Hills and thought I'd stop by Renee's apartment and peek in the window to see if she got a couch. It was a cheap futon—interior decorator, my ass. Anyway, I saw Renee come down the stairs and walk out the front door without locking it, so I kind of hid behind a bush, and after she drove off, I went into the house."

I came to a sudden halt. "You did what?!"

"I know it's bad. David, I don't know what came over me."

"Jordan, where are you *now*?"

"I left her place, and I'm driving to your house."

"I'll meet you there in fifteen minutes."

"Okay," I heard her mumble as I started running toward my car.

"I don't know what came over me," Jordan said more slowly this time, as if her adrenaline had melted into shock. "It was like I was outside of myself, in a trance, and I couldn't control what I was doing."

On a lounge chair in the backyard with my elbows on my knees, I asked in a low, urgent whisper, "How long were you in there for?"

"Fifteen minutes maybe."

"I don't understand. What were you doing?"

"Just looking around. I spent most of the time going through her closets."

"Looking for what?"

"Proof she's full of shit, I guess. And I was right—one of her boxes had all her bank and credit card statements and unpaid bills, letters from her landlord saying she's six months behind on rent and from utility companies threatening to turn off her power and water."

"Jesus," I moaned. "Jordan, you do realize going into her apartment is a felony, right? Breaking and entering or criminal trespass. I'm not a lawyer, but I don't think the fact that you're supposed to move in there in two weeks would make a difference."

Jordan lowered her head in shame.

"Tell me you didn't take anything?" I pleaded.

"No, I put everything back where I found it."

I found myself about to say, "That's good" but bit my tongue; there was no part of this conversation with a silver lining. And, it occurred to me, I wasn't sure if I should believe Jordan. After all, she'd been liberal with my medicine closet before we'd gone to Mexico. Trying not to get her on the defensive, I asked, "Did you look through Renee's bathroom?"

"No, and I swear, this has nothing to do with drugs. You know I'm off everything."

Almost disappointed—that would have been the simplest explanation for this mess—I put my hand on her knee. "Then what happened?" I pressed.

Jordan's eyes began to glisten as she admitted, "It's hard to explain, but it's happened before."

I inhaled sharply. "You've broken into *other people's homes*?"

"Not exactly. But I have stolen things."

"Okay..."

"It's something that began right after I moved to New York. I was working as a personal assistant and nanny to this really wealthy family, and the woman was a nightmare. She had me on call night and day, paid next to nothing, and was verbally abusive."

Jordan stopped herself for a moment. "I'm not trying to blame her or excuse my behavior. Just explaining what goes on in my head."

"I understand."

"Well, part of my job was bringing her clothes to the dry cleaners. But it was ridiculous—she had this walk-in closet with every designer label shoe, handbag, and dress, and she'd try things on and toss them on the ground because it was easier than hanging them back up. So once in a while, I'd take something to the cleaners but not bring it back. She had so many clothes, I knew she'd never even miss them."

"And she never found out?"

"No. The only reason she let me go was because her kids went off to boarding school, and she didn't need as much help."

I waited a few seconds, but she seemed to have finished that story. "You said it *began* when you got to New York?" I asked.

Jordan closed her eyes, a habit I knew she had when overwhelmed, then opened them slowly. "A really good girlfriend of mine and I were part of this circle of girls who worked out together every day. One day, I was in her loft bathroom, and I noticed she'd left a bottle of Adderall by the sink, so I took some. This was right after Ray dumped me, and the stuff was the only thing that gave me enough energy to get through my day. I begged my psychiatrist to switch me from Vyvanse, but she wouldn't, so whenever I went to the loft, I'd take a few more. Eventually my friend caught on."

Jordan's face contorted as she tried to fight her tears. "She confronted me, and I stupidly denied it, so she sent a text to everyone in our group, telling them I was drug addict and a thief. I guess it was another reason I wanted to start over in Los Angeles."

Her tears won, and I moved over to her chair to slip my hand into hers. "Losing your friends must have been traumatic."

"It's humiliating, David. I'm sorry I didn't share it with you, but I thought they were isolated events—just another stupid impulse that happened a few times when I got angry. Even my therapist said she didn't think it was kleptomania—it's not like I get a rush stealing things. It's kind of a blur...I was sitting outside Renee's place and thinking, 'I hate this woman so much. I'm going to go in there and make her pay for that *ugh* and take back my dignity.'"

Jordan's laugh of self-hatred overtook her tears. "But I've royally proved I'm a fuck-up."

It does sound like she lost her mind, I thought. "Jordan, this sounds like a lot more than impulsivity. Have any of your doctors suggested you have some underlying problem, like bipolar?"

"No, and believe me, I've researched it myself over the years."

I nodded—Jordan certainly didn't have those extreme emotional highs and lows I'd seen in films and television shows about people with bipolar. Her moods were generally so stable it was hard to believe she struggled with *depression*.

"But I'll ask Doctor Browning when I see him next," Jordan added. "I know he treats Bipolar with TMS."

I bumped on this—I understood the connection between depression and self-medication but had a hard time believing TMS was this miracle cure that could fix the desire to commit felonies.

"Maybe we should find you a regular therapist," I suggested. "Someone you can see once or twice a week and talk about everything you deal with."

"I need that. I'll go online and find a list of therapists who take Blue Shield."

"Why wait? You can't even apply for insurance again till November. I'll pay whatever it costs."

"David, I hate the idea of paying for something when I know insurance will cover it."

She probably wouldn't have a moral objection to me paying for liposuction, I thought.

I found myself standing, feeling lightheaded, sensing that if I took a step backward, I'd fall into the pool.

"Jordan, you broke into someone's apartment today!" I vented with more anger than I usually allowed myself. "I'm not qualified to know the difference between kleptomania and impulse control. Add that to the eating disorder and drug issues. You need professional help. If you have a problem with how it's paid for, okay—I'll put it on my insurance and go with you, and we'll call it couples therapy."

Jordan looked up at the canyon, as if she was searching for some better excuse but couldn't find one. "Of course, I'll go with you. I'm sorry I'm such a mess."

I sighed and offered her my hand. "Come here."

She stood, went past my hand, and wrapped her arms around my back. As I hugged her, I heard her exhale and felt all the energy drain from her body, and I knew if I let go, she would collapse under the weight of gravity.

❧

I LEFT JORDAN AT Rosewood and drove out to Malibu to be with my kids. Considering the weight of what had just happened, it felt odd to up and leave, but Elizabeth already had the kids waiting for me there, and Jordan had earlier suggested she spend the night at Rosewood by herself, to give me and the kids a rare night alone together.

I found the kids playing on the sand, and of course the first thing out of their mouths was, "Where's Jojo?"

"Jojo's not feeling well," was the most truth I could share.

We took a walk down the sand to the reef exposed by the low tide. And as we explored the tide pools, our bare feet dancing between prickly anemones, I suddenly felt pangs of guilt. *My girlfriend broke into someone's apartment and rifled through her personal belongings!*

Should I tell Renee? I wondered. I assumed if Renee had any clue Jordan had been there, the police would have already contacted us. And I was confident Jordan hadn't stolen anything. Whatever bad decisions Jordan made, she'd always been brutally honest with me.

No, you're keeping your mouth shut and renting the apartment, I told myself. Jordan might have committed a felony, but as far as crimes went, this one was relatively victimless.

I swallowed my guilt well enough, but there was another problem gnawing at me—the problem of perspective. As much as I believed Jordan was being honest, I was beginning to feel like her apologies might be hollow. Since we'd met, our relationship had been one long song-and-dance routine of fuck-ups and apologies. *When does a man admit his girlfriend is seriously troubled? What would she do next? Would she hurt my children?*

Another pang of guilt hit me. How could I even think the woman who loves my children so much would ever harm them? For God's sake, she turned "Slug Bug" into "Hug Bug." No, I knew instinctually Jordan would never hurt them in any way. Herself, she'd hurt; me, maybe; but never my kids.

I felt like there was an argument going on between the right and left sides of my brain. The left side told me my friends and family would say Jordan adding a felony to her resume of issues would be a deal-breaker, while the right side reminded me she'd brought love, joy, and intimacy into my life after decades of feeling romantically cursed.

Would therapy be enough to fix Jordan? Stop her habit of making the worst possible decisions? Or should I take my lumps and end the relationship before she has another problem to apologize for?

As corny as it sounds, I recall literally looking to the sun starting to drop below the horizon and thinking, *I need a sign.*

And wouldn't you know it, my phone pinged with a text.

Look who came to visit!

A video popped up. I tapped on my screen and watched. Jordan had filmed two deer nibbling on spindle plants in my backyard!

I went wide-eyed. I'd been at Rosewood for four months and had never seen so much as a lizard come down from the canyons.

"Hey, little fellas," Jordan whispered off camera.

They bobbed their heads up, saw her, then went right back to their meal.

I was instantly reminded of the scene in the Disney version of *Snow White* where the beautiful, dark-haired princess asks the birds in the Enchanted Forest, "What do you do when things go wrong?" and breaks into song, bringing every animal out of the woods to sing along with her.

Forget Cinderella, I realized, *Jordan is the goddamn Snow White of Bel Air!*

And I reminded myself that all fairy tales have dark sides. After all, in Grimms' stories, Pinocchio spends half his life lying through his teeth before he becomes a real boy. Cinderella is abused by her stepmother for years before she meets her fairy godmother. Little Red Riding Hood is swallowed whole by a hungry wolf before she cuts her way out. And the woods in them are always haunted with ogres, trolls, and witches.

I had my sign. The universe—or whoever or whatever was writing my Once Upon a Time was telling me, *If you want a happy ending, David, you have to make it through the woods.*

22

HOT THIRTY-YEAR-OLD IN MY BACK

"WHAT BRINGS YOU TWO here today?" asked Debra. She was only ten years my senior with russet curls, but her benevolent brown eyes and wool shawl clinging to her shoulders reminded me more of a kindly Jewish grandmother than a psychotherapist. But she'd come highly recommended by Kendra, and I'd been to enough therapists to know their style didn't necessarily indicate their substance.

Where do I even begin? I wondered as I glanced around the office Debra had converted from a garage behind her Santa Monica home. My eyes settled on Jordan sitting beside me on the couch, our hands interlocked. In the three weeks since "ugh," Jordan and I had found our fairy-tale forest enchanted again. She'd moved into the Crescent apartment but still spent most of her days and nights at Rosewood; we'd hiked to the top of the Hollywood Hills under a total solar eclipse and attended a twilight Dodgers game during the World Series with my father and brothers.

I looked to Jordan, offering her the first chance to speak, but she smiled in deference, so I turned back to Debra.

"Well, I suppose it's important you know Jordan and I met on a website called Seeking Arrangement. Do you know of it?"

Debra nodded. "I've had several clients who've had experiences on there."

"Oh, great," I sighed. Jordan and I had some pretty big emotional fish to fry here, and this gave me the confidence we were in the right kitchen.

I spent the next five minutes telling Debra a little about ourselves, how Jordan and I had fallen in love and negotiated our open relationship.

"Open relationships are tricky to manage," Debra remarked, exercising profession-trademark diplomacy.

I laughed at "tricky." I realized I was still a little stung by how Jordan had blown up at me about Colette after she'd seen Paul, but I wanted to steer the discussion toward what was obviously more important—Jordan's escalating self-destructive habits.

"But other issues have come up in our relationship," I said.

"What kind of issues?" Debra asked.

I looked to Jordan again, and this time she acquiesced.

"I've been diagnosed with severe clinical depression..." Jordan said, then recounted her mental health history and the myriad of ways it had come to light in our relationship—her disappearance in New York, the revelation of her drug use in Mexico, and most recently, the trespass into Renee's apartment. Brave as always, Jordan spared no detail. I stayed quiet and held Jordan's hand the whole time. Jordan dissolved into tears, and I used my free hand to reach for a box of tissues on the coffee table. Sensing it wouldn't be compassionate enough to *hand* her the tissue, I dabbed Jordan's eyes myself.

"It's obvious how genuinely you love each other," Debra commented with a sincere smile. "Jordan, can you tell me a little about your childhood?"

Jordan obliged, telling Debra what I already knew about her idyllic Midwest upbringing, marred only by her depression and eating disorder.

"The reason I ask," Debra said, "is that in my experience, women who struggle with challenges like yours sometimes have unresolved traumas in their past."

I perked up—I'd once read that a good percentage of escorts had sexual abuse in their history, and Jordan and I had often discussed if there were deeper reasons for her wanting to be a sugar baby beyond finding her own Richard Gere. But Jordan had repeatedly denied she had ever been sexually assaulted in any way.

"No, none," she insisted. "Honestly, the biggest challenge in my life is my depression. It's why I'm so excited about the prospect of TMS."

"I've heard the therapy can be quite helpful," Debra said, then glanced over my shoulder—at a clock, clearly. "I'm afraid we have to stop now."

"Oh," I said. I wasn't exactly surprised by how fast the hour had gone by, but disappointed maybe. I wanted a little validation, to be told Daddy Fix-It was doing a good job keeping a train wreck of a relationship on the tracks.

"Do you have any practical advice for us?" I asked Debra. "Anything we should be doing differently?"

Debra paused for what seemed like an eternity. "There's a lot to unravel here, but I'd say the most important thing you both need to do is keep working on *yourselves*. There's an old saying: If you want a healthy relationship, change your own behavior."

I bit my tongue to keep from laughing. *That's it? We came in with all these issues, and the most advice she has is a cliché?*

And of course, then Debra asked, "Would you like to make another appointment?"

Jordan and I exchanged glances—by her strained smile, I could tell she wasn't brimming with enthusiasm either.

"We'll talk about it and get back to you," I politely told Debra.

She smiled, not at all offended. "Of course."

"WHAT DO YOU THINK?" I asked Jordan as we walked down Debra's driveway to my car.

"I don't know," Jordan sounded unusually whiny. "She was clearly biased toward you."

I looked to her with surprise. It was beyond me how anyone could detect a preference for *anything* from Debra's meticulously parsed responses. "Really? What gave you that idea?"

"Well, we spent the entire time talking about *me*."

Duh, I thought. "Okay, we did spend most of the time talking about you, but why would she be biased?"

Jordan gave me a bemused look. "Come on, David. You're a man, and a big, Hollywood producer—she knows who's buttering her bread."

"Well, I wasn't impressed with her either, but I think she's at least worth seeing one more time?" I suggested.

"Why?" Jordan asked.

Because you broke into a house three weeks ago, I wanted to yell. But thankfully a ridiculously old Jewish joke came to mind. "You ever hear the one about the actor who keels over on stage, right in the middle of a performance?" I asked.

Jordan looked at me like she couldn't believe I was telling a joke in the middle of all this. "No…"

"As the lights go on and a doctor rushes to the actor's side, this old, Jewish woman stands up and yells, 'Give'm zum chicken zoup!'"

Jordan chuckled at my accent.

"The doctor says, 'Ma'am, he's having a heart attack—that wouldn't help,' and the old woman says, 'It vouldn't hoit!'"

Jordan cracked up. "Debra *did* look a little like a Jewish grandmother."

"That's what I thought!"

"I guess it couldn't hurt to come back one more time," Jordan relented. "But next time *you're* doing all the talking."

"That's fair," I conceded as I opened the car door for her.

I SCHEDULED OUR NEXT session two weeks out because I planned to take Jordan to Lake Tahoe the following weekend for her thirty-first birthday.

"All I want is you, me, and a cabin in the woods somewhere," Jordan had requested.

I loved how unmaterialistic that sounded. The last time I celebrated a romantic birthday had been with Tessa, the woman who introduced me to Sanctum. I rented us a suite at the Hotel Bel Air and had gone on a shopping spree for her. (I remember as I went to check in, weighed down by bags from Chanel, Gucci, and Louboutin, a woman passed by and said to me on the sly, "Aren't you a keeper!")

But a wrench was thrown into my plans for Jordan's birthday when that Monday morning, I woke with a pain in my lower back I'd never thought possible—it throbbed like I'd been stabbed, and stinging waves of pain shot down my sciatica nerve. I managed to crawl my way to the chiropractor, but even the slightest adjustment made me howl, so I called my doctor, who sent me for an MRI.

It revealed I had a bulging disk between two of my vertebrae.

"Your basic wear and tear from decades of surfing, tennis, and golf," my doctor called it when he showed me the images. But I saw a more psychosomatic culprit. I took a picture of the scan, and that night when Jordan came over, I asked her, "Do you know what this is?"

"What?" she asked.

"A hot thirty-year-old stuck in my back."

"I'm breaking your back!" Jordan said with a goliath laugh.

I laughed too, but had to wonder...*Are psychosomatic injuries real?* I hadn't had an accident, and I'd never broken a bone in my body before this. And no, it wasn't because we had so much sex. Jordan and I made love maybe twice a week, and we weren't kinky gymnasts.

Over the next few days, I tried everything to ease the pain—stretching, massage therapy, and herbal CBD oil. The only thing that helped was the prescription for Vicodin my doctor gave me, but when I took one, I got so high I couldn't function.

Finally, my doctor suggested an epidural injection of steroids, which would theoretically block my nervous system from reporting the pain to my brain, lowering the inflammation in my back so it could heal itself.

I went in for the procedure. I lay face-down on a table while an anesthesiologist used an X-ray to guide a six-inch needle into my back. They gave me a local anesthetic, but I'm here to tell you that any time someone puts a long needle in your back, it's scary as fuck.

Thankfully, the day of the trip I woke up free of pain.

Almost *too* free of pain.

Over the course of the morning, I noticed a subtle side effect—I started to feel, well, robotic. It was as if the steroids were slowly overtaking my nervous system and turning me into an android, disconnected from any emotion whatsoever.

Jordan picked up on my mood (or lack thereof) as we packed to head to the airport. "You seem a little distant..."

I explained, and she put it astutely, "Soft David's gone, huh?"

"Don't worry, he'll be back," I said as I manufactured a smile. I was determined not to let an epidural block of my nervous system get in the way of her birthday celebration.

WE FLEW TO RENO, rented a car, and drove to Tahoe. The cabin turned out to be exactly what Jordan had asked for—built of rustic logs and painted forest green with red shutters and a view of the crystal-clear lake.

And I had plenty of surprises in store.

The biggest was a hot-air balloon ride at dawn the next day, her birthday morning. Neither of us had ever ridden in one before, and we drifted on silent wind currents as the towering yellow balloon lifted us in a wicker basket out over the lake. She was overjoyed and awed by the beauty of the immense mountains surrounding us, but I found it difficult to be present with that wall of steroids between my feelings and me. Even so, I kissed her and murmured, "Happy birthday, Jordan."

That night, I took her to the nicest (really, the *only* nice) restaurant in Tahoe, a lodge dining room at the Ritz Carlton Hotel. Naturally, I wanted to spoil her a little, so I brought along a bag full of presents and doled them out between courses. I gave her a slew of gift cards for stores I knew she loved— Ralph Lauren Polo, Addiction Nouvelle Lingerie, Barneys New York.

And over dessert, I gave her the pièce de résistance.

"Check your email, please," I said, somehow managing to feel a little pride break through the steroid wall as I took out my phone and sent her a PDF file labeled *JD MESSAGES*.

I'd compiled every text message we'd ever sent each other. And I mean *every single one*—going all the way back to the first message she sent me on Seeking Arrangement: Hello there, I quite enjoyed reading your profile, you have a very infectious smile!

"This is incredible!" Jordan said. "How did you do this?"

"I downloaded a program to my computer to suck the data out of my phone—it even saved the hundreds of pictures we've sent each other."

"Look at this text," Jordan said as she scrolled through the file. "I was talking about how I couldn't wait to snuggle up with you on your couch after two dates!"

"Our love story would make a great book," I mused. "An older man falls in love with his sugar baby."

"Write it!" Jordan beamed with pride.

"It's funny. My whole life I've wanted to write a book, but I never thought I had a personal enough story to tell. Screenplays—at least mine—have always been formulaic and calculating. But God, I don't know if I'd want the whole world knowing the crazy things I've done."

"Who cares what people think?"

"You wouldn't mind if I shared our secrets?" I asked.

"Not at all," she said. "Maybe it would help start a conversation about mental health and monogamy, and how money is an important aspect of every relationship, like it or not."

Though it would be several months before I decided to write this book, that conversation would turn out to be one of the most prophetic of my life.

❧

THE ONLY BLIGHT ON that night happened when Jordan and I went back to the cabin, shed our clothes, and dove under the quilted down duvet on the bed. As always, we were buzzing for each other, but as we kissed, I found myself not getting hard.

This was the first time since February when Jordan's kiss had cured my romantic anxiety that I wasn't rising to the occasion, though I had no doubt it was from the steroids. Zero. Yet, as I pulled back from kissing Jordan, I couldn't help but feel emasculated—somehow, humiliation penetrated the steroids.

"I'm so sorry," I whispered to her. "I mean, what kind of man can't have sex with a woman on her birthday?"

"Baby, you've given me the best birthday ever," Jordan soothed. "Whether you have sex with me or not, you're the love of my life."

❧

"How was your trip?" Debra asked as Jordan and I settled into her couch a few days later, our hands intuitively clasping again.

This time, Jordan was eager to answer first. "It was the most incredible birthday I've ever had," she gushed. "Although I don't know if David had as much fun…"

I laughed and told Debra about the steroids, which thankfully had done their job—as my feelings had returned, my back pain remained minimal.

"I'm glad you're feeling better," Debra said. "But tell me a little more about how those steroids made you feel?"

I wasn't sure why Debra was focusing on this, but I'd promised Jordan I'd do most of the talking this session. "It was an interesting experience. I think feeling like a robot might have been worse than the pain."

"In what way?" Debra asked.

"Well, being on the steroids reminded me of how unemotional I was before I met Jordan, and it scared the hell out of me. We call how closed I was before I met her 'Hard David,' and I'm afraid if I lost her, I'd go back to being shut down emotionally."

"That's insightful," Debra remarked.

But then I noticed Jordan glancing at me inquisitively. "Why would you lose me?"

I paused. "Well, last weekend was humbling…In all my years of golfing and surfing, I've never had any kind of injury. Now my back is acting its age. And I guess it makes me feel old and weak. I guess deep down I have this fear one day you'll wake up and realize you want a younger man, maybe want children, and leave me."

It was cathartic to vocalize my insecurities in front of Jordan and another person. My chest expanded, as if a surgeon had pried my chest plate apart and stepped back to let the operating room observe my steadily beating heart.

But then Jordan's hand slipped out of mine.

Debra leaned her head to the side. "Jordan, you seem upset by this?"

She nodded. "He's clearly having second thoughts about me moving in with him."

"Wait, what?" I stammered. "I didn't say I was having second thoughts about you moving in with me—I said I was afraid of *you leaving me...*"

Jordan wouldn't look in my direction. "I'll tell you this, there's no way I'm moving in with him *now*," she growled. "I don't know why he had me move to Los Angeles if he wasn't going to make me a part of his family."

My mouth gaped. *My kids sat on her lap at family birthday dinners, for God's sake.* "Debra, did *you* hear me say I didn't want Jordan to move into my house?"

Debra paused to choose her words. "Jordan, it didn't sound to me like David was indicating he wanted to end the relationship."

Jordan shook her head vehemently. "Either way, I'm not moving into his house now. I need stability from a partner."

I stifled a laugh. "*You* need stability?! God knows I'm not perfect, but how have I caused instability? I had sexual issues that disappeared in a day? I don't believe in monogamy. But neither do you. And how does my shit compare to what you do on a weekly basis? *How am I the unstable one?*"

I stopped, realizing I didn't want add anger management to my failings. "Jordan, I was being Soft David. But even if I *was* second-guessing us moving in together—I don't know, in some unconscious way—after all the things you've done, who'd blame me?"

Jordan's face quivered, loosening tears.

I reached for the tissue box, but this time, pulled out a few tissues and just handed them to her. *She can wipe her own tears today.*

Debra chimed in, "Jordan, maybe it would be helpful if you told David how his words make you feel?"

Jordan wiped her runny mascara and turned to me. "I feel like you're throwing me out on the street. Just like Ray did."

"How am I throwing you out on the street?"

Jordan ignored the question. "Don't worry, I'll survive. I'll just go back on the site. There's plenty of men who will take care of me."

I reeled. *What the fuck is happening?* Only minutes ago, I was chuffed with pride at my transformation into a man who could easily articulate his feelings in a therapy session, but now it was pretty clear Jordan was breaking up with me. *In therapy, of all places. For God knows why?*

"Are you really doing this, Jordan?" I stammered. "You're breaking up with me because I said I felt old?"

Jordan picked up her purse from the floor and placed it in on her lap. "I may be saying the words, but *you're* doing this to us! But don't worry, I'll go to a hotel or find an Airbnb, then come by and clean out my stuff while you're at work this week."

I shot Debra a pleading look. *Help me out here, lady?*

"Jordan, I understand you want to leave," Debra said. "I also understand something David said triggered you. But I think it would be a mistake to end the session prematurely."

Jordan shook her head defiantly. "I have nothing else to say."

The room went silent. I'd seen Jordan nearly lose her mind in Mexico, but only because she was on drugs. This time it seemed like she'd simply gotten so emotional she'd lost control of her sense of reality and her ability to communicate sensibly.

"Jordan, David..." Debra cut into the silence. "Can you both say something positive to each other? I know it's hard in the moment, but if you can find something to say to each other from the heart, maybe we can cut through the negativity and get to the root of what's going on between you?"

That's all you got? I thought. *Another cliché?*

I waited, but Jordan wasn't answering, so I turned to face her. "Jordan, let me be as clear as I can here. I love you beyond words. I *want* you to move in with me. *I want to spend the rest of my life with you.*"

Staring at the door, Jordan managed only a nod of receipt.

Debra prodded, "Jordan, can you say something positive to David?"

"Not really."

I couldn't believe what I wasn't hearing. "Jordan? You can't even say *one* positive thing to me?"

"No," she said, then got to her feet and fled to her car.

I rotated to Debra, in utter shock. *How could a professional therapist let a therapy session get so out of control?* But she commiserated with a grimace and a shoulder shrug that once again reminded me of a Jewish grandmother, this time saying, *I'm so sorry, Bubalah.*

23
MY SIDE OF THE BED

THAT NIGHT, AS I PACKED for a work trip to Vancouver first thing in the morning, I felt surprisingly calm. Jordan breaking up with me in therapy seemed too absurd to take seriously, and I was sure it was only a matter of hours before she'd call and dole out yet another of her perfect apologies.

But right before I went to bed, I glanced at Instagram. The first image in my feed was a meme Jordan posted. It was a picture of the New York skyline, hashtag #letsgo!

Jesus, I thought. *She's already making plans to go back to New York.*

❧

AND OF COURSE, THE next morning, as I emptied the contents of my pockets into the TSA screening bins at LAX, Jordan called. For no reason other than to prove myself eternally polite, I answered quietly, "I'm going through airport security, so I can't really talk."

"You're really going to Vancouver today?" she asked.

"Jordan, I have an important meeting. But I'll call you as soon as I'm through security, I promise."

"David, I'm literally begging you not to do this," she pressed.

"Not to do what?" I quietly seethed. "You break up with me, then act like a teenager on Instagram. Well, I have news for you, this is how adults handle things—we don't let crazy drama stop us from working."

"Okay," she mumbled and hung up.

As soon as I had my sneakers back on, I called her—but it went straight to her voicemail.

"My flight leaves in an hour, so call me back," I said in the message. And then, because I'm so damn obsessed with good communication, I texted her, Tried you back.

She didn't call back. She didn't even text me—I knew because I bought Wi-Fi on the flight just in case she might. But frankly, I wasn't really shocked she was ghosting me this time. I was simply past caring what the hell this unpredictable woman said or did.

AFTER A NIGHT AT the Granville Island hotel, I had my breakfast meeting and went to the island's public food market. I walked through the market, thinking I'd get some bites for the plane ride home, but instead I wandered from stall to stall in a daze. For some reason, nothing looked appetizing; I'd stare at the foods in their glass cases but couldn't bring myself to buy anything.

I left the market and headed down the quiet path along False Creek back to my hotel when my phone buzzed in my jeans pocket: Jordan had finally texted me. I could see it was a long paragraph, so I parked myself on a bench and read it.

I want to thank you. Thank you for making me feel seen and accepting me in my totality—gorgeously flawed and, though sad at times, always with hope. Thank you for opening your heart to me. You shared pieces of yourself that made it safe for me to do the same. And thank you for letting me meet your children. They are, without question, the most beautiful gift you've given. I feel lucky to have known them for the short time I did. I will not soon forget all our days by the pool in Bel Air.

And I started to sob.

Jordan was showing all the compassion and gratitude I'd needed in therapy, but it was far from a pledge to love me forever. She wasn't even asking if I'd see her to try to repair the damage. She'd written me the most beautiful note, but it was basically a Dear John.

Tourists walked by, and I couldn't even pretend to hide my tears as I wrote back, words pouring from my heart, through my fingers and into my phone...

Tears are dripping down my face. I can't even begin to thank you and share all that you mean to me. I am beyond grateful. You've taught me to love and be loved again. My heart was hard before we met. Now it's filled with blessed emotion. And though it's confused right now, I know I'd hate if we are not friends, and able to call upon each other for whatever reason, night or day.

I sent it, wiped my eyes with my shirtsleeve, got up, and walked back to the hotel to check out.

IT WAS ALMOST MIDNIGHT when I walked into my dark house. I went into my bedroom, dropped my carry-on bag on the floor and turned on the light. It was immediately obvious Jordan had come and cleared out her belongings. Rarely a day had gone by where she hadn't left an overnight bag, gym bag, or pair of sneakers on the floor, or a bathing suit on the handle of the door that opened to the backyard. But now, there was just a note on my bedside table. Jordan had written "Always and Forever, Amen." It was the title of the Randy Travis song we'd sung together on our drive back from Colorado.

And beside the note was her house key.

My heart sank to a depth I didn't know existed.

I couldn't take it anymore. I didn't know if I was being weak or strong. All I knew was Daddy Fix-It had to put all the absurdity and blame aside and fix this.

I sat down on the bed, took out my phone and dialed Jordan on FaceTime.

I was surprised she answered. She sat on her bed at Crescent, her face puffy from crying but still managing a welcome if sad smile.

"I can't believe all your stuff is gone..." I uttered.

"I came over last night," Jordan whispered. "It was so depressing being there. I laid down on your side of the bed and cried myself to sleep."

I closed my eyes, overwhelmed.

"I'm so sorry about what happened in therapy," she continued. "You had every right to share however you feel…I acted out of total fear and insecurity. My abandonment issues were so triggered."

I should have felt relieved by her apology, but I was desperate to admit my own mistakes.

"Jordan, I'm so sorry I went to Vancouver in the middle of this," I said. "I should have turned around. You're more important than any fucking meeting. But I don't understand. Why didn't you call me back at the airport?"

"Because I knew it was futile—I could hear it in your voice."

I could only nod—she wasn't wrong. I had been determined to make the point that I couldn't be pushed around.

Jordan was quiet a moment. "Maybe I have no right to ask because technically we broke up…but did you see someone while you were in Vancouver?"

I, of course, knew this was her way of asking if I had sex with someone, so I answered with my usual, unhesitating honesty, "Yes, I did."

THERE WERE ONLY A few seconds of silence between us, but the pause was enough room for me to flash back over the last twenty-four-plus hours.

First, I was back on the flight to Vancouver. The plane reached cruising altitude and the seat belt sign flashed off, so I reclined, pulled out my phone and signed up for Wi-Fi. I checked my phone to see if Jordan had reached out, but she hadn't. *Face it, David. You're officially single.*

I recall putting my hand to my neck, feeling as if some noose I hadn't even known was wrapped around my neck had been untied. The symbolism was obvious—Jordan and I had started as a no-strings-attached relationship, but she'd bound those strings into a rope and tried to strangle me with it.

This sudden urge came over me—a powerful aching in my chest. *I really want to get laid tonight,* I thought. *And why resist?* After all, Jordan said she was going to go right back on Seeking Arrangement, so why shouldn't I?

I pulled up the Seeking Arrangement app on my phone and logged in; I hadn't been on the site much in the last few months, so there were dozens of messages piling up in my inbox, but I ignored them, clicked on the search function and typed in "Vancouver." Hundreds of profiles of beautiful young women popped up—I hadn't used the site in Canada before, but clearly finding a sugar baby there was as easy as finding a maple tree.

"Hi there," I wrote to several of the prettiest girls. "I'm in Vancouver for tonight and need some company. Here are my private pictures. If you think we'd enjoy each other's company, leave me your number, and I'll text you right away!"

The responses poured in. A naturally curvaceous, dirty blonde named Lindsay seemed the most enthusiastic, and right to the point. "Hey, you seem really normal and cool, and I'm free tonight!" she wrote. "What sort of allowance are you looking to give?"

"Glad you think so! How is five hundred?" I responded, knowing from experience even girls who were used to getting a thousand dollars a date wouldn't find that insulting—at most they'd try to negotiate up to seven or eight hundred. But Lindsey answered, "That's perfect, where should we meet?"

"How is nine p.m. at the Granville Island Hotel bar?" I asked. "We'll have drinks, and if we hit it off, can hang out after in my room."

"See you there!" she answered.

I met Lindsay in the bar, and over martinis, she told me she was a freelance personal wardrobe stylist. I got the impression Lindsey didn't have many clients beyond the type she met on Seeking Arrangement, but she was classy, sweet, and intelligent enough, so I invited her back to my room.

As I write this, what jumps out at me about sex with Lindsey that night is just how unmemorable it was. I can usually recall a lot about my dates with women—the way they dressed; the way they smelled; the way they kissed or made me feel. But the only thing I recall about Lindsey is that when we finished having sex, I couldn't wait for her to leave. Again, that's unusual; I liked pillow talk—it made me feel like a gentleman and helped me to see the woman as the three-dimensional human being she was. But on that night, I guess I simply had an itch to scratch, and once scratched, I wanted her to leave.

I do remember the goodbye. It involved slipping quickly into our clothes, me putting Canadian bills into her purse, her giving me a light kiss at the door and making me promise to call her if I ever made it up to Canada again. Then me throwing the used condoms into the bathroom trash can and taking a shower.

And then, sitting on the bed at home, I was having a flashback to walking through the Granville Island market and reading Jordan's sweet goodbye on the bench.

And I understood the reason I'd lost my appetite that afternoon was because my stomach was turning over with guilt. But I'd buried those feelings deep down to hide my anger toward Jordan, to distract myself from feeling the utter loneliness her betrayal had wrought. Without even being aware of it, I'd become Hard David all over again. And it didn't matter that technically I hadn't cheated because we'd broken up—Hard David had snuck back up on me and been horribly cruel and insensitive.

Only reading Jordan's sweet goodbye text had penetrated that hardness. And now, back to Soft David, I was overcome with guilt. *Not once*, it occurred to me, *did I stop to think about how Jordan might feel about me getting laid in Vancouver.* If I'd stepped out of my righteous indignation for even a moment, I'd have known that given a day or two, we would have made up. How had I let Jordan's Instagram post convince me she was going back to New York? She'd told me so many times her social media posts were fake. Why didn't I remind myself that lately every time I broached the subject of sleeping with another woman Jordan turned into a cauldron of jealousy? How could I not have predicted me fucking someone last night would make her feel replaceable? Hell, in therapy I'd told her *that* was exactly how *I'd* feel if she went back on Seeking Arrangement.

And suddenly I remembered the argument Jordan and I had after I nearly slept with Colette. Before she'd admitted she was overreacting out of jealousy, she'd called me sexually "insatiable." "You're fifty-three years old!" Jordan had said. "I thought by now you'd have had enough of fucking random women."

Sure, she'd backed down after I pointed out her hypocrisy in fucking Paul and Broken Foot, but now I saw there was a difference between her fucking for money and my fucking for fun. My desire for casual sex *did* border on insatiable. I'd used being a sugar daddy as an excuse to sleep with countless women since my divorce. I might have slowed down a little since falling in love with Jordan—but only because I'd been afraid of how she'd react. Given free rein by her, I had to admit, I would probably continue sleeping with other women as often as I could find the time or money.

How much sex does a fifty-three-year-old man need? I probed myself. *Why do I still want to sleep with other women when I'm in love with a woman who fulfills me sexually in a way I never dreamed a woman could? Something must be broken inside of me.*

I started to cry, heaving for breaths, tears dripping from my eyes as I said to Jordan, "I mean, what kind of man fucks a woman twenty-four hours after a breakup?"

Jordan was silent, as if she knew the answer but needed me to say it first.

Voice cracking, I confessed, "I think I'm a sex addict."

JORDAN AND I FACETIMED FOR hours, in what felt to me like a reversal of all the conversations we'd had about *her* issues—her depression, eating disorder, drugs, and theft. This time I was the one making the apology.

"I'm so sorry I treated you this way," I said. "You must hate me now…"

"I'm not mad at you," she responded. "I feel sorry for you."

I shook my head. "All this time I thought you were causing all the problems in our relationship—you were the crazy one of us. But now I realize I'm sick, too. And you've known since we met, haven't you?"

Jordan pulled a bedsheet up and wiped her eyes. "I knew you struggled with it more than you liked to admit. And I knew you were going to see someone in Vancouver. That's why I begged you not to go."

Guilt forced my eyes shut for a long second. "Do you want me to tell you what happened?"

"I don't think I could stomach the details," she answered. "But thank you for admitting it."

"As if that's any consolation," I muttered.

Jordan looked like alarm bells were going off in her mind. "Have you seen other women without telling me?"

"No! On my children's lives."

She seemed settled by my sacred oath, but I wasn't done probing myself.

"How bad of an addict am I?" I asked Jordan. "Do you think I need to go rehab?"

"I'm no expert in sex addiction either," she answered, but I had no doubt she knew a hell of a lot more than I did about anything addiction-related—she'd gone through rehab for her eating disorder and had lived with a sober alcoholic.

I was relieved that she said rehab might be overkill, though.

"Even though I'm hurt by what you did, in Twelve-Steps terms, you're a highly functioning addict," Jordan said. "You're a great dad, have a great career, and God knows, you've been a rock every time I've needed one."

"I needed to hear that," I said, lying down and holding the phone above me. "Everything about this would humiliate my family."

"Well, I don't see any reason to disclose this to them right now," Jordan said. "But we should get you some help."

"I guess we can discuss this in therapy," I offered.

"You don't want to go back to *Debra*, do you?"

Jordan's tone answered *that* question. And since Debra hadn't navigated our last therapy session well, I didn't disagree. But I knew finding a new therapist was something that might take days or weeks, and Daddy Fix-It wasn't going to be lazy about fixing himself.

"I guess the first thing I should do is go to sex addicts anonymous or something?" I suggested.

"I'm sure they won't be hard to find in *this* town," Jordan chuckled with irony.

That she had a sense of humor about any of this made me feel even guiltier.

"I can't believe you're being such a saint," I said, fighting back tears. "I'm so sorry. I promise I'll do whatever it takes to get help and change. I love you so fucking much."

Jordan hesitated for only a heartbeat. "I love you, too."

But her pause was telling—she wasn't as eager as I was to declare us a couple again.

"Can I see you tomorrow and apologize in person?" I asked timidly.

Jordan let out an exhausted sigh. "I don't know. I'm brain dead and need to sleep on this."

I looked at the clock—it was close to three in the morning. "I understand. Goodnight, Jordan."

"Goodnight, David."

I let Jordan hang up first, then put the phone down on the bedside table, atop her note and key. I peeled off the clothes I'd worn to Vancouver, turned off the lights, and climbed into bed, on the side I always slept in, right where Jordan had cried herself to sleep the night before.

24
SPEAKING TO ME

I WAS SITTING DOWN at my breakfast table with coffee and my iPad to search for Sex Addicts Anonymous meetings when a meeting found me. No sooner had I typed *Sex Addicts Anonymous* into Google when my phone pinged with a message.

Good morning! How was Vancouver? Kendra wrote.

Don't ask...

Perhaps alarmed by my ellipsis, she called right away.

I started the conversation by telling Kendra about our therapy appointment breakup and tried not to make her feel bad about having recommended Debra.

"Wait, you broke up *in* her office?" Kendra said. "Wow, just...wow."

Kendra had never judged my lifestyle before, so I dove into my sordid trip and tearful confession.

My "...so I think I might be a sex addict..." landed with silence, then a little laugh from Kendra.

"So am I," she said.

"You are?" I asked incredulously.

"Well, technically, a love addict," she clarified. "But sex and love are obviously intertwined. I used to go to SLAA—Sex and Love Addicts Anonymous meetings all the time."

"How did I not know this about you?" I asked.

"Well, it is a little embarrassing," Kendra admitted. "Four years ago, I became obsessed with a guy who had broken up with me. One night, after a couple of glasses of wine, I found myself outside his house, throwing rocks at his window like a crazed teenager...I was thirty-four fucking years old."

I laughed out loud for the first time in a day.

"He called the police, but thankfully they just calmed me down and drove me home. When I told a few friends about it after, they thought the wine was the problem and suggested I go to AA. But at my first meeting, I got up to speak and couldn't stop talking about how heartbroken I was over this guy. Afterward, the guy who ran the meeting pulled me aside and said, 'I don't think alcohol is your problem. You should try SLAA.' I went and realized he was right. My whole life I've obsessed over men. I lose myself. I don't eat enough; I drink a little too much; I don't go to the gym; and I ignore my job—I'm too busy chasing that next fix of dopamine or oxytocin or whatever hormone gets released when you're in love."

The idea that love induced a chemical reaction wasn't foreign to me. I hazily recollected reading an article comparing brain scans of people in love to those under the influence of cocaine—they were eerily similar. But love addiction didn't seem like my problem—before I met Jordan, I'd avoided love like the plague.

"Sex is clearly my chemical," I told Kendra.

"Well, it's time we introduce you to the twelve-step program," she suggested. "What is it, Wednesday? There's a great meeting close to your house at noon, I think. I'll text you the address and meet you there."

Of course there's a meeting close to me in a few hours. Of course one of my closest friends has a few secrets of her own. Since meeting Jordan, my world was upended with such magic and drama I felt like I was living in a movie, but the plot twists came so fast they were hard to believe. If I were to pitch my love story to a studio, they'd probably tell me I needed to make things less coincidental. But the magic of it all didn't make me more excited to go a twelve-step meeting. *What if someone I know sees me there?* Yes, it might mean *that* person was also a sex addict, but it could still be humiliating, and gossip spread all too easily in Hollywood. If word got out, my family would be mortified. "See, we told you the prince was a pervert!"

But then it hit me: going with Kendra was a perfect idea. It came with a built-in alibi. Some years ago, I went to an AA meeting as the guest of a friend celebrating their "sober birthday." If I ran into someone I knew at SLAA, I could always say I was there to support Kendra.

I took Kendra up on her offer. "And thank you, really, for being a good friend."

"You're welcome," she answered. "And hey, it will be good for me, too. I haven't been in a while and could use an emotional tune-up."

I laughed but I was miserable inside. "An emotional tune-up? Fuck, I need a new engine."

A FEW MINUTES BEFORE noon, I entered the parking lot of the Westwood Village Church. The small, ivy-covered brick church was on a quiet street only a five-minute drive from my house.

"I cannot believe I'm here," I said as I climbed from my car and embraced Kendra at her Audi.

"It's a very mellow meeting," she said as we walked toward the building. "You don't even have to speak if you don't want to."

I stopped in my tracks. Images from movies and television shows where a character stands up in an AA meeting, tearfully recounts their sins, and declares themself an addict flooded my head.

Kendra turned back. "What's wrong?"

"I am not speaking," I declared.

"I said you didn't have to."

"I know."

"So, what's the problem?"

I shook my head. "What's the problem? Twenty-four hours ago, I thought I had my shit together. I was Daddy Fucking Fix-It. I had the answers for everything. Now, I have all these questions flying through my brain."

"Like?"

"Like 'Just how fucked up am I?' Like 'How do I get better?' Like 'How the hell is walking in there and branding myself as a sex addict for life going to help?' Wouldn't it be easier to go see a shrink and handle this by myself, privately?"

Kendra waited a moment to make sure I was finished, then took a step toward me. "Listen, David. Why don't you come inside and listen? Maybe you'll relate to what you hear. Maybe the things you hear will *speak to you.*"

I sighed. Even in my state, her logic was inarguable.

We entered through the side door of the church, into the community room. About a dozen men and women were milling amiably at mismatched and well-worn couches and chairs—donated by parishioners, I guessed. As if Kendra was in a hurry to get a good seat at a concert, she wound her way through the furniture to the front of the room.

Can't we sit in the back? I thought as I sat next to her on an ancient, plaid polyester couch.

Kendra waved hello to a thirty-odd-year-old brunette woman across the room, and everybody else was chatting like old friends, but I kept my head locked in place so I could escape eye contact. I don't know what I expected (men in trench coats?) but nothing about them screamed "sex addict." In fact, it occurred to me, I was probably the only person here who looked at all somber.

"Let's get started," baritone-d a man sitting into a folding chair at the front of the room, black notebook in hand. He was in his early sixties, fit, tall even in his seat, with a full head of silver hair and weathered crow's feet; he reminded me of Gary Cooper in the 1952 western *High Noon.*

He just needs a tall horse and a white hat.

"Welcome to this meeting of Sex and Love Addicts Anonymous," he said as everybody sat. "My name is Jeff, and I'm a sex and love addict."

I was surrounded by a chorus of, "Welcome, Jeff."

"Please join me in the Serenity Prayer," he said, and the room joined him aloud. "God, grant me the serenity to accept the things I cannot change..." I recognized the prayer and chimed in, "...the courage to change the things I can, and the wisdom to know the difference. Amen."

Jeff pulled out a few pages of crinkly laminated paper from his notebook and, since we were in front, handed them to Kendra. She took one and passed it to me. I did the same to a man on my right without looking at him. The title of my chosen page read SLAA CHARACTERISTICS.

"We'll start with the SLAA preamble," Jeff announced. "No need to introduce yourself at this time."

Kendra lifted her page and read aloud, "Sex and Love Addicts Anonymous is a twelve-step-oriented fellowship drawing on five major resources to counter the destructive consequences of sex and love addiction."

Thank you, Kendra, I silently lamented, now realizing that by sitting front and center, she'd guaranteed even if I didn't have to stand up and speak, I'd have to read aloud.

"Number one—Sobriety." Kendra continued. "Our willingness to stop acting out in our own personal bottom-line behavior on a daily basis. Number two—Sponsorship, our capacity to reach out to fellowship..."

As Kendra preambled, I found myself ruminating on the words "bottom line."

What are my bottom-line behaviors? I asked myself. *What exactly are the destructive things I do on a daily basis that I'd need to give up to be sober?*

It seemed to me I could rule out the idea that I was addicted to the physical act of sex. I might have masturbated a healthy amount and cheated an unhealthy amount during my passionless marriage, but since becoming a sugar daddy, I enjoyed going weeks without touching myself—I liked saving my sexual energy for a woman. And if I weren't in an arrangement, I would go weeks without sex. And though my sexual relationship with Jordan was the most consistent of my life, it wasn't like we fucked like rabbits.

But maybe, I asked myself, *my bottom-line behavior is paying for sex?*

This hit closer to home. I had been in one kind of arrangement or another almost constantly since my divorce. But my fuck-up in Vancouver hadn't shaken my core belief that sex work was ethical, and however

I might have used money before dating Jordan, giving her four thousand dollars a month had helped both of us ease into the love of our lives.

Now there's a quandary, I realized. I had a strong suspicion the die-hards in this room would say that to be fully sober I shouldn't even pay Jordan, but I was sure taking away her monthly allowance would not go over well. If anything, she deserved a raise for putting up with me.

"We need protect with special care the anonymity of every SLAA member," Kendra read. "Additionally, we try to avoid drawing undue attention to SLAA as a whole from the public media."

She placed the paper on the couch and smiled at me, but my return smile was for show. So far, I was unimpressed—SLAA wasn't speaking to me as much as I was speaking to myself.

"Thank you, Kendra," Jeff said. "We'll now read the Twelve Steps of Sex and Love Addicts Anonymous."

I perked up. *This I want to hear.*

"Twelve Steps of SLAA," read the man to my right.

I snuck a better look at him now. He was in his late twenties, wearing running shorts and Nike sneakers speckled with hill dirt from some recent hike.

"One," he continued. "We admitted we were powerless over sex and love addiction—that our lives had become unmanageable."

I don't know if my life has become unmanageable, I thought. Even Jordan had said I was "high functioning."

"Two. Came to believe a power greater than ourselves could restore us to sanity."

I'll take whatever help I can get, I admitted to myself.

"Three. Made a decision to turn our will and our lives over to the care of God as we understood God."

Thank God he clarified that with "as we understood God," because this Jew did not come to a church to be converted.

"Four. Made a searching and fearless moral inventory of ourselves."

They want me to search my soul without being afraid? That was a lot to ask. I always believed that bravery meant doing the things you *were* afraid of.

"Five. Admitted to God, to ourselves, and to another human being the exact nature of our wrongs."

What was I thinking coming here? I cursed myself. *Admitting I was a sex addict to Jordan wasn't enough? Couldn't I just go to another damn shrink?*

"Six. Were entirely ready to have God remove all these defects of character."

Why do they keep coming back to God?

"Seven. Humbly asked God to remove our shortcomings."

What's the difference between defects and shortcomings?

"Eight. Made a list of persons we had harmed and became willing to make amends to them all."

Oh, I'm going to have to make amends to Jordan, that I know. But who besides her have I harmed? Every girl I slept with was consensual, sober (usually), and well paid. I've certainly apologized to my wife a thousand times over. And I'm still friends with every girl I had an arrangement with!

"Nine. Made direct amends to such people wherever possible, except when to do so would injure them or others."

So I make a list of all the girls I've been with, call them and apologize? Wouldn't they be insulted? Isn't that injury?

"Ten. Continued to take personal inventory and promptly admitted it when we were wrong."

Whoever wrote the twelve steps needed an editor.

"Eleven. Sought through prayer and meditation to improve conscious contact with a power greater than ourselves, praying only for knowledge of God's will for us and the power to carry that out."

There's that God thing again. I'm starting to think this is a cult.

"Twelve. Having had a spiritual awakening as a result of these steps, we tried to carry this message to sex and love addicts and to practice these principles in all areas of our lives."

How do I carry the message to other sex addicts if they're anonymous?

He put his page down on his tanned knees. Mine were still shaking, but I was hearing only my own voices, far from convinced I belonged here.

"Thank you," Jeff said. "I'll now ask someone to read the Characteristics of Sex and Love Addiction."

I glanced down at my page. *Okay, let's see if I can relate to what I'm reading.*

"Characteristics of Sex and Love Addiction," I read aloud. "Having few healthy boundaries, we become sexually involved with and/or emotionally attached to people without knowing them."

I heard another faint voice in my head—it sounded like mine, but wiser, calmer—saying, *David, you have had a problem with getting sexually involved with people you hardly know.*

For a long time, I conceded to the Characteristics voice. *But haven't I changed since I met Jordan? I've only had a few one-night stands. And you can't say I'm not emotionally attached to her.*

But you fell right back into the habit as soon as you were single again, it pointed out.

Vancouver was all too easy, I conceded as I read on.

"Fearing abandonment and loneliness, we stay in and return to painful, destructive relationships, concealing our dependency needs from ourselves and others, growing more isolated and alienated from friends and loved ones, ourselves, and God."

The voice quickly probed, *Why have you concealed your life as a sugar daddy from just about everybody you love?*

Because they'll shame me and think I'm, well, a sex addict!

How do you know that? What have your family and friends ever said to make you think they'd disapprove?

You're right, I thought begrudgingly. *I have alienated them.*

"Fearing emotional and/or sexual deprivation, we compulsively pursue and involve ourselves in one relationship after another, sometimes having more than one sexual or emotional liaison at a time."

I don't know if I'm afraid of emotional or sexual deprivation. And I object entirely to the idea that having more than one partner is addiction. I'm in an open relationship. I don't believe in monogamy. I've been HONEST about that over and over again!

Honesty is only a part of being healthy, the voice challenged. *Deep down you know Jordan doesn't want an open relationship. Your heart of hearts knows she only wants you.*

Well, my heart of hearts is fucking confused! I can BE monogamous if I have to, but I don't know how to make myself WANT only one woman.

These past few days haven't changed that?

I wish they had, I pled with sincerity. *I wish I were like everybody else. I wish I were born with a belief that monogamy is natural.*

Homo sapiens rise above their instincts, it argued. *That's what makes us different than every other species.*

I don't have time for this debate, I answered the voice as I pressed on. "We confuse love with neediness, physical and sexual attraction, pity and/or the need to rescue or be rescued."

No woman has ever called me needy, I was happy to retort. *I've encouraged Jordan to be independent and make friends. And I've never confused love with sex—before Jordan I'd even forgotten what love felt like.*

But you feel like you're breaking your back trying to rescue Jordan, right?

It was a joke! Wouldn't you go to the ends of the earth to help the love of your life?

You don't think this is an overly turbulent relationship?

I don't like where this is going! Sounds like you're trying to tell me I'm a sex addict AND love addict!

Just encouraging fearless moral inventory, the voice parried.

Annoyed with the voice, annoyed with myself, I read, a little quicker "We feel empty and incomplete when we are alone. Even though we fear intimacy and commitment, we continually search for relationships and sexual contacts."

I do enjoy the search, I thought as a memory sprang into my head. It was a few years ago, and I was having a glass of post-coital wine on the deck of the Malibu house with Lacey, a black-haired British lingerie model. We'd met on Seeking Arrangement, of course, and were spending a few nights together before she returned to London.

"The site is overwhelming," said the model with two-million-plus Instagram followers. "I get hundreds of messages a day."

"I can't imagine," I answered. "I get dozens, and it's hard to keep up with them."

"It's become sort of a fun hobby though," Lacey said. "Like shopping for money."

I laughed. "We both need better hobbies."

Clearly your hobby got out of hand, the Characteristics voice pointed out.

It was true, I couldn't begin to count the hours I'd spent on Seeking Arrangement in the past decade, scrolling through profiles, sending and responding to messages.

Great, I'm a sex addict, love addict, AND online dating addict.

"We sexualize stress, guilt, loneliness, anger, shame, fear, and envy. We use sex or emotional dependence as substitutes for nurturing care and support."

We call this 'acting out,' the voice explained.

I've acted out, I acknowledged, recalling how I said to myself "fuck Jordan, I'm getting laid" on the plane to Vancouver.

When else might you have acted out? the voice gently prodded.

The night I went to Sanctum, I answered. *Jordan ghosted me so I rushed to a party and had a threesome in front of a room of strangers. I felt ignored so I used sex to distract myself. I do that a lot. When I was married, I used sex with strangers to distract myself from the unhappiness and anxiety. After my divorce I used sex to distract myself from intimacy. And in Vancouver I was distracting myself from feeling the pain and loneliness creeping up on me.*

You're starting to understand, whispered the voice. And then I read this: "We stay enslaved to emotional dependency, romantic intrigue, or compulsive sexual activities."

Suddenly time stood still in my mind. It was as if those three words, "compulsive sexual activities," unlocked a sordid screening of the women I'd had arrangements with...going down on Colette on the swan in my pool...fucking Helena in her blindfold...a dozen eyes on me while Serena and Haley fucked me in the basement at Sanctum... Tessa doing that lap dance...Allison and that tattoo model in her Santa Monica apartment. Then others came to me as names and faces—women whose stories made them memorable...Tandy the US Pole

Dance Federation champion, who, after our first sushi date, took me to her apartment and showed me her routine on the pole mounted in her living room...Janine, the twenty-three-year-old fashion boutique salesgirl, who, after our first lunch date, invited me to the underground parking lot and fucked me in the back of her Toyota Prius as a "test drive"...Alexa, the masseuse who told me while I was on the table she moonlighted as a porn star and gave me more than a happy ending... Lisa, the "dating and male intimacy coach," who admitted after we had sex that she moonlit as professional dominatrix...Natalie, the travel blogger...Angie, the fashion blogger...Kristine, the tantra teacher...Hannah, the painter...Alice, the food commercial producer... Bren, the makeup artist...Sonya, the Persian vegan chef...Sally, the corporate flight attendant...Kimmy, the esthetician...Orly, the boudoir photographer...Devon, the jewelry designer...Patty, the tech code writer...Alicia, the surgical nurse...Kristy, the dermatological nurse... Janet, the neurological science major...

And there must have been countless escorts I found online before I was married, I admitted to myself as the flashes ended.

Countless? The Characteristics challenged me. *Approximately how many women have you slept with in your life?*

After a beat of resistance, I admitted, *Two, three hundred maybe.*

How much money do you think you've spent on sex altogether?

Hundreds of thousands of dollars, I guessed.

Does Jordan know about all these women?

Maybe not the breadth of it, but I've never lied to her.

But you hurt her in Vancouver. You've hurt yourself, too.

You're right. I feel so guilty and ashamed it's painful.

Because?

Because I always thought of myself as the 'rare gentleman'—a man who'd been 'born lucky' and 'just had a very big secret.'

But the secret wasn't that you were a sugar daddy, was it, David?

I drew a deep, deep breath.

No. My big secret was I was a sad, middle-aged man with a compulsive desire to fuck strangers.

The voice went silent. It had made its point. My world was shattered, my pride and self-image in pieces.

"Thank you," Jeff said.

I glanced down at the page in front of me, stunned to realize my list of one-night stands had been so long, my inner dialogue so intense, I must have read the last two characteristics without even knowing. I slid the piece of paper onto the couch then stared at my knees; they looked still but felt like they were shaking uncontrollably.

"I'll open the meeting to sharing now," Jeff read from his notebook. "In order to provide a safe environment for everyone, we avoid cross talk in our meetings. Cross talk is interrupting someone when they are sharing, commenting on what someone shares, talking to someone directly in the meeting, or excessive detailing of our acting out behaviors. Raise your arm if you'd like to speak."

To my own surprise, my right arm went right up.

"One second," Jeff said as he reached into his pocket for his iPhone.

I glanced nervously at Kendra—she was staring at me, maybe even more astonished than I was. The man who insisted no matter what happened he wouldn't stand up and speak was not only going to, but first!

"Everyone has three minutes," Jeff said as he tapped on his screen to start a stopwatch. "Introduce yourself, using your first name only please."

I stood up but pressed the back of my thighs against the couch, thinking this would save me if I fainted, then took a half turn so I didn't have my back to the room.

"I'm David, sex addict," I declared.

"Welcome, David."

I took a deep breath. "This is my first meeting, and it's a little overwhelming, so forgive me if I don't make complete sense." I looked down at my feet. "I came here today because two days ago I made a big mistake—maybe the biggest of my life—and hurt someone I really love." A rush of guilt came over me. "I'm hoping she can forgive me," I said, swallowing the urge to cry. "But if she doesn't, it made me realize I've had a problem with sex for a long time, and if I don't admit it and do something about it, it's just a matter of time before I fuck up again in some way."

I caught Jeff's eye—he seemed to be listening with compassion—and was reminded he said not to go into too much detail. "I guess what exactly I did, and have done, isn't what's important here. But there was something important in what my friend Kendra read that really made me ask what my 'bottom-line' behavior is. I couldn't answer that at first, but now I think I know what it is—it's not paying for sex or having casual sex with strangers. Yeah, I did those things, but I think they're the symptom of my disease. My disease, my bottom line, is that I used sex to distract myself from uncomfortable feelings."

I took a breath and wondered how much time was left was in my three minutes. Either way, I knew I had to wrap it up soon. "Thank you all for giving me a safe place to talk about this."

I let the back of my thighs pilot me down to the couch. The room was silent for a few seconds.

Did I do that wrong? I wondered. Then I recalled Jeff's instructions about not "cross talking" and felt Kendra's hand take mine with a reassuring squeeze.

"I'm so proud of you," she mouthed.

And then I began to cry a little because, to my surprise, I felt proud of myself, too.

OVER THE HOUR, ALMOST everybody in the group shared. Of course, I can't go into *their* stories too much (that whole anonymous thing) but a few made an impression on me. I felt incredible sadness and compassion for their miseries yet couldn't help comparing myself to them. Most of their lives had become far more "unmanageable" than mine—a few of them had literally lost house, home and family to sex addiction, while the main thing I was afraid of losing was Jordan. But I had little doubt that I belonged among them.

The meeting ended (with everybody holding hands and reciting the famous Twelve-Step chant, "Keep coming back, it works if you work it!) and Kendra and I again walked through the parking lot. I felt very connected to my feelings—all of them—my pride, shame, guilt, humility.

"So, what do you think?" Kendra asked. "Are you going to come to more meetings, or do the Steps? Obviously, I'll be your sponsor, if you want?"

I held a "Newcomer's Packet" pamphlet I'd found on a table on the way out. "Thank you, but I really have no idea what steps I have to take next. I mean, I have work to catch up on, then I have to get the kids from school, then do their homework with them and make dinner…"

"As we say in the program, get through one day at a time," Kendra answered. "But I guess the meeting spoke to you, didn't it?"

"You have no idea," was all I could tell her.

25
YES DAY

DYING TO SHARE THE meeting with Jordan, I speed dialed her as soon as I pulled out of the parking lot. Her dial tone rang on my speakerphone, but I quickly disconnected the Bluetooth and pasted the phone to my ear; I didn't want Jordan to think I was being even remotely casual about this call.

"Hi," she said cautiously as she picked up.

"Good morning," I nervously fumbled—it was almost two in the afternoon.

"You sound like you're in a good mood?"

"I don't know if I'd call it *good*. I went to my first Sex and Love Addicts Anonymous meeting."

"Already? Wow, you didn't waste any time."

"I want to tell you all about it, but I'd rather do it in person. I have to pick up the kids in an hour, but I could get a sitter tonight…"

"Can I come with you to get the kids?" Jordan asked. "Whatever happens between us, I don't want them to feel like I disappeared from their lives."

She wants to say goodbye to the kids? My hopes that my first step would bring us back together sank, but at least I had a lifeline. "Of course," I said. "Why don't I come pick you up first, and we can take them for ice cream?"

"I look like a wreck, but okay. I'll be waiting outside."

I sped toward Crescent, the back of my T-shirt sticking to the seat with nervous sweat. Jordan stood on the sidewalk, her hands pressed in the back pockets of faded black jeans with holes in the knees, her hair in a ponytail, and not a stitch of makeup. But of course, I melted looking at her. I put the car in park but before I could get out to open the door for her, she climbed into the passenger side.

Our eyes met, and we both broke into tears.

I leaned across the armrest and wrapped my arms around her.

"Everything's going to be okay," I whispered, then wondered why I was reassuring *her*. I wasn't sure everything was going to be okay, and the hug felt unromantic, as if we were already ex-lovers consoling each other.

"So, tell me about it?" Jordan asked.

I started to drive. The school was only five minutes from her apartment, so I grappled with how to sum it up succinctly.

"Very telling," I answered. "It really made me see how I've used sex in unhealthy ways."

I took a breath and was about to go into detail when she saw the Newcomer's Packet on the console between us.

"Where was the meeting?" she asked.

"At a church a few minutes from my house. And listen to this— Kendra went with me. She called me this morning, and when I told her what had happened, she admitted she was a love addict."

Jordan turned to me, surprisingly irritated. "You went to a co-ed meeting?"

I felt a little wounded; I'd thought she'd be proud of me. "Yeah, why?"

"I thought for sure you'd go to a stag meeting."

"Oh, I didn't know I had a choice."

Jordan nodded. "All Twelve-Step meetings do. Think about it. You're new to the program, sharing your most personal problems, vulnerable, and someone takes advantage of that. They even have a term for what happens when people in the program date—the Thirteenth Step."

"Interesting," I said. "But who would go to a Sex Addicts Anonymous meeting to get *laid*?"

I knew I'd asked a stupid question even before she answered, "A sex addict."

I'd have laughed if I weren't the butt of the joke. "I guess it would make sense—Alcoholics Anonymous doesn't have meetings at bars, I'm sure. I'll go to a stag one next time."

Jordan still didn't seem appeased. "Just be careful you don't turn the program into a lifestyle."

"What do you mean?"

"Ray would go to at least one, sometimes two AA meetings a day; spoke on the phone with his sponsor for hours on end; sponsored other people; worked part-time as a sober buddy; and didn't have a friend besides me outside of the program. And he'd run a meeting almost every night, like it was his night job."

"Sounds like he turned being sober into another addiction."

"Exactly."

"Hey, if meetings bother you, I don't have to go. I'm sure I can handle this on my own."

Jordan raised a brow. "That's your addict mind, they'd say in the program. Addiction is the disease that convinces you that you don't have a disease."

"Twelve Steps has its own language," I noted as I pulled into a parking space on the street outside the school. "To be continued?"

Jordan shrugged, noncommittal, then held up the pamphlet. "I'm putting this in the glove compartment—I don't think you want the kids seeing it?"

"God, no. Thank you."

❧

"Jojo!" yelped Chloe as she ran across the playground—her pink backpack bouncing on her little shoulders—Eli behind her, slowed only by his rolling bag.

"Hi!" Jordan beamed, dropping to her knees to hug them. "Who wants ice cream?"

"I do!" Chloe yelped.

"I'd rather get a cupcake," Eli said.

Chloe groaned. "It's so hot."

"I'm sure you both have homework, so we can go to one place," I said. The kids began arguing, and Jordan jumped in. "You know what? I was driving by Sprinkles cupcakes the other day and saw they opened an ice-cream shop next door, where I think you can get ice cream *on top* of a cupcake!"

"Oh my God!" Chloe squealed.

I laughed. *Only Jordan would know of a place that heaped sugar atop even more sugar.*

We all hustled into the car and headed to Beverly Hills, where the kids ran from the parking lot to Sprinkles, bypassing the lines of tourists waiting to enter the cupcake shop and take pictures beside its famous pink cupcake ATM.

My hand ached to grab Jordan's as we followed them into the ice cream shop.

Eli and Chloe craned their little necks to stare up at the menu on the wall and its pictures of every kind of concoction of ice cream, cupcake, cookie, and soda imaginable.

"I can't decide between the cupcake sundae or sandwich," Eli deliberated.

"Should I get the waffle cone or root beer float?" Chloe asked Jordan.

"Get both," Jordan joked.

"Really? Can we, Daddy?" Chloe asked.

Jordan grinned mischievously at me.

Submit to a higher power came to mind. I knew this wasn't exactly what they'd meant in the Twelve-Steps, but I decided to let go of my control of the situation.

In that moment, Jordan was my higher power.

"Today is Yes Day," I proclaimed. "And on Yes Day, adults are not allowed say 'no.'"

The kids cheered, then placed their double orders. Jordan ordered a salted caramel ice cream in a red velvet cone, but all I asked for was an extra spoon, knowing the kids' eyes were bigger than their stomachs.

Delivered our treats, we sat on the wide, low bench by the window facing the street. Of course, the kids were unable to eat even half of what they ordered before complaining of hurt tummies. Jordan and I avoided smiling at each other—she maybe because she was afraid to trust me, me because I didn't want to pressure her. And, predictably, the kids started bouncing off the walls—dancing and singing on the bench with such sugar-fed glee that one of them knocked over what was left of Chloe's root beer float. I laughed, ran to the counter, and grabbed a handful of napkins to clean it up.

"Better get them home," I said to Jordan.

As we headed back to the car, the kids bounding ahead of Jordan and me, I wasn't sure if "Better get them home" meant "*I* better get them home" or "*We* better get them home."

Then, as if Jordan had read my mind, she asked, "Can I come back to Rosewood and swim with you guys?"

"It's Yes Day, isn't it?" I answered, a flower of hope blooming in my chest.

And back at Rosewood, Yes Day continued. The kids asked if they could swim before doing homework? "Yes." Stay in the water until the sun went down? "Yes." Would Daddy drive to In-N-Out and pick up Double Doubles for dinner? "Yes." Dessert, even though we'd been to Sprinkles? "Yes." Movie night even though it meant staying up way past bedtime? "Yes." Read in bed, too? "Yes." Sleep in Daddy's bed? "Yes." Can Dad and Jordan snuggle with us until we fall asleep? "Yes."

The kids passed out in seconds flat, and Jordan and I shared a smile across their bodies. I used my fingers to mimic a talking mouth and pointed, and she nodded. We carefully extricated ourselves and headed toward the living room, closing the bedroom door behind us. We took our favorite positions on the couch—each at one end of it, facing each other, knees touching, our cashmere Neapolitan stretched over our legs.

"I'm beyond exhausted," Jordan said.

"I can't tell you how much I appreciate you," I answered. "I don't know how many women could handle what I threw at you in the last few days. And listen, if you don't want me to go to meetings, I won't..."

"You do whatever you need to do," she answered. "I was a little triggered."

"I don't blame you," I said. "But listen, no matter how often I go to meetings, I'm not letting my addiction come between us."

Jordan smiled wryly. "Speaking of us..."

"...What?"

"I can't imagine it would be smart to have an open relationship while you're going to SLAA meetings."

I blinked—I'd been too afraid there wouldn't be an *us* at all to think about how the last few days might change our relationship in a concrete way.

"I guess it's time to close it," I said, asked, wondered.

"Not exactly a ringing endorsement of monogamy," Jordan noted.

I knew she'd see right through me if I pretended to have become a different person overnight, so I chose my words carefully. "I can't say I wouldn't struggle with it conceptually..."

But Jordan wasn't sold. "Listen, I want you to *want* to be monogamous, not just do it for me. And I certainly don't want you to do it because going to one meeting scared the hell out of you."

I was awed that she wasn't holding the past two days over my head— that night, she could have asked for my right hand, and I'd have cut it off.

"Well, I am sure seeing another woman anytime soon would not be a good idea," I said. "I need to focus on us, and myself."

She thought about it a moment. "Why don't we not make any decision right now? Maybe see where we are with it in a couple months?"

"Are you sure?" I asked. "Because if you really want to be monogamous, this is the perfect opportunity to say so."

"Yes, our deal is still the same—we're monogamish. End of story."

"A couple months..." I sighed with awe. Though I couldn't imagine that after this, either of us would ever give each other another hall pass, I couldn't believe how open-minded she was. Once again, we were negotiating our relationship.

Jordan read my mind and grinned. "We're still pretty unconventional, aren't we?"

"Very," I agreed.

"Okay," I said, then glanced at my phone, sitting beside hers on the side table. "But there is something I need to do now."

"What's that?"

It occurred to me that showing her might be better than telling her, so I reached over, got my iPhone, and scrolled through my apps.

"One of the things I realized today is how much I've used this thing as a distraction…" I said as I clicked the Seeking Arrangement app and logged in. Out of the corner of my eye, I could see forty-six messages waiting for me, but I quickly clicked on the Settings tab, scrolled down to the bottom and found the words, Delete My Profile.

I clicked on it and a pop-up appeared.

Warning! If you delete your profile, any messages, premium memberships, profile verifications, and background checks will be permanently lost.

They certainly don't make it easy on a guy, I thought, then pressed DELETE.

The screen read, Sorry to see you go.

"Goodbye, Rare Gentleman," I said as I showed Jordan the screen.

"Wow," Jordan finally seemed impressed. "How long have you had that profile?"

"Four years."

"That's quite a statement," she remarked, then reached for her own phone. "Okay then, I'll delete mine. God knows I've probably let it distract me too much, too."

I sat agape as she deleted her account, then showed me her screen.

"Goodbye Seeking," she announced. "For now, anyway."

I laughed, put my phone down on the blanket, leaned forward, and kissed her lightly. She took my face in her hands, held the kiss for a few seconds, then pulled back a little.

"Is it okay if I spend the night in bed with you and your angels?" she asked.

I was amazed she thought she had to ask.

26

LOOKING AT ME, TOO

To reassure Jordan I wouldn't make the Twelve Steps my night job, I went to meetings only during the day, mainly during my lunch hours. And I tried to attend mainly stag meetings, but they were surprisingly hard to find on either the SLAA or Sex Addicts Anonymous website schedules. I found little difference between segregated and mixed meetings. If people who met in the program were taking that Thirteenth Step—dating or hooking up—I didn't see it. All I saw were men and women of every age and color sharing their stories of lives destroyed by addiction, crying over the struggle of recovery, physically shaking as they described the anxiety of withdrawal.

I was incredibly moved with compassion and sympathy for their stories, but frankly, after that first meeting with Kendra, I never again felt the need to get up and share. The closest thing I experienced to withdrawal symptoms was a lingering sting of guilt for having treated Jordan so terribly, and deep regret that I'd abused sex for so long before realizing the power it had over me. I found I got more out of the many books I read about addiction. I pored over *Out of the Shadows* by Patrick Carnes, who, in the early 1980s, pioneered the idea that dopamine from sex was as addictive as any drug. I was moved by Carrie White's memoir, *Upper Cut*, about how her addictions nearly ended her life and career as a hairdresser to Hollywood stars (Carrie had come to my mother's house every Thursday since I was a teenager and was a close friend of the family). And I really identified with Russell Brand's *Recovery* about his sex (and drug and alcohol and shopping, you name it) addictions. It gave me comfort to know there were men who took pride in being vulnerable and admitting their failures publicly.

After about a month, I found the meetings repetitive. I discussed it with Jordan, and she had no concerns with how I was addressing my problem, so I stopped attending. But I took the Twelve Step program to heart. That voice in my head kept reminding me to *take fearless moral inventory*.

❧

ONE AFTERNOON IN EARLY October when the famous Santa Ana winds blew in ninety-degree weather, Jordan and I went to the Malibu house. A late season south swell had brought giant waves, so getting her out on a surfboard was out of the question. Instead, I stood on the deck, taking pictures of her on the stairs in a bathing suit and white yoga tank top, screaming with joy as the ocean crashed at her backside.

After she dried off and got into sweats, we parked ourselves on deck chairs. Jordan went through all the pictures, selecting which ones she wanted to share on Instagram.

It all started here, didn't it? I heard myself think. My heart suddenly sank with shame and guilt as I looked back at the house. It transformed before me, becoming the one-story, wood-shingled, shag-carpeted shack it had been before my parents tore it down and rebuilt it in 1990. In those days, there wasn't much of a deck; we'd had to build and rebuild one several times due to beach erosion. You could basically walk right out from the house to the sand.

Her name was Susie. How do I remember that?

Before me now, I saw a rail-thin girl with straight blonde hair down to her ass pulling off a shiny pink bikini to reveal bolt-on fake breasts.

"You're so fun," Susie said in a high, squeaky voice as she tip-toed to a brown and white striped cushioned chaise lounge that I'd pulled close to the house, so nobody walking by on the sand would see.

"I didn't expect you to be so sweet," I said as I pulled my surf trunks down over my legs, tanned golden brown from surfing—I was twenty-six and surfing every morning before going to work at my surf shop.

"I didn't think you'd be so cute!" Susie chirped as our bodies met, and she kissed me on the lips without tongue.

Fully erect, I sat on the chaise as she grabbed her purse and pulled out a condom.

"I'm a little nervous," I said while she clambered atop me. "This is my first time with a..." I trailed off, unsure if she'd be less offended by "prostitute" or "professional" or "escort."

"You'd never know it," Susie laughed as she slipped the condom onto my cock with her mouth—it was clearly a trick of her trade, but it felt so good, wet, and warm.

I closed my eyes, feeling my nerves dissolve as a breath later, she lowered herself down my shaft.

"Where are you?" I heard Jordan say.

I blinked and saw my love watching me, off her phone.

I felt myself gulping, my chest heaving, fighting tears.

"Baby, what's wrong?" Jordan asked softly.

I took a breath and released it so I could speak about my flashback coherently. "I don't think I've told you, but the first time I paid for sex was right here."

"No, you didn't."

"I think I was twenty-six," I said. "I'd googled escorts and found one of those sites for The Girlfriend Experience, and invited the woman down here. She was dumb as a doorknob but so sweet and sexy. And we had a great time. After she left, I didn't feel shame or anxiety. I just thought, this is how I'll get what I need."

Jordan must have sensed that I had more to say as she silently watched me.

"But thinking about it now, I'm just so sad for myself," I admitted. "It's so obvious I was just distracting myself from the anxiety and fear that I'd never have a relationship. But all I was doing was keeping the possibility of having one out of reach. And I wonder what would have happened if I'd dealt with it some other way? What would have happened if I'd met someone like you when I was twenty-six, someone who could help me understand what was going on inside me?"

I stopped and casually wiped the tear from my cheek. These days I cried so easily, it didn't bother me. Nowadays, I was proud when Soft David made an appearance.

"David, you shouldn't regret the things you've done," Jordan answered. "You have two perfect children, have led an amazing life... and if you'd met me when you were twenty-six, I'd have been, what, five years old?"

"Ha!" I laughed while exhaling. It reminded me of Jordan's breathy laugh, and I thought, *I'm starting to sound like her.*

Jordan smiled and slid closer to me. I buried my head in her neck.

"God help me if I ever lose you," I whispered.

"You never will," she promised.

OF COURSE, I WASN'T the only man examining his behavior in 2019. By then, the #metoo movement was in full force.

One night, Jordan and I were watching a CNN report outlining the accusations against Producer Harvey Weinstein, and how women were coming out of the woodwork and naming other men in the industry who abused their positions for sex.

"This is horrible," I said to Jordan.

"Have you worked with him?" she asked me.

"I've never even met the guy. I mean, I have a few friends who've worked with him, and he's famous for yelling and throwing phones, but I haven't even heard rumors about him doing any of *this* shit."

"Well, I've been hit on by just about every man I've worked with," Jordan said.

I gave myself a gut check and wondered if I ever took advantage of women I had worked with? But for the life of me, I couldn't think of a single instance in which I'd dangled a role to an actress if she'd sleep with me. And I hadn't dated anybody—not a writer, producer, not an agent, while working with them; I'd *never* needed a Harvey Weinstein moment to learn right from wrong.

"But you know what I don't understand," I said. "This guy must be worth hundreds of millions of dollars—why couldn't he just hire escorts?"

Jordan shrugged. "It's not about that. Men like him get off on power and control."

I shook my head. "And I thought I had a problem with sex."

"There's a huge difference between a sex addict and sex offender, David."

I trusted Jordan's distinction between a sexual transaction between consenting adults and men who forced themselves on women in pursuit of control, but my own statement, "why couldn't he *just* hire escorts" made me feel sad with regret. After all, the casualness of being able to scroll through Seeking Arrangement and pull a date for the night because of my access to money is part of what landed me in SLAA to begin with. Paying for sex might not be an outright sin, but for too long I'd used that as an excuse to sleep with women who were probably suffering in some way or another—even if I hadn't forced them to have sex with me, circumstances had.

How many of my sugar babies really wanted to have sex with me? I wondered. How many women saw sex with me as Jordan saw sex with Broken Foot—soul-killing? Women like Lindsey in Vancouver, who I immediately intuited was on the site because her wardrobe consulting business hadn't taken off. If I had truly wanted to be the Rare Gentleman, I would have taken the time to get to know her and figure out if she really thought being a sugar baby was a healthy, fun way to get out of debt, or if she would be taking a hot shower to clean off my smell after being with me. And if it was the latter, I should have helped her in some way without the expectation of sex. It might not be my responsibility to help these women get out of their financial woes, but if they saw sugaring as an act of desperation, I was contributing to the emotional damage of their situations.

There was no practical way to contact each of the women and apologize, but I owed them all a psychic apology. And I vowed—for a second time, but with deeper understanding—never to disrespect another woman by having such casual, careless sex with them. And though Jordan and I were taking a break from the site, if I ever had another arrangement, it would be with a woman who I knew for sure was making the choice to sleep with me from a healthy place.

Jordan, as always, read my face. "David, you've never been and never would be a Harvey Weinstein."

"Thank you," I answered. "But if women ever start calling men out for being sugar daddies, I'm going down hard."

Jordan raised one eyebrow, as if she thought I was being overly dramatic. "Trust me," she said. "Women will never complain about men paying their rents."

ALL THE WORK I PUT into that fearless moral inventory and saving my relationship with Jordan paid off. To my surprise, our love life flourished. Considering her jealous streak and ever-changing moods about monogamy, I wouldn't have blamed Jordan if she held my mistake over my head and withheld sex from me. She would occasionally express some minor trust issues. (Once, when I went to see an afternoon movie for work, she panicked. "Wasn't this what you told Elizabeth when you cheated on her?" Jordan asked once. Thank God I'd kept the popcorn butter-stained ticket stub in my pocket.) But with my history, it was hard to blame her. And when the lease on Renee's apartment was up, Jordan agreed to "officially" move in with me. (I say "officially" because really, she hadn't spent more than ten nights there in the two months we had the place—she was always at Rosewood.)

I called Elizabeth first. I was a little tense as I told her—I knew if she had any idea how turbulent my relationship with Jordan had been, she might be worried. But Elizabeth, who'd met Jordan several times by now, was genuinely happy for us.

Then I sent texts to my family and friends.

Great news! answered my brother, Adam, in the Winkler Family group chat.

We love Jordan! added my sixteen-year-old niece.

She's a wonderful young lady, echoed my father.

Your love story with Jordan inspires me, waxed Megan.

But the best response of all came from my children.

Jordan and I had gone together to pick them up at school and tell them the big news, and as soon as they climbed into my car, I turned to Eli and Chloe in the back seat.

"Guess what? Jojo is officially moving in with us!"

"Yay!" Chloe screamed and stretched her seat belt to its limit to hug the equally gleeful Jordan.

But Eli stared at us, as if we'd told him a bedtime story he already knew the ending to, and said, "I thought she already lived with us!"

27

THE BLOODY BODY BAG

With Halloween fast approaching, the next order of business in the Rosewood household was decorating—and I took this business *seriously*. The holiday was my kids' favorite, next to their Hanukkah/Christmas hybrid of course, and every year we turned our home into our own version of The Addams Family house.

Being the self-described "big kid," Jordan was naturally on board, so we started by taking the kids to every pop-up Halloween store in Los Angeles. We filled my trunk three times over with props, and every day after school for two weeks, we went to work. (If you doubt the gravity of this task, consider that we literally wore construction helmets and gloves!)

We strung white and black cotton cobwebs over every hedge, placed two-dozen Styrofoam headstones on the lawn, hung black rubber bats and enormous hairy spiders from the rain gutters, and covered the windows with stick-on bloody handprints, as though someone had been brutalized inside and was clawing to get out. We impaled fake skulls on rebar hammered into the grass to surround a life-sized haggardly witch and ghostly pirate "having tea" on wooden crates. Under the eucalyptus trees on the other side of the driveway we arranged a pair of skeletons lying side by side on chaise lounges, holding hands connected by fishing twine; the kids poured fake blood all over their plastic bones, and I inserted a pirate's dagger into one of the skeleton's chest plate.

But what put the display over the top was the life-sized body bag we hung by the front door. The bag was translucent plastic to showcase dismembered body parts soaked with blood inside—gruesomely realistic.

One morning, I found a handwritten note in my mailbox:

We love your decorations. But the body bag is scaring my children every time we drive by. Would you mind removing that? Thank you—a neighbor.

"Somebody needs a sense of humor!" I said when I showed Jordan the letter. "And it's anonymous—they didn't even have the balls to write their name!"

Showing more sensitivity than her stubborn boyfriend, Jordan asked, "Is it too much?"

Imagining some little girl in her car seat wailing in horror made me cringe, but I thought, *It's Halloween, for God's sake.*

I suggested we ask Chloe what she thought (I knew my boy would say the grosser, the better); and read the letter aloud to the kids at dinner that night.

"Chloe, what do you think?" asked Jordan. "Should we keep it up?"

"The thing *is* disgusting," Chloe whined sweetly. "But it's *Halloween!*"

Jordan and I exchanged grins. The bloody body bag would stay.

A few days before Halloween, I drove home from the office and found Jordan on the front lawn, spray-painting wood planks with stencils to make "Beware" and "Keep Out" signs.

"Spooky!" I complimented as she stood and shook the can to get the last of the paint. I tried to give her a kiss, but she backed away.

"I'm sweaty and dirty."

"Any man who won't hug his sweaty girlfriend isn't worth a damn," I joked but didn't force it. I squatted, picked up a spray can and squirted a little gray on the edge of a sign.

"What are you doing to my sign?" I heard Jordan carp.

"I thought this would age it a little."

"Well, you're fucking it up," she said, dropped her can and marched into the house.

I stood slowly, sensing this wasn't about me; whatever conflicts Jordan and I might have gone through, we didn't *bicker*.

"What was that about?" I asked when I found her inside at the kitchen sink, scrubbing her hands.

She turned off the water. "I'm sorry. I got an email from Blue Shield. I didn't qualify for special enrollment."

"Oh, no. Baby, why didn't you call me?"

"Because I was on the phone with customer service all day."

"Did they explain why?"

"Nope. They said the underwriting department denied it, it's final, and there's no appeal process."

"I wonder what the hell happened."

Jordan leaned against the counter and crossed her arms. "They obviously turned me down because of my history with depression."

"Obamacare made that illegal," I said. "Even republicans say they want to keep that part of the law."

Jordan scoffed. "Don't be naïve; these companies find loopholes everywhere."

This sounded on the paranoid side to me, but I didn't argue. "Anyway, you can still apply for open enrollment, right? When's that?"

"November first."

"Oh, next Tuesday."

"If they didn't accept me now, why would they ever?" Jordan said, her voice cracking. "I did everything I was supposed to…I got every document…I went off benzos…but now I don't know if I'll ever get TMS."

Tears began to well in her eyes, and I stepped toward her to put my arms around her waist. "Honey, I promise we will get you insurance—one way or another. If they turn you down next week, we'll figure it out. We'll talk to an insurance broker or something. Maybe now that you're living with me, I can get you on my company plan…"

"Daddy Fix-It never gives up, huh?"

I laughed, and she located a smile.

"Still," she sighed, "this means TMS is months from happening. Last time I saw Browning, he said if we didn't get approval by November first, I'd have to wait until January to start. He doesn't like to break it up over the holidays."

"I understand how frustrating this must be for you," I said.

"Thank you," Jordan answered, then stood up tall. "I'm getting TMS if it kills me."

That was the second time she made that vow in my kitchen, and I loved and respected her resolve.

WHAT MADE OUR HALLOWEEN dedication all the more impressive was the fact that we didn't plan to trick-or-treat at Rosewood. The neighborhood was a hilly canyon, and I doubted there would be many kids going to door-to-door. Besides, I was excited to introduce Jordan to the Winkler Family tradition of Halloween in Malibu Colony.

"I can't even do it justice," I said when I told Jordan about it. "They close the streets to cars so it's safe for kids to run around, and the whole neighborhood transforms their homes into haunted houses. And since the neighbors are either rich or famous, they go to crazy lengths to out-do each other."

I wasn't trying to boast—I just wanted Jordan excited. Not that I needed much of a sales pitch.

"This all sounds amazing!" she gushed. "I wouldn't miss Halloween in Malibu Colony with you guys for the world."

The plan was that I'd leave work early, pick up Jordan, then we'd meet Elizabeth, the kids, and a few of Elizabeth's friends and their children down there. After trick-or-treating, Elizabeth would head back into town, and Jordan and I would spend the night, then drive Eli and Chloe to school in the morning.

"I'm home!" I yelled as I arrived at Rosewood and hurried to the closet where I'd been keeping our matching costumes. I was going as an Egyptian pharaoh (weren't they all bald?) and she as Cleopatra (complete with fake hieroglyphic tattoos and snake-headed arm bands.) I transferred it all to the trunk of my car and went to corral Jordan.

I found her asleep in bed, the shades drawn, room dark.

"Honey, we need to hit the road," I said as I sat in front of her.

She batted her eyes open and swallowed. "I feel horrible…"

I felt her forehead, years of fatherhood having turned me into a human thermometer. "You don't have a fever."

"I'm fighting something…my stomach is in knots…I'm sorry, I can't go to Malibu…"

"Are you sure?"

Her answer said it all. "Can you get me a trash can?"

I hurried into the bathroom, got a small one, and rushed it back. She pulled it toward her but just held onto it, prepared if not ready to heave.

"I'll run the kids' costumes out there and come right back," I said. "I'll ask Elizabeth if she can cancel her morning appointments."

"Please, don't…it's bad enough I'm letting you down. I don't want her annoyed with me."

"Are you sure?"

"Just tell Eli and Chloe that I'm sorry."

"They'll understand. But text me if you get worse, and I'll come back, one way or another."

She nodded and closed her eyes.

Obviously disappointed but more concerned, I drove to Malibu. When I walked into the house, the kids were too eager to start candy-hunting to give more than a little "aw, bummer" to Jordan's absence. They jumped into their costumes, but when I started to put mine on, I couldn't. It felt like, after all our planning, I'd be betraying Jordan in some way. *What's a pharaoh without Cleopatra?*

We headed out to trick-or-treat, leaving behind a large plastic pumpkin with candy for kids to grab from. Hundreds of families in costumes wandered the half-mile long road. Because beach house front lawns, are, well, beaches, the garages of the homes face the main road. Almost every garage was opened and decorated so outlandishly, it was like walking through New Orleans on Mardi Gras. The kids bolted for a garage. It usually kept a pair of Porsches, but tonight the luxury cars were replaced with Mexican folk art and a skeletal mariachi band playing spooky music. Eli and Chloe emerged with life-sized candy skulls that barely fit into their bags! Another garage was decorated—no, set-designed—into the famous Mos Eisley Cantina from Star Wars, complete with aliens playing boozy jazz on strange instruments. At a more traditional haunted house, a dad dressed as a scary clown asked all those who entered if they wanted it "scary," "really scary," or "deadly." My kids wisely chose "scary" and as they headed in, I lingered outside to text Jordan.

Hope you're okay?

Same, she reported.

Love you, I'll come home after I drop the kids off at school in the morning.

Love you too, turning off the phone to sleep.

THE NEXT MORNING, I TEXTED Jordan but didn't hear back. Hoping she was just sleeping late but worried, I dropped the kids off at school and rushed home. As I parked in the driveway and climbed out of my car, Jordan came out to greet me, clad in Adidas work-out clothes.

"Hi!" she said cheerfully, then gave me a quick kiss.

"Somebody's feeling better," I said.

"I woke up feeling great. Thank God. I have a Model Fit class in half an hour, then I'm coming home and applying to Blue Shield. Oh, and I want to see all the pictures you took from last night!"

"I'll show you when I get home from work," I offered.

"Can't wait!" she said and headed to her car.

Huh, I thought as I watched the Hug Bug drive down the canyon. Last night, Jordan had been so sick she missed what she said she wouldn't miss for the world. This morning, she was headed to a workout class? *Talk about unpredictable.*

"OFFICIALLY APPLIED THROUGH OPEN enrollment!" Jordan announced when I walked in the door that evening. She sat on the couch, laptop beside her, blue eyes beaming with optimism. "I even called customer service to confirm they got it—they said it should only take a day or two to hear back."

"Fingers crossed," I said as I slipped off my shoes and sidled up next to her.

"I want to see last night!" she urged.

"Thank God you recovered so quickly," I said as she scrolled through the dozens of pictures and videos from the previous night on my phone.

"I've never seen anything like this," she said, then sighed. "I feel terrible for disappointing everybody."

"I feel bad for *you*. I thought for sure you had the stomach flu and would be down for days. I'm kind of surprised how quickly you recovered."

Jordan lowered my phone, suddenly flush with embarrassment. "I might have binged on candy a little yesterday afternoon."

I blinked, realizing I'd never actually *seen* her eating disorder in action. "It makes you pass out like that?"

"No..." she turned solemn, "I passed out for the same reason I binged—I got hit with really bad depression."

"Oh. I'm so sorry."

"I'm sorry you had to see it. It's one of the reasons I've never lived with anybody before. It was easier to hide it..."

"You shouldn't have to," I said. "But when did it happen? You were fine when I left for work yesterday morning."

"Around noon. It was like a bus came out of nowhere and ran me over. I thought maybe if I ate it would help, so I had some salad—and then some candy, obviously...and then more candy." Her jaw quivered from shame. "The wrappers are in the outside bin."

I made a mental note *not* to humiliate her further by looking in those bins next time I took out the trash, but asked, "Honey, why didn't you call me at the office?"

"I don't know why I do *anything* when I'm depressed, David. It's what people without chemical imbalances don't understand—when it happens, I'm not in control of my actions."

"Did something happen to bring it on?" I asked.

"Again, I really don't know…I know I was more upset about having to push back TMS than I let on. And the idea of being down in Malibu with Elizabeth and her friends was a little intimidating."

"I can understand that," I said. Jordan had never complained before, but I knew my close relationship with my ex-wife was almost as unusual as my relationship with Jordan.

"Honestly, I'm so fucking relieved it was gone when I woke up this morning," she said. "Sometimes it lasts for days, even weeks…but I guess it's a good reminder of why I'm so desperate for TMS."

I gave Jordan a sympathetic hug, then she pulled back with a smile.

"You know what I'd like?" she said.

"What?"

"To not make a big deal out of this. Let's not cry and spend all night discussing and dissecting it. We've had enough drama for a lifetime. Can we order Postmates and watch something mindless, like Celebrity Rehab or Dateline?"

I laughed. "Sounds like a perfect night."

WHILE JORDAN ORDERED DINNER, I decided to get a jump on taking down the house decorations. I had the sense my household's enthusiasm for cleaning would be a tenth of what it was to make the mess, so I figured I'd go about it a little every day over the next week. Thinking there was no reason to terrorize the neighborhood children longer than necessary, I started with the bloody body bag. I stepped up the ladder and used an Exacto knife to cut the string that held it to a nail in the roof, and the bag landed at my feet with a thud. And for some reason, I was suddenly overcome with an incredible sense of disappointment.

I understood why Jordan had missed Halloween. And I was sure she was more upset about not showing up for the kids than anyone. But I couldn't hide from myself the fact that it concerned me her depression had found a way to ruin a night we'd looked forward to for weeks.

Will this happen again? I wondered. She and I could hope for the miracle cure of TMS, but what if that didn't work? Although Jordan's bout with depression had been thankfully short, I'd seen how it had haunted her in other ways, from ghosting to drugs and theft.

Maybe I'd become complacent—the spotlight had been so hot on my problems lately I'd almost forgotten about hers. But Halloween night was a reminder Jordan's issues hadn't magically disappeared. And now that she was living with the kids and me, whatever drama those issues might create wouldn't be so easily ignored or fixed.

And frankly, that scared the hell out of me.

28
WHERE RELATIONSHIPS GO TO DIE

JORDAN AND I BOUNCED BACK from the disappointment of Halloween as fast as always, but in November, new problems arrived at our emotional doorstep.

First, our sex life started to wane.

Inexplicably.

I hadn't lost my "buzzing" for her in any way, and my romantic anxiety was ancient history, but for no reason I could put a finger on, Jordan lost interest. I'd make an advance, and she'd make an excuse, "I'm not feeling sexy tonight," she'd say. I'd press for an explanation—had some lingering mistrust dislodged itself from its hiding place after Vancouver? Did she miss our open relationship and need a trip to New York to have some fun? "No, I'm just not in the mood," she'd say. I felt so unusually rejected, I began to be afraid of climbing into bed with her. I told myself even couples with normal, healthy sex lives have ebbs and flows. Maybe we'd left the infamous honeymoon stage and needed a few date nights to spice things up for her.

But one night, I climbed into bed—she was naked but for her black-rimmed glasses, watching a show on her computer, and I shuffled up next to her and began kissing her shoulder, then her neck.

She manufactured a yawn. "I'm sorry, I'm tired tonight."

"Jordan, we haven't made love in two weeks," I said, careful not to sound too whiny. "I'm desperate for you, like you always wanted."

She smiled. "I love you, but you know I've had issues opening up sexually in the past."

I blinked. Jordan and I had dissected my romantic anxieties and intimacy issues ad nauseam, but she'd never mentioned any of her own. "What do you mean?" I asked.

"It's late, David. I really don't want to get into it now."

"Okay. I'm going to go to the couch and take care of myself," I said and planted a kiss on her forehead.

She stared a hole in me. "What the fuck? You're going to go masturbate?"

I felt unusually shamed. I'd never had to masturbate during our relationship but didn't think there was anything wrong with it. And it was inexplicable to me how sexually controlling Jordan suddenly seemed. I'd known her to change her moods about monogamy, but she'd turned into a regular school marm.

"Jordan, I don't know what's going on with you, but if you don't want to have sex, I'm not going to be controlled like this."

"Do whatever you want," she said. She pulled off her glasses, put her laptop away, and shut off the lights.

I went into the living room and lay on the couch but didn't dare touch myself. Being right wasn't as important as being in a relationship. And of course, in the morning, I woke to Jordan sliding under the Neapolitan cashmere blanket.

"I'm sorry about last night," she whispered as she reached her hand down, sliding off my underpants.

I sighed with grateful pleasure as she climbed atop me and pulled me inside her.

And for the next week, we made love almost every night.

I asked Jordan a few times what she meant when she said she'd always had trouble opening up sexually, but she never wanted to talk about it. I was left with no idea what had switched her libido off but was so relieved it was back, I didn't force the issue. On any given day, Jordan and

I had such bigger dramas to discuss that I was happy to have a relatively "normal problem."

⁂

BUT DAYS LATER, A new problem…Jordan's vaginal infection.

(Isn't this a little too intimate? you're asking. Trust me, this story is one I do NOT want to share. But it's hugely important, so I ask you to reserve judgment until you reach the end of the chapter.)

Jordan's vaginal infection first appeared back in June, while she was coming and going to San Diego for yoga teacher training. We were making love when suddenly she had a thick, white discharge down there. Obviously, this ruined our moment, and Jordan was horrified, but I took it in stride—having been in the delivery room twice, nothing that came out of a woman's body shocked me.

Daddy Fix-It went into action. I found a gynecologist in San Diego who had great reviews on Yelp, and Jordan went to see him after class one day.

"He was one of the best doctors I've ever seen," Jordan said after the visit, then added with the glee of someone who has just joined a club, "He's Jewish, of course."

The gynecologist told Jordan she either had a bacterial or fungal infection. (Female readers will know how such issues are often difficult to diagnose.) He prescribed Jordan an antibiotic cream, and in a day or two, the discharge was gone.

Except, over the next few months, it ruined a few more moments. But since it would go away so quickly, we weren't that worried, and even turned it into a joke, naming the discharge "Pulp."

"Something a little off down there to you?" Jordan might ask as I kissed my way down her stomach.

"Yeah, Pulp's back."

We'd laugh, she'd use the cream, and we'd be good to go in a day. But lately, Pulp had come and stubbornly refused to leave; I suggested a few times we head down to San Diego to see the doctor or find another one closer to home, but Jordan wouldn't go.

"I'm not letting you pay for another doctor, and I'm not paying until I get good insurance," she insisted.

Despite Jordan having applied during open enrollment, she hadn't been approved, and I began to wonder if she wasn't so paranoid for thinking the insurance company was using her depression against her.

"But this is your health we're talking about," I pleaded. "I can afford this out of pocket."

"Stop worrying!" Jordan would answer. "I just need to balance my pH or something."

But one afternoon, the opportunity to fix the problem presented itself to me in such a way I couldn't refuse.

It was the second week in November, and Jordan and I were grocery shopping at Whole Foods. We had been discussing a little furniture shopping in advance of a trip New York, where she wanted the two of us to do a mini renovation on her Manhattan apartment in order to attract someone to sublet it for the entire next year.

"Would you believe I've never been to Ikea?" I said to her as we walked through the produce department.

Picking out an organic frozen burrito, she turned, amused. "You're kidding me."

"No. I mean I ordered furniture from the catalogue back when I was in college," I explained. "But it was cheap and always fell apart while I was building it."

"Ikea has come a long way since the Stone Age," she teased. "Not all Ikeas are alike, you know. I went to one in Orange County, and it was by far the best I've ever been to."

"Then why don't we take a trip to Orange County?" I suggested. "See the doctor you love in the morning, then go to Ikea."

"That's a great idea!" she answered to my surprise.

I can't believe I had to bribe Jordan with Ikea to get her to go to the doctor, I thought. *But whatever works.*

※

WE DROVE SOUTH A few mornings later and visited the gynecologist first—he prescribed Jordan a stronger antibiotic and a different cream—then headed to Ikea.

Walking hand in hand through the arena-sized store, Jordan and I followed the arrows painted on the floor and wandered through the maze of departments. We spent a good three hours shopping for a new bed, armoire, couch, shelving, and bathroom décor for her apartment. Our tastes were gleefully in sync. I'd point out a wall mirror I liked, and she'd coo, "I love that." She'd ask what color room-dividing curtain I liked; I'd say, "the gray," and she'd beam, "That's what I was thinking!"

"We're like the Olympic team of Ikea shopping!" I joked.

Amazed at how inexpensive everything was, I was ready to buy whatever she needed, but Jordan insisted she wanted to wait until she could get to New York to measure her space and make sure everything would fit perfectly. The only things Jordan wanted to take home to Rosewood were small things—bathmats for our bathroom, blown-glass flower vases, and spiraled bamboo dracaena plants for the kids' bedrooms.

As we stood in line to pay, our clerk putting the items into the biggest, bluest polyester shopping bag I'd ever seen, Jordan seemed happier than she had been in quite some time. I had never understood why Jordan was obsessed with shopping at modest places like Target or Ikea but buy so little. But now it struck me that Jordan's shopping habit wasn't about making purchases—it was about the act of nesting. No matter what eccentricities she had, what she wanted most in life was a calm, safe place—to be part of my family.

"I had so much fun today," Jordan said. "It's hard to believe Ikea has a reputation for being the place where relationships go to die."

"What?"

"Oh, it's totally a thing. There's even a *30 Rock* episode where Tina Fey and her new boyfriend almost break up at Ikea. They're like, a perfect match until a disagreement over some chairs becomes a metaphor for their relationship."

"Well, *we* clearly beat the Ikea curse," I laughed.

But Ikea wasn't done with us. After we exited the check out, Jordan eagerly pointed out a whole *other* section, a food market where they sold Scandinavian specialties. So, we spent another ten minutes wandering through the aisles of packaged food, laughing as we pointed out their odd names like "Allemensratten! and Gronsakskaka!" And then there was an entire *other* section of candy. Jordan took a plastic bag to fill, then stopped at the wall filled with containers of candy and chocolate in every color and shape.

And stood there.

Staring up at it.

"I'd like to hit the road before traffic gets too bad," I gently prodded her.

Jordan turned and glared at me. "You ruined the entire day."

"What?"

She tossed the baggie into a trash bin and headed toward the exit without looking back to see if I was behind her. With a shopping bag over my shoulder so large it was banging on my knees, I rushed to catch up with her in the parking lot.

"Jordan, I didn't mean to rush you, but we've been here for hours."

Too furious to answer, she marched to our car and climbed into the passenger seat.

I put the shopping bag in the trunk and got into the driver's seat. "Can we talk about this?"

"I need a minute," she seethed.

I bit down on my own growing anger, started the car, and pulled out of the parking lot.

We sped north on the 405 freeway, traffic had yet to slow to its inevitable rush hour crawl, when Jordan finally turned to me.

"I can't believe how fucking selfish you are," she hissed.

My jaw dropped. "I took the entire day off work, drove you down here to take you to the doctor, then spent four hours helping you find furniture for your apartment, and I'm selfish?"

"You didn't come down here for me!" she barked. "You only give a shit about my infection because it ruins sex."

"That's…" I stopped myself from saying *crazy*. "First of all, if that were the case, I would have insisted we go to the doctor months ago when it started cropping up all the time. Second, how is being worried about your girlfriend's health *ever* a bad thing?"

Jordan shook her head angrily then switched tactics. "You manipulated me into coming down here by saying we go to Ikea."

"Manipulated seems a little harsh, don't you think?"

"That's exactly what a narcissist would say," Jordan barked.

"I'm a narcissist?" I answered with a laugh. I knew the term was used to describe anyone who was egotistical to the extreme, but this was the first time Jordan, or anybody else, had used it to describe me.

"Let me out the car," Jordan suddenly demanded.

"What? You want me to pull over on the freeway?"

"Let me out of this fucking car!" she yelled, unbuckling her seat belt. The car started to beep as she grabbed the door handle.

"Don't you dare touch that damn door!" I screamed at the top of my voice.

Jordan recoiled her hand.

Her body started to shake, and she began to cry and wail in a way I hadn't heard since Mexico. My eyes darted between her and the road—I was scared to hell she'd try it again.

"Pppullll ovvverrr," she uttered.

"NO! Just sit there and be quiet till we get home!"

Jordan scrambled over the middle console and jumped into the back seat. I turned over my shoulder to make sure she wasn't reaching for the door, but she rolled onto her side and pulled her knees to her chest, face turned from me. I looked back at the road and angled my rearview mirror so I could watch Jordan with a flick of my eyes. She took several deep breaths to calm herself, her body growing stiller, her wails softening to a nearly imperceptible moan.

But horrible images flashed through my mind, a waking nightmare of what could have happened if I hadn't stopped her from opening that door…

Jordan tumbling out of the car, onto the freeway.

Me, slamming on the brakes.

Jordan, being struck by one car, rolled over by the next.

Cars swerving and hurdling into mine.

My airbag going off, slamming me into my seat as my car spun to a stop.

Running across a smoke-filled freeway through wrecked cars and people climbing from them screaming, toward Jordan's lifeless body...

The prattle of my tires bounding over freeway line dividers told me I was drifting, and I forced myself to concentrate on the road. I noticed a dreadful silence in the car. I glanced in the rearview mirror. Jordan had gone so quiet that if it weren't for her slow, shallow breaths, I'd have never known she was alive. I guessed she'd fallen asleep but couldn't imagine *how?* I was so wired with adrenaline, I couldn't think straight. It was all I could do to drive. At one point, I thought maybe if I put on some music, it would help break the dreadful silence, but when I tried to peel a hand off the steering wheel, it wouldn't budge. I had a death grip on the thing.

It was getting dark when I pulled into my garage. I'd barely parked when Jordan was unfurling herself from the backseat, climbing out, and rushing into the house. Taking a breath to force myself to keep calm, I unloaded the trunk.

I dropped the shopping bag in the kitchen and walked into the living room. Passing that long shelf above the fireplace, I noticed one of the picture frames was overturned.

This struck me as more than happenstance—on her way through the house, Jordan actually stopped to place it face-down? I righted it and saw it was a picture of Jordan and me—a selfie we'd taken of us kissing on the Malibu Pier. I shook my head, unclear what message this sent, but sure it was a foreboding one.

I headed into our bedroom, where Jordan was slipping out of her sneakers and grabbing her laptop.

"Jordan, we have to talk about this," I said as I stopped at the foot of the bed.

She ignored me at first and sat on the bed to open her laptop. Then, as if waiting for the computer to come out of sleep mode gave her a moment to consider, she said shortly, "I'm sorry I called you selfish."

I shook my head. "Jordan, I'm more concerned with what happened in the car."

"I shouldn't have called you a narcissist. You're anything but. Thank you for taking me to the doctor."

I crossed my arms. "Jordan, you nearly jumped out of the car on the freeway..."

"What?"

"You tried to open the door."

"I don't know what you're talking about...I may have pushed myself off the door or something when I was climbing into the back?"

I shook my head vehemently. "I know what I saw—I even yelled at you to stop, and then you sat there before you climbed into the back."

"You're imagining shit."

"*I'm* imagining this? You don't remember half the things you say and do when you're upset."

Jordan clambered off the bed. "I don't need this fucking harassment!"

"You need help, Jordan."

"Fuck you!" she yelled as she swung her right hand at my face.

I reared my head back just in time. "What the fuck?!"

She swung again—I raised my left arm, and her wrist rebounded off my elbow.

"Jordan, stop!"

She swung a third time, this time slapping an open palm against my left shoulder. It only stung a little.

I stared at her. "Am I imagining this, too?"

"Fucking asshole!" she shouted and stormed past me.

"I'm an asshole? Fuck, you tried to hit me!" I yelled as I followed her into the hallway. "Do you realize if I'd hit YOU, I'd be arrested for assault or domestic violence?!"

I let out a sarcastic cackle. She slammed the door to Chloe's bedroom shut behind her. I marched to the door and turned the handle, but it was locked.

"How dare you lock this fucking door!" I yelled.

I used all my might to push down, breaking off the fragile 1950s L-shaped handle. The door flew open. Jordan kneeled at my daughter's empty bed, crying, grabbing tissues from a box on the bedside dresser.

I didn't take a step into the room. I felt like I didn't need to—I'd stood my ground.

"We don't lock doors in this fucking house," I muttered. "But sleep wherever the hell you want tonight."

I picked up the broken door handle, turned, and walked into the living room. Seething, I lay down on the couch.

I was in a state of shock. This was the first time in my entire life *anybody* had hit me—man or woman. Then my shock turned to shame. In breaking that door handle, I'd lost my temper. And it didn't matter if Jordan had tried to hit me. Hell, it had made me laugh, perhaps cruelly. And though I'd basically accused Jordan of domestic violence, I knew there was a double standard when it came to women hitting men. I wasn't really afraid of Jordan's temper. But I was scared and confused by what had happened in the car. Jordan might have diminished it, but I knew what I saw.

She had tried to climb out of a moving car on the freeway.

I didn't think Jordan intended to commit suicide or to hurt herself. She'd lost control of her emotions—wanted out of the car, out of the situation—and acted impulsively. But dangerously so.

I wracked my brain, trying to find an explanation. "Is Jordan on drugs?" was always the first question I asked when she did crazy things, but in this case, it didn't make sense. If Jordan was taking Xanax, she'd have been less reactive to our argument in Ikea. Xanax calmed people *down*, not riled them up. Jordan had only gone off the rails in Mexico because she combined the Xanax into that pharmaceutical cocktail.

I knew what Jordan would blame for today's emotional explosion. The same thing she blamed everything on: depression. I knew tomorrow she would probably calmly apologize and say something like "depression causes anxiety" or "depression causes exhaustion and the inability to control my emotions."

The problem was, I didn't know if I believed her anymore. I hated to play dime-store psychologist with Jordan's mental health diagnosis. But seeing her switch from being the happiest girl on the planet to this volatile, violent creature made me wonder if the problem was something else completely. *Does Jordan have multiple personalities? Is she bipolar?*

Multiple personalities seemed like a stretch of the imagination, but then so did bipolar. Jordan told me that her doctors, including Doctor Browning, had ruled it out, and as I understood it, people with bipolar disorder underwent long periods of manic highs and depressive lows. But with a few exceptions, like in Mexico or when Jordan broke into Renee's apartment or today, Jordan seemed even-keeled, far from manic. She had good days and bad days like every person.

But deep down I knew *something was wrong with her*. We weren't some "normal" couple who broke up at Ikea because of an argument over metaphorical chairs. We weren't dealing with typical sexual issues like the end of the honeymoon stage. No, I was a man in love with a sick woman, and the idea that she'd tried to jump out of a moving car on the freeway told me she might be sicker than I'd ever imagined.

29

OF ALL THE THINGS

I PEEKED INTO CHLOE'S room the next morning—Jordan was still sound asleep. There was so much to untangle about what had happened yesterday, but I had back-to-back meetings, so I texted her as I walked out the door.

Hope you're okay. I'll come home from work at lunch, and we can talk about yesterday. Love you.

Love you more. See you then, Jordan calmly answered an hour later. That left me sanguine, confident we'd work things out without too much drama. What that looked like this time, I didn't know. More therapy? I knew something had to change in our relationship (okay, she had to change) for us to have a future together.

I walked into the house that afternoon and saw Jordan out by the pool on a chaise lounge, naked except for my Dodgers cap. She was on her stomach, perched on her elbows as she read a book, no trace of the venom from last night on her face. Her beauty disarmed me, as always.

"And I thought *I* had a good life…" I said as I walked outside.

She laughed. "Doesn't suck."

I bent down and lightly kissed her tanned butt. "I'm going to get changed and come right back."

"Okay," she said and went back reading.

I came back a few minutes later in my swim trunks and sunglasses. As I settled into the chaise beside her, my phone rang with a FaceTime call from my son. I glanced at Jordan—she hadn't even looked up from her book, so I tapped "accept."

"Hi, my boy!" I said as Eli's face smiled at me from his computer at his mom's house.

"Dad, did you call School of Rock about drum lessons?"

I laughed—he'd sent me a link to the music school only an hour ago. He wasn't spoiled—he just knew I rarely put *anything* off until the next day.

"You start this Saturday at eleven forty-five," I reported.

"Yay! Thank you!"

I spent a few minutes giving Eli the details (mainly, that he'd be getting his cousin's hand-me-down electric drum set with soft pads, so as to not torture his parents and the neighbors) then hung up and noticed Jordan sitting and wrapping a towel around herself.

"Why would you do that?" she demanded.

I tensed, sensing a downward mood shift. "Do what?"

"I'm lying out here naked, and the first thing you do when you get home is take a *call*?"

I sat up and took off my sunglasses. "I'm sorry, I didn't think taking a call from Eli would upset you."

"Well, I feel like you came in and ignored me."

"Jordan, the first thing I did was kiss your ass."

I smiled, thinking that would stop the argument in its tracks, but Jordan shook her head.

"I guess I'm starting to realize everything we do is on your schedule, your timing," she hissed.

I squinted, trying to follow her logic. But alarm bells were going off. We clearly weren't going to discuss yesterday, because she was already creating new problems. "Jordan, what is this about?"

She shrugged her tan shoulders. "You've been ignoring me lately. I haven't felt love in your touch in months."

I stopped myself from laughing. "Jordan, I came home to talk about yesterday, to work things out, not to continue fighting..."

"I don't want to fight either," she answered. "But I've been so starved for affection, I've been thinking of going back on the site."

"You're thinking of doing what?" I said, feeling like I'd been slapped. "Jordan, you're clearly unhappy. I'm pretty unhappy these days, too. But threatening to go back on the site is not the way to talk to me about it."

She gave me something short of a full nod.

I felt a rising panic. She wasn't being logical or sensitive. *Maybe she does have multiple personalities.* I stood, thinking it would be a good idea to cool off and start this whole conversation again. "Look, I'm going to get something to eat. Let's take a minute and come back to this, okay?"

She nodded begrudgingly.

I walked toward the house, but as I opened the glass sliding door to the kitchen, she was on her feet, following me.

"I'm always alone in this house!" she yelled at my back.

I stopped by the kitchen table. "Jordan," I said with a warning tone, "there's a limit to how many things I can handle in one conversation, so I think we should stop talking."

She folded her arms. "You're always in the driver's seat, and what do I have to show for it? I move to Los Angeles and have no career at all."

Anger overtook me, and I shot back, "And that's *my* fault? I've literally begged you to teach yoga! I gave you Kim's number ages ago, but did you ever call her?"

"You know it's hard on my body," she answered. "Teacher training nearly killed me!"

"That was eight hours a day! You can handle a class or two a week. Jesus, stop using your depression as an excuse for everything!"

Jordan stared daggers. "I don't even know how I ended up being a damn yogi."

I couldn't believe my ears. "Jordan, do you know ungrateful you sound? I spent thousands of dollars on teacher training."

"I never said I wanted to teach. I wanted the experience."

"What are you talking about? You said you wanted to teach in Fiji! You said you had a friend who ran retreats—did you ever contact *him*, either?"

Jordan's face suddenly seemed brittle, as if she was cracking under the strain of logic. "I wanted to be an actress..."

"Oh, my God," I said. "I offered to help you get a commercial agent so many times, but you kept saying you needed to redo your book and take new pictures...I offered to pay to make a short film with you, hire a songwriter, pay for a website! But have you had *one* photo shoot since you've been here? Have you let me help you in any way? And more importantly, have *you* done anything to get your acting career going?"

Jordan sank into a chair. "I don't fit into Los Angeles. All the girls have fake tits like your friend Megan. Or that cunt, Kendra. She never stops talking about herself. Please don't invite her to any more pool parties."

My eyes widened. Jordan had dropped a few slightly disparaging comments about Megan and Kendra in the past that I chalked up to insecurity, but now I saw she truly hoped to isolate me from my friends.

"You're attacking my friends?" I moaned bitterly. "At least I have some. I mean, you haven't made a single one in Los Angeles. And Jesus, I can't believe you'd say anything insulting about either one of them. Kendra helped introduce you to the kids, and if she hadn't dragged me to that SLAA meeting I'd have been too scared to go! And you're talking trash about Megan? The woman was so kind to you—do I have to remind you that she told us about TMS!"

"Which I'd have by now if you'd helped me get insurance!" Jordan yelled.

That was her answer? Would I also have to remind her that I was her moral support through all those calls to Blue Shield, stood in line with her at the DMV, committed fraud for her by letting her use my house as an address before she'd even moved in...?

"I cannot believe you're giving me a list of my failings," I uttered. "But hell, go on. What else *haven't* I done for you?"

Jordan seemed to be scanning her most ancient memories. "I asked you for guitar lessons months ago, but you did nothing."

Guitar lessons? What the fuck is she talking about? Then I remembered—she'd mentioned it only once, in passing, a few months back while we'd been shopping for Renee's apartment.

"First of all, I told you to google teachers and I'd pay for them," I said. "But did you ever do that? No."

Jordan looked out at the pool and pointed to the chaise lounge where we'd started this conversation. "When Eli asks for drum lessons, you make it happen immediately."

"Because Eli can't make his own appointments," I blurted out. "Jordan, he doesn't even have a phone! He's a ten-year-old child, for God's sake!"

Jordan went mute.

"Of all the things…" I whispered.

Because of all the crazy and nonsensical things Jordan had ever said and done to me, the fact that she was complaining that I hadn't scheduled her guitar lessons while I'd handled drum class for my son struck me like a lightning bolt. Suddenly, I saw Jordan in a different light than I'd ever seen her. A moment before, she had been a woman with some psychological problems, but now she was a child—incapable of taking care of herself and possessing so little self-control that she was jealous of my ten-year-old son!

"I'm sorry, that didn't…didn't…come out right…" Jordan stuttered. "I'm sorry about what I said about your friends. I sit at home and get so jealous. You know I don't mean the things I say…"

But in this moment, I realized it didn't matter what she meant. And I understood that no matter how much love I gave, no matter how many therapists or doctors I took her to, no matter how well I supported her financially—none of it would help her. None of it would turn her into a healthy young woman who made good decisions. And as much as I liked being her sugar daddy, I didn't want to be her damn father.

"I'm so tired of this, Jordan," I uttered. "You can't keep saying horrible things, then backtracking. It's as if you think if you apologize, nothing you say or do matters. Well it matters, and I can't do this anymore. I can't be in this relationship anymore."

Jordan blinked. "You're breaking up with me?"

I was shocked by my sudden and calm conviction. "I'm sorry. I don't see any other choice."

She started to cry. "But why? Because I said something stupid? I'm sorry. I don't even know why I brought up the guitar lessons."

"It's not about the guitar lessons, Jordan. That was just the straw that broke the camel's back. Do you realize what you've put me through for the past ten months? I think you took it for granted that I had no limits or boundaries. You figured because I love you so fucking much, I'd never say 'no' to you. I've given and given, and here you are giving me a list of everything I've done wrong. I've never felt so taken for granted, so utterly unappreciated."

"I'm sorry; I'm sorry; I'm sorry," she repeated as she bawled. "Can't we go back to therapy? Or give it through the holidays?"

"No. I'm sorry. It's over."

"Please…" Jordan began to cry. She slid off the chair, onto her knees on the floor, putting one hand on each of my thighs. "I'm literally begging you…"

"Get up, please," I whispered.

She stayed there, weeping. "What do I have to do?"

"For us? Nothing. It's over. You need to figure out how to help *yourself*. You need to get healthy. And don't wait for TMS—get your own therapy, get a job, make some friends…"

"You're right—I know."

I reached to the kitchen counter to pull a few tissues from a box and handed them to her.

"How are you going to tell the kids?" Jordan asked as she wiped her cheeks.

My chest felt like it was caving in, overwhelming my heart with insufferable sorrow—and the thought that my children might have to feel even a portion of that made me cry. "I don't know. But I know I still want you to be in their lives somehow, a friend…"

She closed her eyes with only the slightest relief. "Thank you."

"And listen," I said, "I'm not going to abandon you like Ray. You can stay here until we find a place for you to go. And I'll give you a few months' allowance, so you can get back on your feet without having to go back to escorting. You know it tears you apart inside."

She nodded. "Thank you. And will you do something for me?"

"I'll try…"

"Don't rush out and get laid."

I stared at her, furious. *She has the nerve to suggest I haven't learned a thing about my sexual behavior since Vancouver.*

"Don't worry," I said calmly. "I'm not going to act out."

Jordan nodded and got back into her chair, then gave a fateful sigh. "Okay, but once I go, I'm gone."

That sounded like a threat. "What does that mean?"

"It means I've been here before. Every man that's left me has tried to get me back. And I don't think you realize how hard it will be for *you*… Do you know hard it is for a man in his fifties to find a beautiful thirty-year-old who doesn't want her own kids?"

My jaw dropped. Jordan was repeating *almost verbatim* what I'd admitted I was most afraid of in that last, horrible therapy session. *She's taking my most existential fear and using it as a knife to stab me in the chest.*

"Maybe you're right," I said with a swallow. "Maybe I'll never find love like this again. But you know what also scares me, Jordan? The fact that no matter what crazy things you do, you never seem to run out of new ideas. You're so broken, Jordan. And I'd rather die alone than keep trying to fix you."

She looked down at her feet and seethed, "This is so fucked. If I get over this, I'll send you the psychiatry bill."

I've been paying them for months! I wanted to shout.

Instead, I stood, feeling my legs shake. Despite all I'd said to her, I didn't know if I really had the conviction and courage to walk away from the love of my life, however unhealthy she was.

One foot in front of the other, I told myself, and did that until I had left the kitchen.

30
THE STORIES WE TELL

BREAKUPS ARE NEVER AS clean in real life as they are in the movies, so naturally, Jordan and I spent that night, and several nights after, talking and crying. It wasn't like I'd fallen *out* of love with Jordan. I'd come home from the office and find her sitting on my couch in sweats, computer open, hair in a ponytail, searching for an apartment and a job, and it took every ounce of my resolve not to crawl up beside her and put my head in her lap.

And I made good on my promise not to abandon Jordan. I wrote her a check for fifteen thousand dollars to cover her expenses through the end of February ("Severance pay?" she joked). We even agreed that with Thanksgiving on Thursday, we wouldn't tell anybody we'd broken up for another week, and Jordan would come to my family's house for dinner.

That was a story in itself: Jordan wasn't a fan of Thanksgiving— she'd often told me her eating disorder made it difficult to watch people gorge, especially at her family's home in Denver, where the holiday was a "weekend of football watching, beer drinking, and leftovers." But I'd promised her ours was a quiet affair, and Jordan warmed to the idea so much that she even offered to make a dessert.

THANKSGIVING MORNING, I WOKE TO a text from my mother, What did Jordan decide to make for tonight?

Jordan had yet to emerge from Chloe's bedroom, where she'd been sleeping since our breakup, so I texted her.

Are you awake? My mom's asking what you're making tonight?

Are you sure I should go? She answered. What do I say if they ask how I am? Lie and pretend we're fine?

Trust me, they won't ask anything personal, they never do, I reminded her.

OK...Pumpkin cheesecake with chocolate ganache.

Sounds good. I'll pick you up at 4.

She gave me a thumbs up emoji, so I got dressed and headed to the office.

I had settled into my chair behind my desk when I received an alert on my phone from Facebook Messenger.

I clicked on the app and saw that Colette the Role Play Queen had messaged me.

Hey stranger! I'm stuck in Paris. I came home for a few months, but when I tried to come back, US Customs went through my phone and found all my messages about BDSM and deported me. I'm on some terror watch list.

I laughed out loud. *Her sexts must have been beyond explicit for customs to deem her a terrorist threat.*

Sorry to hear that, I quickly typed back. I think the Trump government will use any excuse to stop immigration.

LOL, she wrote. And how are you?

Been better, I admitted. Jordan and I broke up.

I'm sorry. Come to Europe and visit me over Christmas.

Maybe, I wrote back. I'm at work, but let's talk soon.

OK, miss you!

You too, I wrote with a small smile. After the last few weeks of feeling like I had been Jordan's punching bag, it felt good to have another woman expressing interest in me. In truth, however, I knew I wasn't going anywhere this Christmas. Jordan and I had discussed taking the kids to Palm Springs for part of the holiday break, but that clearly wasn't happening.

My cell phone rang. Jordan was calling.

"Hi," I answered.

"So you're going to Europe to see Colette?!" Jordan spat accusingly. "You couldn't even wait until I was out of the house to start contacting your cheap sluts?"

"Hold on," I said as I closed my door behind me. "First of all, how do you even *know* I talked with Colette?"

"Your iPad was going crazy with alerts, so I was curious and looked."

"You went through my iPad?! That's a total invasion of my privacy."

"Well, I had a feeling I couldn't trust you, and I was right."

"Because I answered a message from someone I haven't spoken to in months?"

"Ha!" Jordan laughed derisively. "I'm sure you've been talking to Colette and countless other women for months."

"I was being polite! Did you see any other messages from her or any other women on there?"

"No, but I'm sure you delete every incriminating text."

"I'll come home right now and show you my phone!"

Jordan went silent. *Why am I defending myself?* But after working so hard to keep myself in check since the Vancouver incident, I couldn't stand to have my honor questioned.

"I don't know if I believe you," Jordan came back at me. "After all, you cheated on your wife. And then there were all those hookers before you married!"

I nearly lost it. "Jordan, you're doing it again! How dare you use my past against me like this? You know how honest I've been with you."

"How do I know that?" she pushed. "For all I know, you've been with other girls the whole time we were together..."

"I have never cheated on you! On my children's lives."

Jordan was slow to respond—even in her state, she knew how sacred my children were to me. "I'm sorry," she finally said. "My thoughts spiral.

And I shouldn't have gone through your messages. It's wrong, and I know nothing good comes from it."

"Thank you," I answered, and as my blood pressure lowered, part of me didn't blame her. I was, after all, a self-avowed sex addict. "Look, I'll come back to the house, and we can talk about this."

"Please don't," her voice shook. "I'm going to find an Airbnb and get out of here."

"What? Today?" I answered. "It's Thanksgiving."

"I'm devastated, David. I can't move forward in life if I'm sitting in your house."

"I understand, but can't you wait till tomorrow or the weekend? It's a holiday."

"Today's not a holiday for me. It's just another Thursday."

"Jordan, I'm coming home right now."

"Please don't," she begged. "It's going to take every ounce of strength I have to do this, and if you're here I'll lose it. Tell Margo I'm sorry I didn't make the dessert."

"Okay…but where will you go?"

"I don't know yet. But don't worry about me, I'm a survivor. Goodbye, David."

As she hung up, I couldn't help but roll my eyes. She had fifteen grand in the bank, and in retrospect, her tales of being so broke that she'd once been forced to jump subway turnstiles seemed ridiculous. I'd met Jordan's family and was sure that if she ever told them she was in financial straits, they'd sell their house before they let her starve. *What did Jordan have to survive, except her own self-destructive impulses?*

Yet, every fiber of my being wanted to grab my car keys and drive home to reason with her. I wanted so desperately for us to remain civil. But then I thought, *What's the point?* Even after the breakup, Jordan was doing crazy things—this time reading my personal messages. I felt idiotic for even being surprised—she'd broken into apartments, stolen drugs, so why *wouldn't* she snoop through my iPad? And her explanation that she'd heard my iPad pinging with messages was *ridiculous*. I'm anal about keeping my ringers off every device. No, since we'd broken up, Jordan had repeatedly asked me to pledge not to "go out and get laid," so she clearly harbored some secret suspicion I was cheating on her. I'd long ago given her all my passwords to my phone and devices, so who knew how long she'd been going through them, looking for incriminating evidence.

I allowed myself the slightest feeling of guilt—*I probably was flirting with Colette*. But I had zero intention of going to Europe to visit her, so did my slight indiscretion justify Jordan's reaction? To pack up and leave the house on Thanksgiving night?

I couldn't help but remember Jordan's story about Ray, her ex, who demanded she move all of her belongings out of his apartment in a single day. "By text, without an apology," was how she'd described the scenario. That story, the way she described his abandonment of her, sounded eerily similar to what was going on today.

I sank into my chair and looked over the wall of framed posters of the movies I'd made, boxing movies, thrillers, dramas, horror movies, comedies, romantic comedies…reminded of the old Hollywood saying, "a movie is only as good as its story," it occurred to me that Jordan had just completely rewritten our breakup in the movie playing in her mind. No longer was she an unhealthy woman who ruined a relationship with her bad behavior. No, with one snoop and the flimsiest of evidence, Jordan had cast herself as the victim, a poor young woman finally making a stand and leaving a philandering sex addict.

Did Jordan *really* believe I'd cheated on her throughout our relationship? Did she really think I was so eager to fuck someone else that I was planning my next erotic adventure? Or was she subconsciously using this to give herself the courage to leave the house she loved so much? Either way, to this producer, her plot twist was a little convenient. "Hard to buy," as we often say.

But I had to give Jordan this much credit. *The girl knows how to make a dramatic exit.*

❧

BUT WHAT STORY DO I *tell my family?* I had to ask myself. *Even they'd notice Jordan's empty place setting!*

Thankfully, Eli and Chloe were spending the holiday in Dallas with their mother, so I had a few days to figure out how to break the news to them without crushing their little hearts too badly. But how was I going to explain Jordan's absence at dinner when my family had no clue how turbulent our relationship had been?

Not only that, but when I arrived home from work to discover Jordan had managed to clean out all of her belongings, probably loading that Hug Bug several times over, I was a wreck. I felt horrible, imagining her huddled on a bed in some Airbnb, feeling abandoned, angry, heartbroken, and depressed.

Staring at the key she'd left on the kitchen counter, this time without that "Forever and Ever, Amen" note, I started to weep so uncontrollably that I didn't know if I'd be able to go to dinner at all. Hyperventilating, I sent a group text to my entire family. I told them that Jordan had moved out, and that I'd rather not talk about it tonight.

I got a lot of "We're shocked" and "So sorry to hear that…" answers, then a text came from my mother on a separate thread.

I'm sad for you, she wrote, but the relationship was volatile from the beginning.

That gave me pause. *How the hell did my mom know things with Jordan were volatile?*

I chalked it up to mother's intuition and went to dinner.

But from the moment I walked into the house, holding my breath so I wouldn't break down in tears as my family greeted me with hugs and sympathetic looks that I never imagined them capable of, another story began to be rewritten.

As much as I'd always known how lucky I was to have been born into such fortunate circumstances, never having to worry about money and being blessed with great health, I lived with some resentment. I had blamed the flaws in my fairy tale—my therapy-proof romantic and sexual anxieties, my introversion, my naivete of the most basic human emotions such as loneliness, and being emotionally stunted to the point I called myself "Hard David"—on my family, my parents in particular. I had this story in my head that my family was guilty of emotional neglect and sexual shame, and if I opened up to them, they would judge and shame me. They'd call their prince a pervert. And if I tried to talk to them about my feelings, they'd call me "too sensitive" and "confrontational."

But on this Thanksgiving night, as I sat quietly and listened to them talk, as always, about politics and current events and movies, it occurred to me I had held onto my story, my resentment, for far too long.

Of course my parents hid their feelings, I realized. My father was of that post World War II generation too poor to be touchy-feely with their children. He'd grown up in a conservative Jewish home, sold shoes at night while going to college during the day. *So what if he'd never shed a tear in public?* That was a privilege few men his age were culturally afforded. For all I knew, he was a bawling mess when he and my mother were behind closed doors.

And yeah, my mother slammed the bedroom door on me and sent me to shrinks. Tonight, that seemed like such a whiny complaint. Maybe I was argumentative? Maybe I was too sensitive for my own good? Maybe she'd realized my emotional needs were beyond her ability to process, so she'd brought in a professional? That was downright progressive parenting in 1976!

And so they never talked about sex at the dinner table? So my dad pickled? So my mom kicked me out of a screening room? My kids were only twelve combined, and right now everything was Disney, but I knew in a few years I'd have to start making hard decisions about what films they could watch. And for how long was I going to blame my parents for society's sexual shame? Again, for all I knew, behind closed doors they were sexually liberated and kinky as hell! (God, that's a scary thought!)

Whatever mistakes my mother and father made, they've set the highest bar when it comes to creating a family. In Hollywood, where everybody was on their second or third marriages, my parents had stayed happily married for almost sixty years now! It was no accident that I was called a "super dad" and was famously amicable with my ex-wife—I'd learned parenting from my parents, and from their treatment of family and friends, I'd learned that the bonds of family stretched beyond divorce.

And I need to rewrite my story, so I don't see myself as an emotional moron. So I was a slow learner! So I'd been sheltered and it took my relationship with Jordan to learn about depression and anxiety, addictions and intimacy. Better late than never. It was time to let go of my resentment of my family's mistakes, of my mistakes, and be grateful for all I had.

And thank God they don't pry or ask personal questions. Because if one person had not respected that text I'd sent, if one person had asked me so much as "how are you?" I'd have broken down in tears and run up to my childhood bedroom and hid. That's how miserable I was.

That Thanksgiving, I don't think I said more than two words to anybody, but I've never been more grateful for my family. And no matter how disappointing Jordan's sudden flight was to my hopes of our remaining amicable, I had to give her thanks once again. Even in our breakup, the relationship was helping me grow.

I only wished Jordan had been there to share my revelation.

31
THE TOP LOCK

RUNNING A FEW MINUTES behind you, sorry!

I read Jordan's text as I sat with Eli, Chloe, and a tray of four miniature key-lime pies between us at Clementine Café.

It was December 2, and after exchanging a few "are you okay" and "yes I'm well, thank you for asking" messages over the last several days, I was making good on my promise to ease Jordan out of the kids' lives on a friendly note. I'd already told Eli and Chloe about the breakup, and though a few tears were shed (mostly by me), the kids handled the news as well as could be expected.

No problem, I typed back to Jordan. Kids are excited to see you.

I'm dying to see them! she answered. Just hope I don't scare them.

Why would you scare them? I asked.

I saw Doctor Cabin this morning, so I have a little bruising.

Oh, what did you get done? I asked, because I knew Doctor Cabin was a renowned Beverly Hills plastic surgeon.

Just some Botox and fillers.

An expensive Beverly Hills plastic surgeon, I thought with irritation. *This is how she spends the money I gave her?* I'd hoped that $15,000 I'd given her would go toward living expenses, but clearly Jordan was more interested in injecting it into her face.

"Jojo!" Chloe yelped when Jordan hurried into the café, clad in her standard black jeans, converse sneakers, and a maroon T-shirt. Both kids rushed to her and into a three-way hug.

"I've missed you guys so much!" Jordan said, then ushered them back to the table.

I stood and looked at her face. She wasn't exactly child-scary, but she wore a thicker coat of makeup than was her habit. But the double layer of foundation couldn't hide dark black and blue bruises streaking her forehead. And her lips were more plump than usual, too, so I guessed Jordan must have spent two to three grand on the plastic surgery. *It will be a month before she's dead broke and escorting again*, I thought sadly.

"Hi," Jordan said as we exchanged polite smiles and sat.

Chloe lifted her fork. "Can I start?"

"Yup," I said.

"What happened to your face?" Eli asked between bites.

"Well," Jordan said, speaking to the kids like an elementary school teacher. "I had some stuff put into my face to help me stay young looking."

Chloe finished a sip of limeade. "Does it hurt?"

"Not really. I've been icing it, and I put arnica on right after I left, so that will help the bruises."

"That's smart," Chloe said, then moved onto the next subject. "Where are you living?"

"I've been bouncing around places…"

I sat back in my chair, figuring the time was best used for Jordan and the kids to catch up. But as I listened to them, I started to notice Eli, an extrovert who never struggled to make conversation, becoming unusually withdrawn.

"How was Dallas with your mom?" Jordan asked him.

"Fine."

"Are you excited for your football game this Saturday?"

"Yeah."

"Which of the private schools you're touring for next year do you like best?"

"Dunno."

I thought he might be tired after a long day at school, but then he suddenly got out of his chair and opened his arms to me. "Can I have a hug?"

"Of course."

He came around the table, and I squeezed him.

"Can we go home?" Chloe whined—she'd stuck her fork in her half-eaten pie. That was odd as well—Chloe seldom left a dessert undevoured.

"Yeah, I have so much homework," Eli moaned.

What the fuck? Eli *never* hurried to do homework.

"We've only been here twenty minutes!" Jordan pleaded with disappointment in her eyes.

I didn't know what to tell her. I couldn't explain why the kids were in a rush to leave. Maybe seeing her did the exact opposite of what I'd hoped—maybe it hadn't reassured them that she intended to stay in their lives, but instead reminded them she was leaving. Either way, I wasn't going to make them sit through this any longer than they were comfortable with.

"I'm sorry," was all I could say to Jordan as I fished for my wallet.

I TURNED MY KEY in the doorknob at the side door by our garage and pushed, but the door wouldn't budge.

"Try the top lock," Eli said beside me, rolling backpack in tow.

"You *know* I never I lock the top one," I said.

He mimicked my adult voice, "What's the point of having two locks on the same key?"

I rolled my eyes—at least he was in a better mood.

Chloe did a little dance behind us. "Hurry, I have to pee."

"Elvia must have locked it," I said as I put the key into the lock above the knob—sure enough, the door swung open.

"Told ya!" Eli teased as he and Chloe headed inside toward their rooms.

I stepped into the kitchen and keyed the alarm pad to quiet its beeping.

Huh, I thought, *Elvia doesn't work on Wednesdays...*

I stood there a beat, trying to work out who besides my maid could have come through the side door since I left that morning. Jordan had been the only other person in my life who both knew the alarm code and had a key, but she'd left the key behind on Thanksgiving Day.

I headed into my living room. Nothing seemed out of place. My television, Apple TV, and cable box were still on their stand. The one expensive piece of art I owned, a Roy Lichtenstein print, still hung on the wall, and my laptop sat on the couch.

I walked to my bedroom and took off my shoes—something caught my eye. Through the open bathroom door, I saw, on the counter next to the sink, a tube of arnica gel. Now, I've never even used arnica—I consider it to be, like most herbal remedies, snake oil. But someone *else* had said she used it, less than an hour ago.

Jordan was in the house today? But how?

Then, I remembered the hide-a-key I kept outside the house, in a small magnetic box. And of course, Jordan knew about it—I told her the location before I'd given her a key, so she could get into the house while I was at work.

But why? I wondered. Jordan had cleaned herself out of the house when she left. If she'd come back for something, I would think she'd ask first, or at least have mentioned it at Clementine.

*Unless she…*Before I could finish the thought, I glanced at my medicine cabinet. *She wouldn't…*I thought. Since Mexico, Jordan had avoided my drugs like the plague. (And since then, I admit that I'd even gone through my prescription bottles on occasion, just to make sure.)

I hated myself for what I was thinking. *But why else would Jordan have come into the house?*

I opened the cabinet, glanced through the bottles and found the Xanax—it was empty. The last time I'd checked, there were at least five or six tabs in there.

Shit, Jordan…

I put the bottle back and found my Ambien. It was empty.

My heart beating like a drum, I quickly went through every bottle with a prescription label, ignoring anything I didn't think Jordan would care about—antibiotics, those unused Viagra, stuff for my (now rising) blood pressure…then stopped as I found the Vicodin I'd been given for my spasming back before our Tahoe trip.

I opened it and found only five or six left out of the thirty I was prescribed. I'd only taken one!

Jordan went fucking drug shopping here!

I hurried back into the bedroom, closed the door so the kids wouldn't hear, then dialed Jordan.

"What's up?" she answered evenly.

Surprised she'd even answered, I took a second—I had zero doubt in my mind she'd stolen my drugs, but knew if I wanted her to admit to it, I was better off not putting her on the defensive. "Listen, by any chance were you at my house today?"

"No, why would I go *there*?" she answered. "I've been too distraught to drive anywhere near your house."

She sounded so convincing it was scary. "Jordan, it's okay if you did, I just need to know. Otherwise, I have to assume someone broke into the house, then I'll need to call the police and change the locks."

"Someone broke into the house?! Oh, my God, how do you know that? What did they take?"

I was so disgusted by how alarmed she sounded I dropped the pretense. "Jordan, you left your arnica in my bathroom."

"What arnica?"

"The arnica you talked about this afternoon! And you smeared makeup on a towel."

She laughed derisively. "I'm sure whatever chick you saw last night left it there."

I laughed back. "I *wish* that explained it! I haven't been with anyone since we broke up."

"Well, forgive me if I don't congratulate you on keeping your dick in your pants while you accuse me of breaking into your house! I mean, why would I even want to go back there after you kicked me out?"

"Well, some of my prescription drugs are gone…"

"And you think *I* broke into your house and took them?" Jordan gasped, sounding so convincingly offended, it occurred to me she might even believe she *was* innocent. "David, I've been spending my days and nights like a nomad, hauling five carloads from one Airbnb to another...so wherever this paranoid delusion is coming from, don't point the finger at me."

Now I was insulted. "Paranoid delusion? Jordan, I understand you're in pain but..."

"I don't have time for pain!" she shrieked so loud I had to pull the phone from my ear. "I'm too busy surviving! And seething! You have no loyalty whatsoever! If you did, you wouldn't be finger-pointing! You were my lover and my best friend! You should have stood by me and helped me get to the other side! The better side! You took everything in my life that I loved! The things that got me out of bed each morning! And I will never forgive you! I *hate* you!"

"Oh, Jordan," I uttered.

I could hear her start to wail as she hung up.

I looked at the phone and saw my hand was quivering. Jordan had hurled some cruel insults at me over the past few months—she'd even hit me. But the anger she'd thrown at me just now was a fury I'd never witnessed from her, or from *any* person in my entire fifty-three years on this earth.

I sat on my bed, utterly violated. Jordan had often been self-destructive, but this felt directed at me personally. The idea that she'd sat at coffee with me and been sweet to my children after breaking into my house was cosmically disturbing. It might have even explained why Eli was so antsy at Clementine. Had my child sensed something about the situation wasn't right? Was he psychic? Child-like intuition?

I needed to process this with someone, but the idea of telling even close friends like Megan or Kendra that the woman I'd loved had broken into my house was too humiliating. But I knew there was one person I *had* to share this with. If Jordan was a threat to me in my house, she was one to everyone in this house, and the mother of my children deserved to know.

※

WITH THE KIDS PLAYING in their rooms, I stood in the kitchen, the alarm manual in one hand as I searched for instructions on how to change the code, phone in the other.

"I had no idea," Elizabeth said with shock; I'd told her as much as I thought she needed to know about my relationship with Jordan, focusing the conversation on her drug use. "Do you think she'd hurt the kids?"

"Who the hell knows *what* Jordan's capable of now."

"You haven't told the kids, have you?" Elizabeth asked.

"Of course not. But I'll find a way to ask them to let us know if they see Jordan's car near either of our houses without worrying them. And I think we should get to pick-up a little early for a few days—they wouldn't think twice if she told them that I asked her to pick them up after school."

"Good idea," Elizabeth said, then added, "I'm so sorry, David. I deal with drug addiction in my practice all the time. You must be so hurt."

"I'm too furious to be hurt."

"I understand. Well, if you need to talk about it, I'm here for you."

"As always," I answered, feeling a lump of gratitude in my throat. Elizabeth could have skewered me for trusting Jordan after Mexico and not sharing this sooner, but she was so calm she almost gave me confidence in therapists again.

"Do you think you should call the police?" she asked.

"I thought about it, but she'd deny it, and what proof do I have other than a bottle of arnica?"

"It might scare her enough, so she doesn't come back."

"I'll call them if I so much as see her face again..." I vowed.

We hung up; I changed the alarm code, then realized there was one last thing I needed to do to protect myself.

I walked out the side door and turned to the box where I kept my hidden key. I kneeled and pulled the little black magnetic box off. I shook the case and could hear the key rattle inside. Then I carried it into the house, closed the door behind me, and locked it—first, the knob lock, and for good measure, that top lock, too.

❧

JORDAN'S CONFESSION CAME AT noon the next day.

I was in my office when my cell screen lit up with Jordan's smile—a picture I had taken of her at one of my son's touch football practices a few weeks ago.

Feeling fenceless rage, I closed my office door and accepted the call, thinking if Jordan's first words weren't "I'm sorry, David," I would hang up on her. I didn't even say "hello."

"I'm so sorry," Jordan said through sobs.

Unmoved, utterly unbelieving of yet another of her apologies, I breathed loudly so she'd know I was listening.

"Can I come see you, apologize in person, and bring you back everything I took?" she forced out an octave lower than I'd ever heard from her.

I weighed my desire to tell her to fuck off against my worry she'd use the drugs and arrived at a compromise. "Come to the office. Text me when you park out front, and I'll come down for *one* minute."

"Thank you," she uttered.

Ten minutes later, I walked out my office building to where her car was parked in the red. I opened her car door and climbed into her passenger seat, intentionally leaving the door ajar—this wasn't going to be a long conversation. I looked at Jordan—her bruises hadn't faded much, but this time she wore no makeup and her face looked wearied from two days of guilt and tears.

"I'm so ashamed," she began, having a hard time looking at me, wiping tears away with a ball of damp tissues. "I went to see if I had any mail…and went into the bathroom to get myself together before I met you guys…but being there made me so upset and angry that I guess I wanted to hurt you somehow. Here, I swear I haven't taken any of them," she said, then picked up a plastic baggie that contained a handful of my pills and tablets.

I took the baggy and stuffed it into my pocket. There was something eerily similar between her explanation of her actions now, and her explanation of breaking into Renee's apartment. In both cases, she hadn't *meant* to steal anything, she was just acting out with unregulated anger.

"I'm going to get healthy," she simpered. "I have an appointment with Doctor Browning tomorrow…and if I can't get TMS, I'll go into rehab, whatever he says…"

I had little reason left to believe her, so I pulled myself out of the car. "I'll let you know if you get any mail," I said as I closed the door.

32

BEL AIR BURNS

"ARE YOU OKAY OVER there?" Kendra's voice fretted.

"Yeah, they haven't even issued evacuation orders for my canyon yet," I said into the phone as I muted my television.

It was Friday, December 7, only five days after Jordan confessed to breaking into the house, and I sat on my couch watching news reports of the wildfire burning through the Sepulveda Pass—two canyons west of mine—threatening to spread throughout Bel Air. Sparked by the dry Santa Ana winds blowing in from the desert every fall, it was one of several wildfires raging across Southern California.

"Well, we got the order to leave Roscomare," Kendra huffed, referring to the canyon where she and her boyfriend, Peter, lived. "We're gathering everything we can fit into our cars!"

"When the LAFD tells me to leave, I'll leave," I reasoned.

"I don't know, I say you get the hell out of there, just in case?"

"Kendra, I appreciate the concern. But I've lived through so many fires in the last fifty years, they don't even raise my blood pressure anymore."

"David, why are you being so stubborn?"

"I'm fine," I grunted—it was less embarrassing than telling her that Jordan had broken into my house.

"Okay, well don't stay there for too long," she pled. "Love you."

As we hung up, my house rumbled with the sound of a helicopter flying overhead. I slid the glass door aside to walk into the backyard and gazed at the sky. Dark, gray clouds of smoke plumed across the horizon, and my verdant canyon was hued an eerie orange. Large flecks of gray ash rained from the sky, peppering my furniture and coating the surface of the pool in a thin layer of what looked like dirty, fake plastic snowflakes. Then a DC-10 filled with fire-retardant flew over my head, only a few thousand feet off the ground. I realized I should cover the outdoor furniture and began the labor of pulling canvass covers out of the garage and battening them down over the sectional couch and day bed. Next, I stomped around the backyard, lowering umbrellas as I went, collecting lounge cushions, pool toys, and floaties and storing them in the garage. Then, guessing that with Jordan out of the house I wouldn't use the pool enough to justify a winter of thousand-dollar heating bills, I walked to the pool heater at the side of the house. I pressed its yellow, arrow-shaped button, changing the setting from 89 degrees to OFF. The whole process of securing the yard felt like an exercise in removing Jordan from our poolside kingdom.

Despite what I had told Kendra, I was anything but "fine." And not because I was all that worried about the house—as much as I loved Rosewood, you certainly wouldn't have seen me standing on the roof with a garden hose if the LAFD told me to evacuate. No, I wasn't fine because I was being burned alive by my own anger toward Jordan for laying siege to my house and heart. And that stubbornness I'd shown to Kendra, I knew was a sign that the old, emotionally hard David was making a return, pretending I wasn't hurt, that feelings didn't matter.

But that's the last thing you want to happen, I told myself. No matter what crimes Jordan had committed, I knew I couldn't allow myself to be so victimized I shut my feelings off.

So, standing right there in front of the pool heater, I decided to admit to myself *how much* I was burning up inside—to not fight it, even if it meant I melted from the inside out. And then, for the first time since Jordan had violated my house, Soft David returned and started to cry. Under all that anger, there lie even worse feelings: devastating sadness, regret, loss, and loneliness.

I was heartbroken.

I wandered back inside my house, trying to recall the last time I'd felt this horrible pain in my heart. I'd ended my marriage on such a painless note it made me wonder if I'd ever really been in love with Elizabeth—or any woman, for that matter. I'd had such romantic anxiety for so many decades that when prior relationships had ended it had been a relief, an escape, freedom. And in the few day-long breakups Jordan and I had endured, I'd suffered, but nothing like *this*.

No, I didn't have to dig too far into my memories to realize the only time my heart had been this broken was when I was sixteen years old. When Michelle had cheated on me. When I'd spent a summer crying into my pillow. When I'd closed my emotional shop and vowed to never feel this sort of pain again.

Just thinking about how this thirty-seven-year-old wound had taken its toll on my ability to be intimate and vulnerable embarrassed me. And though I was proud I'd overcome it with Jordan's help, I was less confident that I could handle it again. Would my romantic anxiety come back? Would I ever find another fairy tale love? It had taken every ounce of my energy to make it through those woods, only to find an ocean of blood and tears.

And so the prince jumped into the ocean of heartbreak...my fairy tale could very well end...and was never heard from again.

I WALKED OUT OF my office and found Jordan slotting quarters into a parking meter. It was a week before Christmas, and though the Bel Air Fire had been contained, a gray haze still lingered in the air.

"Can you believe it finally came?" Jordan said as she turned to me with a broad smile, enthusiastic and optimistic in a way I'd forgotten she was capable of.

I smiled, hoping Jordan wouldn't see how miserable I'd been. *After all she's done, why do I still buzz when I see this woman?*

"You never gave up," I said as I handed her the short stack of envelopes, atop which was a letter from Blue Shield.

Jordan quickly opened it with her finger, pulled out the insurance card, and showed it off like it was a game show prize. "And I thought it was a conspiracy."

I put my hands in my pockets and looked around awkwardly, as if I were attending a party I wasn't sure I wanted to stay at.

She glanced at her phone. "Do you have time for a coffee? Real quick—my friend Sandrine is in town, and we're going to a Clippers game."

*Now she has friends…*I thought as I said, "Sure."

We walked across the street to the outdoor courtyard café in the Montage Hotel.

"How are your angels?" Jordan asked as her chai tea latte was set before her.

I opened a pink packet of Sweet'N Low and tapped a bit of it into my cappuccino. "They're handling it well, but they miss you."

"You have no idea," Jordan lamented. "These past few weeks without them, I feel like I've lost a piece of my heart."

I've lost all of mine, I kept myself from saying.

"Can we get together when I get back from Colorado after Christmas? I have little gifts for them."

"They'd like that," I said, slightly noncommittal. The kids *had* been asking about her—Eli even cried to me at bedtime once that he felt like "Jordan's forgotten about us." I'd even discussed the idea of letting Jordan see them again with Elizabeth, who'd been surprisingly open to the idea as long as Jordan was getting help.

"So, when do you think you'll start TMS?" I asked.

"As soon as Blue Shield approves it. I called them right after you texted the news this morning, and sent my ID number to Browning's office."

"Couldn't even wait for the actual card, huh?" I asked, as impressed as I was amused.

"Nope," she proudly beamed.

I gently pried, "Have you told Browning about what happened at the house?"

"Yes," she said without taking her eyes off me. "He's totally confident once my depression is under control, I won't be such a slave to my impulses. And again, I'm so sorry…"

"Thank you," I said, but in truth I wasn't even angry at her anymore; I'd forgiven her when I saw her face at that parking meter.

"Are you going away for the holidays?" she asked.

"I'm taking the kids to San Diego for a weekend," I said with little enthusiasm.

"So, you're not going to Europe to see Colette?" she led with a smile, as if she wanted to pretend it wasn't a serious question.

"No, and I'm really sorry I answered her on Thanksgiving—that was insensitive of me."

She smiled her thanks. "And how have you been handling *things*?"

Jordan's emphasis on "things" suggested she wasn't asking if I was heartbroken—she was asking if I'd gotten laid since we broke up.

"I haven't seen anybody, if that's what you're asking."

"Really? You must have been tempted."

I sipped my coffee with a shrug. *Of course I've been tempted.* But as proud as I was of myself for not burying my misery between the sheets with strangers, not distracting myself like an addict, that was none of *her* business now.

Jordan tapped her iPhone to bring up the time. "I have to head home and get ready—I also have a job interview this afternoon."

YOU have a job interview? I thought but asked, "Oh, what kind of job?"

"Nothing exciting. To be a receptionist at a law firm in Century City called Perkins Coie. I've already had two interviews there this week, and they say this should be the last one." She laughed at herself. "Can you imagine *me* working in an office nine to five?"

I really could not and batted away the urge to say, *Jesus, you could have taught two yoga classes a week!*

"How'd you find it?" I asked instead.

"Craigslist—oh, and I found an apartment there, too."

"Really? Where is it?"

"Brentwood. It's tiny. Two bedrooms and I have roommate—makes Renee's place look like a castle."

I laughed away my shock. *Friends, a job, AND an apartment?*

"You don't mind if I run, do you?" Jordan said as she got up. "Thank you for coffee and for bringing my mail. I'll let Blue Shield know about my address change right away."

"Thanks," I mumbled as she gave me an awkward hug and headed back to her car.

I signaled the waiter for the check and sat there a moment, doubt creeping in.

I wasn't sure if I believed *anything* she'd said.

Jordan could have won an Academy Award for her performance trying to convince me that she hadn't broken into my house…could she have just lied to my face again? But why? She hadn't made any attempt to get me back after leaving the house, so what did she have to gain? Was this some twisted way of her trying to prove she wasn't suffering like I was? If so, it was an awfully elaborate ruse—how long can a woman pretend to have a job, friends, and their own apartment?

Back at the office, I kept checking Jordan's Instagram. There was no way in hell Jordan would go to a job interview or basketball game and *not* post about such a significant event in her life. And sure enough, at about 4:00 p.m., she posted a short video story. In it, she exited a mirrored elevator wearing a pantsuit and heels, then she entered the reception area of a plush office with two receptionists sitting behind a video mural of the Los Angeles skyline.

An hour later, I had to text her and ask, How was your interview?

They gave me the job in the room!

Congratulations! When do you start?

January 8 at 8:30 a.m. Oh! And I start TMS January 10.

Santa came early! Good luck!

Jordan texted me back the "Amen" emoji, but I still thought it would have been divine intervention if all this were coming to pass so quickly for her. So that night, I checked her Instagram again…and again…and again…each time scolding myself for acting like a teenager obsessed with social media. Jordan posted at around 8:00 p.m.—this time from the Clippers game—as she, seated in expensive courtside seats, cheered alongside another woman's whistles as she filmed power forward Blake Griffin shoot a three-pointer. In other words, she'd have to be a special effects wizard to have faked these stories.

I felt guilty for doubting her. *But who would have thought Jordan would get her life together while mine burns to the ground?*

33
THE GIFT OF A LIFETIME

CHRISTMASTIME WAS NO HOLIDAY for my heartbreak.

To begin with, I rediscovered where my long-lost loneliness had been hiding all those years before it returned while surfing. Except now I wasn't so grateful to feel it. For weeks my chest ached with the stuff, soothed unsubstantially by listening to Sinatra songs.

I tried to distract myself in healthy ways, like holiday shopping. But as I walked through Beverly Hills or the malls, I'd find myself buying Jordan things. At J.Crew, how could I *not* pick up a charcoal cashmere V-neck sweater she casually mentioned are only released once a year? And at James Perse, why not toss a few "daddy T-shirts" for her? And there was this gray and white alpaca blanket I hoped would look good in her new apartment and replace the Neapolitan one we'd always huddled under.

Each time I put my credit card down, I realized how pointless it was to buy her things. *I'll never see her again! I'd be crazy to ever see her again!*

I spent a few days with the kids in San Diego at the famous Safari Park, walking each trail and seeing every animal in the 1800-acre zoo. I pretended to enjoy it but fought tears the whole time. The highlight of the excursion was supposed to be a Jeep ride to a herd of friendly giraffes; I posted a picture on Facebook of one nibbling acacia leaves right from my hand. I smiled goofily in the picture but felt like a complete fraud, reminded of my irritation when Jordan posted ebulliently in the midst of our Mexico disaster.

Now who's pretending to be a picture of health?

We ended the trip with a day and night at the Lego Land theme park, which *should* have been fun for a father who spent many Sundays on the carpet building Lego, but again, I was despondent. I remember checking out of the hotel while my kids played in the lobby in a giant pool filled with tens of thousands of plastic bricks, and thinking, *How did I end up a single father in a cheesy place like this? A year ago, I was in Costa fucking Rica, a happy sugar daddy unwittingly about to meet the love of his life.*

And, because when it rains it pours, I woke up on Christmas morning with a raging sinus infection. (I knew that Lego pool would come back to haunt me!)

I spent the next five days at home, alone on my couch, coughing up evergreen mucus, and of course, crying my eyes out.

Now, NEW YEAR'S EVE had never meant much to me. I'd never needed a reason to pop champagne and kiss a woman at midnight, and always thought it pointless to make resolutions that would be abandoned before hangovers were cured. And I liked to think I did a good deal of self-reflection every day of the year. But this year, I found myself doing some deep introspection.

For God's sake, I asked, *why am I so heartbroken?*

The answer was obvious. Though I'd been betrayed and angry for weeks after the break in, from the minute I laid my eyes on her at our coffee date, I knew I was still in love with Jordan. Deeply, madly, frustratingly in love with her. *Why* was a complete mystery to me; no matter how transformational the relationship had been, wouldn't her destructive acts make me want to run for the hills? Instead, I was looking for any excuse to crawl back to her.

I found myself asking over and over: *What could I have done differently to save the relationship?*

Practically speaking, I knew I'd made many Daddy Fix-It gestures to help her. If anything, I might have been *too* giving, *too* understanding. Would we have fared better if I'd used tough love and demanded she go to rehab after Mexico? Or found a new therapist after she'd discarded Debra? But I was also tortured by doubt. Would we have had a happier ending if I'd been even *more* patient, or, as she'd begged, gone to therapy again, given it through the holidays, or waited to see if TMS fulfilled its promise? I consoled myself with the knowledge that since Jordan was so unpredictable, nothing would have guaranteed us our happily ever after.

But of course, I knew I hadn't been the perfect boyfriend, so I asked myself, *what do I regret about my own behavior?*

I regretted Vancouver, obviously. I tried not to be too hard on myself—I'd been honest and made every attempt to accept my sex addiction and prove to Jordan she could trust me. But maybe I'd been too demanding that she communicate as well as I did? Maybe I'd been blind to Jordan's abandonment issues and not realized that constantly renegotiating an open relationship wasn't the smartest way to build a *lasting* relationship?

And then, at exactly 12:59 a.m. on January 1, watching New Year's festivities from all over the world, I was jarred into sitting up. Because I realized there was one thing I'd done during our relationship to doom it.

Something I've never shared with Jordan.

A voice as strong as the one that directed me in those SLAA meetings asked, *How could you have been this stupid, David?*

I didn't even bother arguing. Every fiber of my being was infused with guilt and disappointment in myself.

For the first time in my life, I had a New Year's resolution, one I needed to share with Jordan. Maybe she would understand it. Maybe it would make her hate me even more than I imagined she already did. Considering she was getting her life together, I doubted it would make a difference—apologizing for this mistake wasn't likely to make her want to move back into my house.

I only knew if I didn't do this, I'd regret it for the rest of my life.

❦

SATURDAY MORNING, I WALKED FROM my car to a small row of one-bedroom cottages on a quiet residential street in Santa Monica, carrying a shopping bag filled with Jordan's Christmas gifts. The sun warmed my shoulders through my black T-shirt, and it felt like nature offering me a subtle squeeze of encouragement.

I needed it. I'd texted Jordan on New Year's Day and asked if we could get together to talk, but she'd been hesitant. She'd said she needed nothing but "positive energy" in her life. Only after telling her I had a revelation about something I'd done during the relationship did she agree to let me come to the Airbnb she was renting before moving to Brentwood. But I had a feeling it was more out of curiosity than the desire to talk to me.

Jordan was opening the door as I stepped up to it, and of course I buzzed at seeing her face.

"What's in the bag?" she asked with a polite, mannered smile.

"Christmas and Hanukkah gifts."

"Oh! I'm sorry," she answered. "I didn't think we'd be exchanging gifts this year. But I did get some things for the kids."

"Of course you did," I laughed.

"Come in, I'll go get them," she pointed to the couch as she darted into the apartment. I obliged, sat on the modern, low-lying couch, and put my bag on the floor at my feet.

"I was hoping to give these to the kids myself," Jordan said as she grabbed two red and white plastic bags from (where else?) Target and handed them to me. "But who knows when I'll see them again..."

I looked inside and saw gift baskets covered in plastic wrapping, containing boxes of candy, chocolate, and microwave popcorn. They had tags attached which read, *Movie Night Snack Bowl*.

"They'll love them," I said earnestly. "But why not wait until you can give these to the kids yourself? We'll make it happen whenever you're available."

"The next two weeks are going to be intense," she demurred. "I have to move, and I start at Perkins Coie on Monday, TMS on Wednesday. Will you take them home and hide them somewhere?"

"No problem."

Jordan sat on the carpet in front of me, cross-legged, and I reached into my bag and brought out the blanket, cursing myself that I hadn't taken the time to wrap the gifts. "For your new apartment," I suggested.

"Thank you!" she said as she held the alpaca to her face.

"The famous 'boyfriend' sweater," I reminded her as I gave the seasonal treasure from J.Crew.

"Oh, I'll wear *this* all the time."

I pulled out the T-shirts. "And some daddy shirts of your own."

Jordan winced with cute confession. "I took a couple out of your drawer when I moved out."

I could only laugh and shake my head.

"Thank you. For all of it," she said.

"No, thank *you* for all of it," I answered.

"All of what?"

"Everything. Loving me, hurting me. I'm grateful for all of it."

Jordan smiled, but clearly, we were in different places—she wanted to move on, and I wanted to dredge up the past. "So, what did you want to talk about?" she asked.

Gathering my courage, I slid off the couch to rest on my knees in front of her. "I made a horrible mistake," I confessed. "And I need to apologize."

"Oh," she said with a vexed frown.

I knew what she was thinking—that I was here to apologize for cheating on her—so I quickly added, "I didn't cheat on you, Jordan. I wish I could find a way to prove to you I was never anything but honest."

"Okay..." she said, unconvinced. "So, what's there to apologize about?"

"Well, for acting like the most stupid man ever put on the face of the planet and wanting an open relationship."

"What?" Jordan said, allowing a laugh.

"I'm totally serious," I answered, then mocked myself. "No strings attached? Who was I kidding? I was in love with you at first sight, but at every opportunity, I kept insisting we be able to sleep with other people. I had this ridiculous idea monogamy wasn't natural, so I'd negotiate my way out of it. 'It's okay to fuck other people if I'm paying for it' or 'if we're not in the same city,' I'd say. I'd pat myself on the back and call myself 'open minded,' or 'progressive.' But Jesus, what arrogance. All I was really doing was negotiating myself out of a relationship."

I shook my head bitterly as Jordan pointed out, "David, I did make those decisions with you."

"Only because you needed money and didn't want to lose me," I reminded her. "Let's be honest, if at any point I'd said I *wanted* to be monogamous, you would have been, right?"

Jordan half-nodded. "Maybe not right away. But yeah, I wanted you to want just me."

"You said it so many times, but I never got it," I sighed with deep regret. "But now I understand. It doesn't matter if monogamy is natural or not. We're human beings. What separates us from every other animal is our ability to be better than our nature. God, I wish I could go back to our first date. I'd have taken out a goddamn second mortgage on my house and given you everything so you wouldn't need other men."

"That's so sweet," Jordan softened. "But my debt wasn't your responsibility, and let's face it, I fucked us up in so many other, worse ways."

"I know, but I can't help wondering how much healthier you'd have been if you felt safe and taken care of? I thought you were being unreasonable the first time you got angry about me seeing Collette, but now I understand it's because you were risking a part of yourself that I hadn't yet—that emotional attachment to me. You needed me to take care of you, but I used the fact that you *had* to see other men to make it okay for me to see other women. If I hadn't spent money on other women or trips to Mexico, or somehow found a way to pay for TMS months ago…"

"You went above and beyond to help me," Jordan chimed in. "I've acted like an ungrateful child and pushed you away."

I smiled, feeling a little appreciated, but noticed my back was starting to ache; I slid my legs out from under me to move to my stomach, propping myself on my forearms.

Looking up at Jordan now, I saw she had her head cocked to the side— she was studying me like I was a jigsaw puzzle, as she'd so often done.

"All of this is amazing to finally hear," she said. "But what made you change? Losing me?"

"No, no," I quickly answered; I didn't want her to think I was this sad case, saying anything I could to win a woman back. "I swear. I was sitting in front of the television on New Year's Eve, and it struck me that I've been living with this gaping wound for decades…"

"Michelle?" Jordan suggested.

I nodded, feeling silly as always for wallowing in this ancient history but still forced to admit its effect. "I think the damage that heartbreak did went far beyond fear of intimacy. It created a deep mistrust of women and love. Seeing other people is a way of holding back a piece of my heart. If I could avoid commitment, avoid giving myself completely, I could avoid getting hurt…"

As I said this, I laughed at the irony. "That clearly didn't work out. I can't tell you how miserable I've been since we broke up."

Before I could even feel my tears, Jordan was wiping them away with her fingertips.

"Come here…" she said as she uncrossed her legs and folded them under herself.

I rolled onto my back and rested my head atop her thighs. Then she bent over and kissed me.

I wasn't expecting it, but I accepted it. Her lips had never felt so soft. Her tongue never so gentle. And when she lifted her face from mine, neither of us were crying anymore. I felt open-hearted, seen, connected to her and to myself. I had never felt so vulnerable yet so safe.

"I *never* want to kiss another woman, ever," I whispered up at her.

"Everyone we know would think it's crazy for us to even *think* about getting back together," Jordan said as she caressed my temples, my head still resting on her thighs.

We'd been talking for hours, but only that—Jordan hadn't kissed me again, and I hadn't thought to ask. We were both too stunned that it had happened at all, and by its significance.

"I couldn't care less what the world thinks," I answered. "It's sort of ridiculous how amazing I feel. So present. And loved."

Her fingers tenderly brushed across my eyebrows, lulling my eyes closed.

"You were right, you know," Jordan said.

"About?"

"Asking me to move out, work. It all needed to happen. For our relationship, for myself…"

I opened my eyes but was speechless. Closing Rosewood's door on her was something I'd second-guessed almost as much as I had asking for an open relationship, but she was validating my decision.

"And I haven't reached for a pill in weeks," Jordan braved. "I was in such denial. I let drugs keep me from so many things. You, most of all."

"And yet, here I am," I pointed out. "And proud of you."

She shook her head in wonder. "Eight thirty to six, and then an hour of TMS, five days a week. Could you have imagined *me* doing this a year ago?"

"A year ago, tomorrow," I reminded her. "Our first date was January ninth."

"Oh, my God, that's right. Do you remember that I spilled champagne in the Uber?"

"How could I forget?"

"The first of many messes I made," she joked. "And you have tried to clean up so many since."

I laughed, more interested in our possible future than our past. "Why don't we have dinner on Tuesday? I'll take you to the Ivy again."

"I'd like that," she smiled cautiously. "But can we take this slow? I don't know if I can handle jumping fully back into anything."

"Whatever you want," I said.

Jordan arched and twisted her back. I took the hint, sat up, and reached for the Target bag.

"I'll hide these."

She smiled even as she said, "Again, I'm sorry I didn't give you anything."

"Are you kidding? Teaching me how to be monogamous is the gift of a lifetime."

We climbed to our feet, shuffled toward the door, and hugged goodbye. And for some reason, as we parted and I took two steps toward my car, I felt the need to stop and turn back to her.

"What a crazy love story we've had," I said.

"Have," she corrected me. "Our story isn't over."

34

THE MAGICAL ALLOWANCE

"YOU'LL MAKE EVEN LAWYERS smile," I dictated to the florist from my office desk Monday at 9:00 a.m. "Love, David."

"Got it," the man said. "A dozen tulips, care of Perkins Coie, 1888 Century Park East, Suite 1700, Los Angeles 90067."

I double-checked the law firm's website on my computer. "That's right, thanks."

I hung up, teeming with pride as I imagined the gleam on Jordan's face when the flowers were delivered. I was also still aglow with romance after our kiss the previous Saturday—so much so I had to temper my urge to send her roses and settled on tulips; I didn't want Jordan to have to field questions about her relationship status on her first day of a new job.

Two hours later my cell phone rang from a number I didn't recognize. Assuming it was Jordan calling from an office phone to thank me, I answered cheerfully, "Hi there."

A young man's voice said, "Hi, I'm here at Perkins Coie trying to deliver flowers, but I can't find a Jordan."

That didn't shock me. "She started there this morning," I explained. "Maybe they didn't recognize her name."

"Dude…" The guy sounded annoyed. "I've been here for half an hour. Human Resources even came out and said there's nobody here by that name."

"That's strange. Let me figure this out and call you right back?"

"Cool. Have to make a few other deliveries in the area, but I can come back in about half an hour."

I hung up and texted Jordan, only a bit chagrined I'd have to ruin the surprise.

Happy first day! Tried to have something delivered, but they couldn't find you. 1888 Century Park East, seventeenth floor, right?

I saw her text bubble light up immediately, No, Baker, Nunn, Smith, 1901 Olympic.

I blinked. *She switched firms?*

I don't understand, I wrote back.

I'll explain later, she answered. It's crazy busy here.

Okay...I wrote. Baffled, I reached to my computer keyboard and googled the new firm's name, which led me to their website. They were a boutique litigation firm in Santa Monica. *But there's something about that name*...I clicked on the "Lawyers" tab. At the top of the list was a picture of a doughy-faced man with brown hair.

I stopped breathing, because I remembered the nickname Jordan and I had used for this man since he'd first come into our lives.

He was the sugar daddy who Jordan had called having sex with "soul killing."

You went back to Broken Foot? I typed, my fingers shaking with fury.

I'm not dating him. He gave me a job.

And I'm supposed to believe that??

I'm sorry. I'm on an errand for the firm at the Santa Monica Courthouse. I'll call you in an hour.

No! This can't wait an hour! Jordan, how could you do this?

It's bad, I know. I'll call soon, I promise.

It's bad? I thought. *That's the best adjective she can find to describe what she's done? How about 'devastating?'* Even on Saturday, while I had my head in her lap and she was kissing me, she'd been lying to me. That struck me as such pathological dishonesty I had to wonder what else she'd lied to me about in our relationship. Had she been fucking Broken

Foot this whole time? While accusing *me* of being a cheating sex addict? Had she been seeing other men, too?

I was overcome with a long overdue dose of raging jealousy. I'd thought I'd been missing a gene or had commitment issues, but now I was on fire, my head filled with flashes of her fucking the doughy lawyer. *What timing*, I bittered. *I finally give one person all of my heart, and this is my reward?*

I'd never felt so betrayed in my life. I recalled Jordan on Saturday telling me "our story isn't over" and was sick to my stomach that I'd taken it as a promise. *The woman was warning me that she wasn't through with me!*

I'd always seen Jordan as a flawed princess, but now she was this film-noir femme fatal, manipulating and conning me. *What else had she lied about?* Had she ever quit drugs? Had she broken into other people's apartments? Had she robbed more from Renee than her self-respect?

Shit, I'm going to need an Ambien tonight, I predicted.

I scowled at the phone for an hour, but it didn't ring. I went to a lunch meeting with a literary manager at a restaurant up the street but placed my phone on the table with the ringer on, politely warning him I was expecting an important call. The phone didn't ring, and I came across as rude for repeatedly checking it.

As I trekked back to my office, a good three hours after Jordan had promised to call, I called her and spoke to her voicemail.

"You don't even have the decency to call me back?" I bled into my message. "Jesus, Jordan, you had to know what this would do to me."

I WOKE UP LATE the next morning, on the couch in my clothes. A thunderstorm had showed up in the middle of the night and the sky had poured all morning, but now the sun seemed to have broken through. I glanced into my backyard and noticed a rainbow covering the sky over my house, stretching from one side of the canyon to the other.

Just when you need a little magic, I marveled as I got up and walked outside. I stood on the grass by the pool, took a few pictures of the sky, then felt my phone vibrate.

Jordan's smiling face was on my caller ID.

Naturally, she'd call at the exact moment there's a fucking rainbow over my house!

Cursing, I pressed the phone to my ear. "I can't wait to hear *this* apology."

"I'm so sorry I didn't call yesterday..." Jordan's voice cracked exhaustedly, as it was wont to do in such confessionals. "I didn't even get a *lunch* break. I was being trained to use the phones and the office manager was watching my every move, and everyone expects me to know to scan and file all these depositions and claims, and then I got home and collapsed..."

"Stop, Jordan, just stop," I moaned bitterly. "I support two kids and an ex-wife, produce movies, and I'm finishing up writing a script, but somehow I always manage to call you when I say will. *Always*. And have I *ever* not picked up one of your calls? Ever?"

Jordan was slow to answer, and it occurred to me she might not even *understand* how hurtful this was to me. At every turn I'd tried to communicate through our problems, to fix them, while she in turn shut down and ran from them, and then created new ones.

"I'm sorry," she finally said. "I couldn't deal with you getting angry. And then I slept past my alarm this morning and had to rush here."

"Where is exactly is *here*?" I asked. "Because for all I know you're calling me from Broken Foot's house."

"I'm at his firm. Google the number and call it in five minutes. I'm in the bathroom now."

"You can understand if I don't believe you, right? You must have told me you were working at Perkins Coie five times over the past month."

"I know, I'm so sorry. I started this in anger, and it spiraled. I went to Christopher right after we broke up, told him everything, about you, about us, and he said he'd give me a job. It's *just a job*—I haven't seen him outside of the office at all. I met him in his conference room and had to go through three interviews that Christopher wasn't even in."

I reeled that she was using his real name now.

And oddly enough, I felt sorry for the guy. Even if she wasn't sleeping with him, she'd probably hustled him for the job—today I wouldn't put it past her to threaten to out him as a sugar daddy to his partners.

And if I was wrong, I was willing to bet the story she'd told him about our breakup and the résumé she'd provided his firm didn't include her drug addiction or theft.

"I didn't know where else I'd get a flexible job, David," Jordan continued. "I start TMS tomorrow, but the schedule is all over the place—some mornings, some afternoons and evenings."

I almost laughed. "This is *Los Angeles*, Jordan—half a million actors work as *waiters*, so they have the flexibility to go on auditions whenever they get them."

"You know how hard that is with my depression," she whined.

I shook my head. "Jordan, how can you *still* use that as an excuse? It's not a catch-all for every single problem. I mean, how can working forty hours a week at a law firm be more flexible and easier on your situation than waiting tables?"

Jordan didn't argue the logic, so I continued. "And even if you *are* working there, why should I believe you're not also sleeping with him too?"

"You have no reason to believe me, I know, but I'm telling you, even if I wanted to date him, he's seeing someone, and after all this Me Too stuff, sleeping with *anyone* in his firm would be career suicide."

I heard some logic in that. The Me Too movement had now exploded, and every boss's behavior was being scrutinized. And, from all of their interactions Jordan shared with me, Broken Foot had come across as a kind and honest man. And, if Jordan were that manipulative, wouldn't she have schemed her way into a hundred grand, not a job as a receptionist?

"So maybe you're not sleeping with him," I allowed. "But why wouldn't you tell me any of this before?"

Guilt lowered her pitch. "It's been eating me up. I guess I didn't think we'd even stay friends long enough for you to find out."

"That didn't stop you from having coffee with me or kissing me... and Jesus, we were supposed to go to the Ivy for our anniversary tonight. When were you going to tell me? At dinner? I mean, what happened to the woman who told me on our first date all she wanted was 'honesty and transparency?'"

"I don't know; I don't know..." she mumbled, starting to cry. "I'm sorry, please, what can I do to fix this?"

One thing immediately came to Daddy Fix-It's mind, and I spat out, "Well, you can start by marching into Christopher's office and quitting."

She hesitated. "It would take me weeks or months to find another job, but if that's what you need..."

I'm not sure what I need, I thought as I looked up toward the sky. I knew what I wanted—I wanted to believe Jordan was telling the truth and wasn't sleeping with Broken Foot. I wanted to accept she'd only lied to me because until Saturday, she had no reason to think we'd ever get back together. I wanted to accept her apology, even if it was late and forced. I wanted her to have this job—even if it had been borne of anger and dishonesty, it was an adult decision. I wanted this rainbow above me to be a sign I should be forgiving, that I should give her and our relationship one more chance.

But then I thought, *How many times have I seen magical signs like this in our relationship and used them to excuse Jordan's behavior?*

I'd seen Jordan sending videos of deer in this backyard as proof she was my Snow White of Bel Air, so I could live with her breaking into Renee's apartment and keeping the truth about her history of theft to herself. I had let Jordan's mystical connection to my children blind me to the fact that she was a drug addict. I was enthralled by the magical coincidences that kept our relationship going—the discovery of Doctor Browning moments after Megan introduced me to the promise of TMS; Kendra being there in my morning of need to take me to a SLAA meeting. And, most of all, I let the magic of Jordan's "true love's kiss" justify her shifting moods, jealous rages, cruel insults, and even her fists...her emotional and physical abuse.

And suddenly I understood *this allowance*—beyond any money I'd given her—was the basis of our *real arrangement*...Jordan brought magic into my world, and in exchange, I repeatedly allowed her to behave in destructive ways.

"You can keep the job," I blurted into the phone.

There was a long pause, as if she couldn't believe I'd backed down. "Are you sure?"

"Yes, I'm sure."

"Okay, thank you for understanding."

"Understanding?" I laughed with disgust. "Jordan, that's the craziest thing about you lying to me. If you'd been honest with me at *any time* before today, I would have probably understood. For God's sake, rainbows appear when you call me! That's how crazy in love with you I am."

Jordan gasped dramatically. "You. Are. Magic."

The fact that she'd used those exact words made me go silent for a second. As she'd done so many times, Jordan seemed to be hearing my thoughts. Except now I felt like she was using her empathy to manipulate me, betting my track record of forgiveness proved I had no emotional boundaries.

"Happy anniversary," I said, trying to not sound spiteful. "But I'm sorry, I never want to see you again."

I saw her mouth gape with surprised disappointment as I clicked off FaceTime.

I bent over to vomit, but I hadn't even had coffee yet, so I dry heaved. Violently.

35

THE HEALING DIAGNOSIS

IT WAS 7:00 A.M. on March 2, my fifty-fourth birthday. Eli and Chloe were still in their beds, and I calculated that I had less than twenty minutes before I'd have to wake them, make breakfast, lunches, and drive them to school.

My phone did a little dance on my bedside table. Seeing Jordan's face on caller ID, I exhaled.

I hadn't seen or spoken to her since that day under the rainbow almost two months ago, but I couldn't pretend I hadn't wanted to. Within a day my heartbreak returned, and there were days when we texted and attempted to meet, but in the end, one of us would come to our senses and cancel last minute. We tried to remain friendly, and Jordan occasionally updated me on how difficult working and the TMS treatments were for her.

TMS is making me Looney Tunes. PMS times 10 gazillion, she wrote to me in early February.

That surprised me. Megan said she'd been able to take *naps* during the treatments and experienced no side effects.

But I put aside my questions and tried to support her. I curated a playlist called "Don't Worry, Be Happy" of calm but upbeat songs for her to listen to during the process. Jordan sent me a selfie in the treatment room from the waist down, black pantsuit and pink closed-toe heels crossed in front of a small computer monitor that showed what looked like an ultrasound of her cerebellum.

I made it through today thanks to your playlist!!!

Impressed to see Jordan out of jeans and converse sneakers, I wrote, Adult Jojo!

And then she vanished. Stopped answering texts, stopped posting to Instagram and Facebook.

After three weeks I knew something was wrong. No matter how inconsistently Jordan's posts might represent her actual mood or health, Jordan had never—or at least not in the year I'd known her—gone a day or two without posting.

So, after my "are you okay?" texts went unanswered, I wrote her again, Hi...tomorrow I turn fifty-four. The only thing I want for my birthday is to hear your voice and know you're okay.

And here she was, only a few minutes past being my wake-up call.

"It means so much to me that you called," I answered with a whisper.

"Happy, happy birthday!" Jordan chirped with a hoarse rasp.

"Are you okay?"

She rattled anxiously. "TMS has been a beast, a fucking nightmare. I had terrible side effects. I was hypomanic, suicidal—I went to the hospital twice."

"My God—"

"Just for a few hours each time, not overnight," she interrupted, rambling so quickly it was hard to follow. "Browning cut all my antidepressants in half and put me on mood stabilizers and is convinced I was misdiagnosed all these years—I'm not depressed. I have bipolar disorder. The TMS shock brought it to the surface."

She took a breath, and I tried to make sense of this. Jordan had told me several psychologists ruled out her being bipolar, and though she sounded obviously manic right now, I'd never heard her like this before.

"Does Doctor Browning say this kind of reaction is normal?" I asked.

"Oh, I bet it happens to a lot of people," Jordan asserted. "But he'd never admit that—it goes against his life's work and everything his medical research and funding is for. TMS may be anti-pharma, but it's still about the money."

I heard in this a jumble of paranoia, but knew it wasn't time to argue; she needed help, even if not from me.

"Does Christopher know what's going on?" I asked.

"Yeah, he's kept me from being fired. I'm barely able to work half days. And these bipolar drugs make me exhausted. I sleep twelve hours a day and when I'm awake, I'm irritable and have no desire to do anything, not even watch TV or read. It's a narrow way to live. I have nothing."

My chest felt heavy with compassion for her. I might have been struggling with heartbreak here and there, but *she had nothing?*

"But I guess it worked, I'm not as depressed," Jordan added with a harsh laugh, her signature breathy "ha-ha" gone.

I felt like I was talking to a different Jordan, as if on the other end of the phone was a strangely animated version of her.

"Jordan, how can I help?" I asked. "I swear, I'll come to TMS with you every day and hold your hand? You don't have to do this *alone.*"

Without anger, as if it was a matter of fact, she answered, "Yes, I do, David. You kicked me out of our home."

I kept myself from reminding her why, and for clarity asked, "So, have you given up TMS?"

"Given up?" she hissed, irate. "How dare you? I don't quit; I never quit."

"I didn't mean to say that you'd failed—"

"I would have done anything for TMS to work, David!" she yelled over me. "I'm grieving the loss of the only beacon of hope I've had for a decade and fighting for my life—there was even a chance I wouldn't be calling you today!"

Fighting for her life? A chance she wouldn't be calling me today? Those sound like suicide threats.

"Jordan, what does that mean?"

She was crying.

"Jordan?"

The line went dead. I dialed her but was sent to voicemail.

I texted her, Jordan, if you're having suicidal thoughts, please talk to me, or to someone?

I pressed send but my text turned green. She'd blocked me.

I spun with dread. I'd seen her nearly jump out of a moving car on the highway, so even if there was the slightest chance she was considering suicide, I had to get her help. But who? Jordan hadn't made a single friend while we were dating. I couldn't call Broken Foot—if Jordan's job was already on the rails, calling Christopher wouldn't help matters. I could call Doctor Browning, but his therapy had already put her in the hospital twice, so he seemed like a last option.

I could call her mother.

I had never spoken to Francis on the phone, but Jordan had given me her number to text her a happy birthday, so I pulled up her contact and wrote, Francis, it's David Winkler. Jordan said something that really concerns me. Please call me as soon as possible.

Hunched over the phone, waiting for her response, I had some serious déjà vu…

Jordan had told me that after her breakup with Ray, he reached out to her mother repeatedly. Jordan described him in stalker-ish terms, insisting his contact with Francis had been nothing but manipulative attempts to get Francis to talk Jordan back into the relationship.

But now I had to wonder how much of that story, or really any of the stories she'd told me about Ray, were based in reality. Had Ray really been a narcissistic alcoholic who "broke up and abandoned her" with a text? Had he *really* been disillusioned by the reality that his "Insta-famous girlfriend had real problems like depression?" Or did Jordan put him through a year of psychological horror? Had Jordan threatened *him* with suicide, so his only option was to call her mother?

I had to fight an urge to find Ray on Instagram and contact him. I could safely bet he'd have a *very* different version of his relationship and breakup with Jordan than she did. I knew I would never invade her privacy that way, but it made me wonder what Jordan—God willing she survived her latest self-destruction—would tell her next boyfriend about me? Now that I knew pathological dishonesty was one of her traits, I doubted any man would ever truly know what came before him.

My phone rang and I steeled myself, vowing not to say anything to Jordan's mother that might give her reason to doubt my intentions—or if it got back to Jordan, give *her* any reason to claim I was stalking her.

The call was as impersonal as one can be when telling a mother her daughter, and someone you've loved, has threatened suicide. I was careful not to ask her what she knew about anything that had happened in my relationship with Jordan, and careful not to tell her anything about it, beyond what led me to believe Jordan might be an immediate danger to herself. And Francis didn't question me, or, for that matter, seem surprised. I wasn't sure if this was because she already knew her daughter had been hospitalized, or because as a lawyer she was trained to keep her feelings out of emergencies. Only at the end of the conversation did either of us get even remotely personal.

"I'll call Jordan immediately," Francis said to me, adding, "And David, I can't thank you enough for everything you've done to help her for the past year. Jordan has told me she regrets the affects her mental health had on her relationship with you."

I choked down my tears. Lately, I'd been struggling to accept that Jordan would never acknowledge the totality of what she'd put me through and realized this was probably as close to an apology as I should expect. I often dreamed Jordan and I might one day have a *The Way We Were* moment, where we'd meet, reminisce, and be thankful for how love had changed us, but now I realized that was a trite fantasy.

"Thank you for telling me," I said, voice breaking as I hung up.

JORDAN BEGAN POSTING TO Instagram a week later, to my great relief. And though I never learned how my call with her mother might have helped, the mystery of Jordan's diagnosis haunted me a little. It was hard for me to believe Jordan had been bipolar her whole life, not just clinically depressed, and that Doctor Browning's machine had jolted the reality out of Jordan.

This was highlighted in April, when I offered Jordan a supportive gesture, emailing her a link to a book (one of the numerous memoirs I'd been reading before beginning to write my own) called *Fast Girl*. In it, Olympic runner Suzy Favor Hamilton details her secret life as an escort and her struggles with bipolar disorder.

Naturally, I expected Jordan to identify with Hamilton's issues, but a few days later she wrote me back.

Thanks, but I'm not bipolar.

What changed in the last two months? I asked, but Jordan didn't answer.

ONE LATE JULY EVENING, I returned home from a day of writing this memoir. Writing was basically all I'd done for the past few months. Reliving the ups and downs of our relationship daily was, at times, torturous. I'd spend six or seven days a week at the office, poring over the thousands of pages of texts I'd printed up and bound into binders, then pour tears of joy and pain onto my keyboard. But it was much more cathartic and healing than torturous. Writing was my therapy, helping me process an extraordinarily complex relationship. For a man who'd once complained he'd never have a personal enough story to write, I had one so personal, so full of meaning, it was often hard to choose what stories to tell.

I opened my glass sliding doors and walked outside, checking my emails, and noticed one from Jordan. It was telling that she'd emailed me—whatever message she had, she wanted to make a statement, something more irrefutable and important than a text.

I took a seat on the warm concrete beside my pool and read.

Hi, David, I hope you are doing well and that the kids are well. I felt like I should end this dynamic of your attempting to communicate with me and me not responding. While our relationship was meaningful to me, I realized we were not right for each other and moved on. But you have contacted my mother, monitored my social media, sent flowers to my place of employment, and other inappropriate emails. I'm asking you to stop, respect my privacy, and let go. All the best, Jordan.

Her tone was polite enough, but as I'd suspected, she was in near complete denial of reality.

We weren't right for each other? That was our problem? But at the same time, I was a little impressed she, not I, had the strength to finally force a curtain-dropping goodbye. I knew she was right—it was time for me to let her go completely.

Damn it, once again I'm learning from the relationship.

I decided to send her a final goodbye, for my own peace of mind—set the record straight. So, with no pride, only sad disappointment, I wrote back.

Jordan, thank you, I will stop reaching out after this. But please don't paint my attempts to communicate with you as inappropriate. I sent you flowers days after you kissed me, to congratulate you on your new job. And I contacted your mother only after you'd threatened suicide. I hope that if I am ever so self-destructive someone will be that inappropriate.

I wish you all the best as well, David.

I sent the email, then looked back at my house. Jordan had been so much a part of Rosewood I wondered if I shouldn't move out of the house for my own emotional health. Instead, I decided to reclaim it as my own.

But I knew I would never fully move on if I didn't make some symbolic act, a grand gesture to myself, to say goodbye. While reading dozens of memoirs and books about love and mental health, I'd read about scientists reporting that brain scans of people in love were similar to those under the influence of narcotics, and I realized a good deal of my lingering heartache was due to withdrawal from the powerful chemicals of Jordan's love.

I was addicted to Jordan.

I'd been using my sporadic contact with her, and so many other things, as my methadone. Every time I looked at her Instagram or her pictures on my phone, or any number of memorabilia throughout the house, I was getting a fix. But if I truly wanted to let Jordan go, I needed to let go of all the objects in my life pulling me toward her. I would need to go cold turkey of Jordan for once and all.

Still sitting outside, I began by pulling up our text threads—over a year of messages and pictures. I needed them off my phone, so I wouldn't be reminded of her every time I used it.

I deleted the whole thread. Then, knowing I'd already transferred all the pictures in my phone to a Dropbox file in case I needed to refresh my memories while writing, I went through my phone and carefully deleted every picture of us together, every picture of her, even a simple picture of me she'd taken.

Then—and this one was hard—I unfollowed her on Instagram and Facebook. Jordan might have been out of line in calling my messages inappropriate, but she was right about one thing—as long as I was watching her life, I would be mired in it.

And finally, I got up and went into the house.

Feeling like I was exorcising a ghost, I moved systematically through the house with a construction-sized trash bag and collected any item that reminded me of her. I tossed in pictures of us I'd hid in a closet; her phone that was installed in the living room; then the gifts her mother had bestowed upon the kitchen; then the Ikea vases, bathmats, and plants still adorning the kids' bedrooms; then that cashmere Neapolitan blanket still on the couch, frayed from being huddled under so often…and I walked outside to the garbage bins and dumped it all.

I cried incessantly as I did these things, but in retrospect, my heart made a giant leap in healing that night.

36
TALK ABOUT HAPPY ENDINGS

"Do you know what's happened to Jordan since that last email?" I heard the therapist ask.

"I know she's alive," I answered, then sipped from a water bottle, thirsty from recounting the highlights of how my fairy tale with Jordan ended. "I'm writing a memoir, and I checked her Instagram the other day. She hasn't posted in almost two years But I got a text from her recently…"

"What did it say?"

"Nothing basically. That she thought of me and the kids often and hoped we were doing well."

"And how did hearing from her make you feel?"

"Truthfully, I wasn't triggered at all," I answered.

"Did you answer her?"

"No. It seemed pointless. 'Hey, been thinking about you?' That's what she writes after everything that went down? Maybe I'd feel differently if she'd said she wanted to talk and apologize. But really, I don't even need that. I've forgiven her. I hope she found happiness with Broken Foot. After all, I'm a producer. Every romantic comedy or love story I'm pitched is about someone falling in love with a person they once found soul-killing."

After a laugh, I heard, "So true. And how's the memoir coming along?"

"Almost done," I reported. "That's why I came to see you. Since I'm writing about mental health, I thought it couldn't hurt to get a professional opinion. And you met Jordan, so I thought you might have some insight into her character."

"Couldn't hurt," repeated Debra, the Jewish grandmother of a therapist.

Having written and rewritten the chapters where Jordan and I broke up in therapy, I had long ago decided Jordan's indictment of the sweet woman as biased was, like many of her resentments against other women, just plain ridiculous.

Debra pursed her lips. "I remember thinking Jordan was very...sparkly."

I laughed, thinking that "sparkly" was a perfect way to describe Jordan's charisma.

"So, what about her mental health can I help with?" Debra asked.

"Well, her diagnosis, to begin with," I answered. "What made Jordan do all the things she did? Do you think she was bipolar?"

"I only met Jordan twice," Debra said with a respectful pause. "But I think she might be more borderline than bipolar."

"I've heard of it," I answered—but of course knew little about borderline personality disorder. I laughed at the repetitiveness of my ignorance. A good friend had recently suggested I was born a "young soul," which I found more comforting than any theory my therapists had proposed. (Although, I'm pretty sure my soul aged quite a bit over *this* chapter of my life.)

Debra smiled, then summarized BPD. It was like bipolar in that the main symptom was mood swings, except those with borderline have far shorter ones, lasting hours as opposed to days, weeks, or months. And borderlines typically have "emotional regulation" challenges—they feel their emotions so intensely they're easily triggered by events, fear abandonment, suffer from low self-esteem, and struggle with compulsivity behaviors such as drug addiction and eating disorders.

"*That* sounds like the Jordan I knew," I agreed.

Debra waited for me to elaborate.

Instead, I said, "I think I'll let that be the last word about what went on inside Jordan's head. In the end, my book isn't about her anyway—it's about how *I* changed. Jordan, the relationship, they were beautiful catalysts."

Debra nodded, impressed. "That's a healthy way of looking at it. So how have you changed?"

"Where do I begin?" I chortled. "In one year, I learned about depression, eating disorders, health insurance, kleptomania, drug addiction, and sex addiction..."

At those last two words, Debra squinted. "You mentioned you went to a few SLAA meetings after we last saw each other. Did you struggle with it after you and Jordan broke up?"

"A little," I admitted. "After Jordan went back to Broken Foot, I went back on Seeking Arrangement, but it took all of three dates before I realized how hollow it felt. Once you've had a taste of real intimacy, random sex gets *surprisingly boring*."

"Interesting how that happens," Debra remarked, as if this were a secret any old soul would know.

"And being back on the site made me ask myself if I was acting like an addict again," I furthered. "So, one day I challenged myself. I decided the only way I'd know how much of a problem I had was to, well, give it up."

"What exactly did you give up?"

"Everything. Sex, paying for sex. For six months I went sober."

"It was that easy for you?"

"Surprisingly so. Actually, it made me wonder if I ever *was* a sex addict."

"Oh?"

I let Debra in on the inner monologue I often had while writing about sex addiction. "Look, I cheated on my wife and had a lot of one-night stands, but the sum total of the mistakes I made with Jordan were wanting an open relationship and one night in Vancouver. That all might have been from an unhealthy fear of commitment, and a little acting out, but did I really need to go to SLAA meetings?"

"You wonder if you threw yourself on your sword to save your relationship with Jordan?" Debra asked.

I crisscrossed my arms, and we studied each other, as if we were in an existential stand-off.

"I'm sure I was torturing myself with guilt," I answered. "But before Jordan, I probably was addicted. Hundreds of escorts and sugar babies do not a well man make."

Debra nodded evenly as I continued, "Not that there was anything unethical about my lifestyle. I know it might disappoint some people who read my book and expect me to make some neat and tidy message about the ethics of paying for sex, but money is just a tool. It's how you use it that matters. Before Jordan I used money to keep myself out of a relationship. Now if I help a woman out financially, it's to get into one."

I expected Debra to pull something out of the SLAA handbook like, "Addiction is the disease that convinces you that you're not sick." But she smiled, encouraging me to continue.

"But I do want to tell people to be careful using sugar daddy sites," I said. "Young women need to be especially careful. There are a lot of broken people on them. I know because I was one of them."

Debra studied me for a moment. "You don't sound broken anymore."

I placed my arms atop the cushions on either side of me, so my chest was unguarded. "I'm happier and healthier than I've ever been. But sometimes I wonder why I put up with Jordan's emotional abuse. Was I codependent or something?"

Debra leaned forward in her chair, elbows to her knees. "David, you dealt with drug addiction, depression, kleptomania, pathological dishonesty...any *one* of those can destroy a relationship. And you got out after a year. The way you handled these problems wasn't codependent—you went above and beyond to help someone you loved."

I tried not to let my heart swell with validation, but let's face it, when any professional tells you there's nothing wrong with you, it *doesn't hurt*.

"Tell you what I'm most proud of," I said. "Through all the heartbreak and pain, I never went back to being that invulnerable Hard David."

"I remember you using that nickname in one of our sessions," Debra recalled. "How did you manage that?"

"By not distracting myself," I answered. "I've learned to accept that pain is normal. Healthy even."

She laughed. "Pain is healthy?"

I smiled. "If I hadn't gone through everything I did with Jordan, I might never have learned so much about myself. My relationship with Jordan *had* to end this way. It might not have been the fairy-tale happy ending, but it was the right ending. I needed to learn how resilient my heart is…I don't want to sound too corny, but I feel like I learned what I was put on earth to learn. Honestly, if it weren't for my children, I could die tomorrow without the slightest regret."

"I don't hear *that* from many people," Debra said, allowing herself to sound impressed.

"I'm so grateful for the relationship," I said. "And I'm grateful to Jordan. Whatever mistakes she made, she loved me. And loving her paved the way for me to be in the relationship I'm in now."

"You're in love now?" Debra asked.

I felt blood rush to my cheeks. "Going on six months now. It's a bit soon to be making announcements, but my kids love her, and I can even see myself marrying her one day."

"That's amazing. Where did you meet her?"

"On Hinge, a 'normal dating site.'"

I expected Debra to ask if it was an arrangement, but she didn't. And though the relationship was anything but one, I appreciated that she respected my stance on money and relationships. *Love is love, wherever you find it.*

But she asked warily, "Is it an open relationship?"

I laughed heartily. "God no! I asked her to be monogamous after our third date."

Debra couldn't contain her laughter. "That lesson stuck, did it?"

"Don't get me wrong," I expounded, "I have *no* existential issue with nonmonogamy. I'm just a fundamentally different person now—the idea of sharing a woman I care for makes me cringe."

Debra smiled approvingly. "And you've prepared her—and your family and friends—for what's in your book?"

"She's already read most of it and is so open-minded and supportive," I said with pride. "As for my family and friends…I'm sure there will be some gasps when they read it. But I'm not ashamed of the things I've done. In fact, the more I tell people, the more I'm surprised by how my vulnerability brings them closer to me and makes them tell me secrets they never thought they could share."

"Anything that opens a conversation about love, intimacy, and mental health is valuable," Debra commented. "But how will you explain it all to your children? Are they going to read the book?"

"When they're old enough, obviously," I answered. "And in the meantime, I've already started talking to them about depression and addiction. I'm sure it won't be easy when the book comes out, but I'll try to communicate with them."

"I'm sure you'll handle it delicately," Debra said, then glanced at the clock over my shoulder. "I'm afraid our time is up. But I have this time available every week if you'd like to come back?"

"Honestly, I'm good," I said. "But thank you for the help. This book has become my life's work."

"You're welcome," Debra said as she got to her feet. "And I can't wait to read it. Do you have a title yet?"

"I do," I said as I stood. "It's called *The Arrangement: A Love Story*."

37

THE LAST OF DADDY FIX-IT

It was a Sunday night in August 2021, when I received a text from Elizabeth.

Bad news. Broken heart in our house.

I called my ex-wife but knew immediately the broken heart belonged to my son, Eli. He was fourteen now, as tall, more handsome, and equally romantic as his father. He'd been the first of his friends to fall in love, almost two years prior, and had stayed true to his girlfriend throughout the pandemic.

But that afternoon, as Elizabeth told me, Eli and this girl saw each other for the first time since she'd returned from her family trip to Nantucket, and she announced to him she thought they were "better off friends."

"Oh, no," I moaned.

I jumped in the car, made it to Elizabeth's house in record time, and found Eli snuggling on the couch with his mom and sister.

"Hi, Dad," Chloe said softly. She was twelve now, still as sweet and sensitive, and clearly knew why I'd come.

I smiled at her as Eli stood, his hair damp from pushing it out of his face with tear-drenched hands.

"Come here, my boy," I said as I led him into his bedroom, closed the door behind us, and sat on the bed with him.

"Tell me what happened," I gently prodded.

Eli did, punctuating the sad story with texts he'd shared with the girl. *Like father, like son.*

I thought of the best way to console him. I could tell him I felt his pain, swear to him that it would go away in time, promise he'd fall in love a dozen times before he found someone to marry. I could explain that every human being has been where he was tonight. Or I could remind him that when I was his age, the same thing had happened to me, and tell him how important it was that he not close up emotionally.

But then I realized Eli didn't need my advice. He didn't need Daddy Fix-It to swoop in and try to fix things. He just needed me to hold him, be sympathetic and understanding—just be good old dad. He, like everybody, would have many problems throughout life, and he'd ultimately be responsible for fixing them himself.

So, I put an arm around Eli and hugged him tightly.

"Eli," I whispered, "I know how much this hurts, believe me."

He began to cry, his body heaving as he fought it.

"Let it out, it's okay," I said.

He sniffled, then let his tears flow like a river onto my shoulder. I felt my own tears well up in my chest. I didn't fight them, I just let them go. And there sat father and son, in a hug, crying together. Despite my sorrow for him, I was filled with love and appreciation that I had the type of relationship with my son where we could open to each other like this. And that I had such a relationship with myself. Five years ago, I'd have probably sat there stiff as a board, awkward, unable to feel these powerful emotions. Unable to understand them, communicate them, share them. Unable to be emotionally vulnerable and connect on the level that every human being deserves.

But love changes people. I'm living proof.

THE END

38
THE WORDS AFTER

WHEN I SAT DOWN TO write this book, I wanted it to read more like a suspenseful love story than a memoir. I wanted to drop the reader right into our first date, and off you go. I tried to avoid the standard memoir tropes like introductions, pictures in the middle pages, etc. I even wanted to avoid an afterword section. *The book ends when the story ends,* I vowed.

But here I am, writing more words.

I guess the good news is, if you're reading this, the suspense kept you until the end.

First, the disclaimers.

Though I tried to write this book with "radical honesty," on rare occasion, I've combined events or conversations for editorial reasons. I've also changed a few people's names and identifying details to protect their privacy. (If I've failed and someone in this book is recognized or embarrassed, I am genuinely sorry; I encourage you to find me on social media so I can correct it in future printings.) Also, I don't portend to be an expert on the mental health issues discussed throughout my book. Depression, borderline and bipolar disorders, eating disorders, kleptomania, and sexual and chemical addictions are serious issues. If you or someone you care for are struggling with any of them, please seek a professional therapist or counselor.

Additionally, though I've tried to explain my own reasoning and rationale in living the "sugar" lifestyle, if you are considering becoming a sugar baby or sugar daddy, I encourage you to research it long and hard before taking that step. The money might seem easy, the sex casual, but the social stigma of being outed is real. Believe me, it took much soul searching, and a few uncomfortable discussions with loved ones, before I decided to use my real name on the cover of this book. And, most importantly, consider your safety when meeting strangers on any online dating app. I have female friends who have met men who were not such "rare gentlemen."

And some words of thanks:

To my editor, friend, and sounding board of three years, Devin, for going down all those rabbit holes with me.

To Al, who interviewed me for thirty hours, then refused to ghost-write this book, turning down a fair sum of money. He told me, "David, only you can write something this personal." His selfless and sage guidance gave me the kick in the pants I needed to sit my ass in the chair for four years.

To my family and friends, some of whom supported my decision to publish my memoir even if they hated the idea. Or maybe I should say, *because* they hated the idea. It's easy to support someone when you agree with them; my phenomenal family does so even while being uncomfortable with the subject matter. (Although, those gasps that I predicted I'd hear on the first page were loud, let me tell you.)

A special thanks to Megan Penn, whose friendship and support stretches far beyond those moments which I wrote about. (And then there were those missing texts you found!)

To Tyson and the crew at Rare Bird Books. They agreed to read it on a Friday and by Monday had become the enthusiastic and courageous publisher I'd hoped to find. In their hands, I know my book will be read by as many eyes as is humanly possible.

To Ciena, for helping me understand what it feels like to be truly loved, desired, and respected. I can't wait to spend the rest of our lives loving each other "more."

And, lastly, words of love and appreciation to Elizabeth, Chloe, and Elijah. As I've said, I know I was born a lucky prince, but the family we've created is the jewel in my crown.

Printed in the USA
CPSIA information can be obtained
at www.ICGtesting.com
JSHW030716180624
64993JS00002B/1